KONG

KONG

GARY ELKERTON
WITH PETER McGUINNESS

ABC
Books

The ABC 'Wave' device is a trademark of the
Australian Broadcasting Corporation and is used
under licence by HarperCollins*Publishers* Australia.

First published in Australia in 2012
by HarperCollins*Publishers* Australia Pty Limited
ABN 36 009 913 517
harpercollins.com.au

HarperCollins*Publishers*
Level 13, 201 Elizabeth Street, Sydney NSW 2000, Australia
31 View Road, Glenfield, Auckland 0627, New Zealand
A 53, Sector 57, Noida, UP, India
77–85 Fulham Palace Road, London W6 8JB, United Kingdom
2 Bloor Street East, 20th floor, Toronto, Ontario M4W 1A8, Canada
10 East 53rd Street, New York NY 10022, USA

National Library of Australia Cataloguing-in-Publication entry

Elkerton, Gary.
Kong : the life and times of a surfing legend /
Gary Elkerton and Peter McGuinness.
ISBN: 978 0 7333 3068 1 (pbk.)
Elkerton, Gary.
Surfers – Australia – Biography.
Other Authors/Contributors:
McGuinness, Peter, 1967–
Australian Broadcasting Corporation.
797.32092

Cover design by Matt Stanton, HarperCollins Design Studio
Front cover image by Simon 'Swilly' Williams
Back cover image by Jeff Hornbaker
Background texture by shutterstock.com
Typeset in Minion Pro by Kirby Jones
Printed and bound in Australia by Griffin Press
The papers used by HarperCollins in the manufacture of this book are a natural,
recyclable product made from wood grown in sustainable plantation forests.
The fibre source and manufacturing processes meet recognised international
environmental standards, and carry certification.

5 4 3 2 1   12 13 14 15

BATTLING THE BEAST

Kong was a larger-than-life character when I was a kid. Already a legend before he turned pro, and touted to win the World Amateurs in California in '84 (I just narrowly missed qualifying at twelve years old), I met him on the beach when he came up and asked me for a pretzel from the bag I was holding. He was larger than life and not even twenty years old. He didn't win that event but he went on to be one of Curren's few real challengers and to hold the line with power surfing when our generation of aerialists and new-school surfers came along. Elko took it as his personal task to take on each of us and quiet the noise we were making. He himself would not go quietly, and we had numerous classic and personal battles between us. I beat him at Bells, he got me back at G-land the day my daughter was born! And there were a whole bunch between those. We ultimately hugged it out. Elko is an epic, legendary figure in pro surfing. I'm glad it's all in the past and I can enjoy the memories now! Ha, ha!

– Kelly Slater

For Keith and Joan

CONTENTS

THE GORILLA ON MY BACK

One perfect summer's afternoon in 2000 on France's Côte Basque, I emerged from Lafitenia's surging shore break, walked a couple of steps, then staggered and fell to the sand. I'd just won my first world professional surfing title – the Masters. At last, I was World Champion. In my mind I would charge up the beach at this point with fists pumping jubilantly, embrace my inner circle of true supporters, fly through the media rounds on a wave of pure joy and then celebrate very long and very hard. I knew myself well. I knew what I'd do in this peak moment. Or so I thought.

In fact, once I hit the beach the thousands of faces in front of me swirled psychedelically, the rumble of the surf fell weirdly silent and I was sweating profusely, despite the chilly breeze. 'Surely you're not gonna faint, for fuck's sake!' I remember trying to talk myself out of it but it was too late.

I was only on my knees for a few seconds, to all appearances immersed in triumph and relief. Athletes do this often enough after big wins in football, tennis and so on. A lovely moment, captured in a memorable photo and immortalised in Quiksilver promotions for the selling season.

But it wasn't a celebration, and it wasn't an expression of relief or of triumph.

Sports pundits reckon that being separated from a deserved Association of Surfing Professionals World Title by a mere couple waves, a few shitty judging calls and some plain bad luck not once but *three* times put a monkey on my back. They don't know the half of it. They *really* don't.

I collapsed because I finally felt the full weight of the one-tonne gorilla I had on my back – not a monkey but a roaring, raging gorilla. I had no idea how heavy he was until I let him go. Until I saw that *I* was hanging onto *him*, not the other way around. I'd been carrying the big bastard around since I was twelve years old, loving him and ignoring him equally, but always feeding him. And second-place finishes feed the beast like nothing else.

So, for those few moments on the sand, as I tearfully opened myself to the rawness of the day's events, way more poured out of me than I was prepared for. Right then and there it became crystal clear that my marathon journey with the gorilla on my back had changed course forever. I no longer needed to keep thinking about him, living up to his legend in the water and out, or wrestling him kicking and screaming into the background.

I collected myself and sprang to my feet feeling … free. This wasn't a finale – it was a beginning. Not just to a career, but to life. I walked toward the approaching throng of wellwishers and beyond them into a brand-new and much improved relationship.

With a gorilla called Kong.

BEAUTY AND THE BULLFROG

At the peak of my pro surfing career, in the heat of a man-on-man battle, I thrived on the fact that my opponents struggled to figure me out. To most of them I was a half-mad ball of pure aggression. They perceived my style of surfing and my personality were one and the same thing. While it's true that I didn't go out of my way to be all cosy with my rivals on tour, I also didn't hide who I was.

Out of the water, the hard charging, big drinking and general debauchery that so characterised public coverage of my early career were simply who I was as a young man. I wasn't after any leadership role as a party animal, I just loved a good time and I was highly competitive. As things turned out, that combination proved a nice fit with my surfing style in the making of a reputation as a wild bastard. Of course, having a nickname like 'Kong' and being a large chunk of a lad in a sport dominated by jockey types contributed to the persona.

I'll admit to being a bit indelicate with people's feelings at times too. Okay, lots of times. But speaking one's mind without engaging a social etiquette filter isn't unusual. There's no Swiss finishing school for young, uncouth arseholes where I come from.

I know it's human nature to be curious about 'different' people and I'm happy that people have always looked on my surfing as being out of the ordinary. Great! That's the objective of a pro surfer's career, because successful surfers need to find a point of difference for themselves in the water. However, it took some time for me to accept that the world viewed me as being somewhat apart from the norm as a person too.

Aside from my surfing, I've never deliberately tried to set myself apart – I've just always done things my own way. Not in a 'look at my radical hairdo and armful of tatts' sense, but out of a deeply ingrained and strict self-reliance.

I hate imposed limits and regulations with a furious passion, yet I've often fucked myself up trying to follow my own set of rigid rules. Maybe that's why I don't see myself as particularly out of the ordinary. I follow rules too, albeit not obvious ones.

Like most blokes finally do, I've started to reflect more deeply on life now that it occurs to me that I've got more yesterdays than tomorrows. I suppose that I *am* a little different and people can be forgiven for being curious about me. I also now realise that I've actually been growing more conventional, more 'mainstream', since the day I was born. Yes, *more*. Which says a hell of a lot about my truly unusual childhood, one that I loved and considered totally normal.

After all, how many kids have their family home at sea on a prawn trawler?

* * *

I'm glad my old man got out of prawn trawling before blokes who'd get crook in the guts on the Manly ferry applied their prissy intellectual arrogance to ruining it as an iconic Aussie industry.

My dad lived on the Tasman and Coral seas at a time when people with good intentions but no idea whatsoever about prawn trawling were contenting themselves with smoking poor-quality dope in university toilets and protesting furiously over other matters about which they had no idea. Somewhere along the line we must have finally rid ourselves of every last war-mongering, animal-testing, tree-felling, V8-driving, burger-chewing, child-vaccinating, gene-manipulating, gun-toting, whale-spearing, imperialistic, materialistic, chauvinistic, homophobic, ozone-wrecking, carbon-belching bastard on earth. Because at some stage the humble, scraggy old Australian prawn trawlerman made it onto the shit-list of the anti-everything establishment. The do-gooders must have run out of other enemies.

Apparently, despite what veteran professionals observe with their own eyes every day, the whole Australian east coast prawn fishery is stuffed. It follows then that Australian prawn trawlermen need the guiding hand of politicians and academics, who've never trawled in their lives, to tell them how to care for their own livelihoods. Therefore all manner of restrictions, surveillance, electronic limitations and prohibitions regulate every aspect of a way of life which was once as free – and as wild – as the sea itself.

And if history ever requires a personification of that life, it could start and end its search with Keith 'Bullfrog' Elkerton. If prawn trawling was as ingrained a part of modern global culture as is surfing, then the Elkerton family member performing the unlikely task of writing his life's story would definitely be 'Bull', not 'Kong'. Any stature I've been fortunate enough to develop over the years as a surfer pales in comparison to the well-earned legend of my father in the world of Australian trawler fishing, from Port Macquarie to the Gulf of Carpentaria to Perth and all points in between.

Bull seems for all the world to have been created overnight as a fully developed crusty sea captain, standing tough as nails in the wheelhouse and roaring through the maelstrom of heaving northern New South Wales river bars. But he was, at one time, a child. So I'm told, anyway.

In fact, Keith was born on 17 March 1939 to Barney and Jean Elkerton, the second boy of four children. The Elkertons split their work efforts between a small farm in Grafton, northern New South Wales, and beach or net fishing nearby from Minnie Water to Wooli. In keeping with the general tone of Elkerton family life for generations, most of Keith's upbringing happened under the flat tin roof of a beach shack in the pristine wilderness of the dunes at Minnie Water. Barney taught Dad just about all there was to know about the gruelling and usually dangerous art of beach mullet netting by the time his little feet could touch the bottom of a rowboat. They fished for both the family table and for wholesale using rods on the beach, and they trapped lobsters and crabs to sell back in the big smoke of Grafton.

By the time Jean convinced old Barne to move the brood up the coast to the naturally protected north-facing trawler anchorage of Evans Head, thirteen-year-old Keith was already built like a brick shithouse and had salt water for blood.

The Bullfrog – or just Bull, as he became known – learnt prawning on Barney's trawler and by crewing for any other skipper who needed a strong pair of hands and an extra set of eyes, with an instinct for the sea. In his late teens an interest beyond a growing devotion to beer and ciggies emerged. Ted Lowe, a towering, patriarchal figure amongst Ballina's hard-bitten trawlermen, had a daughter who was a really good sort. Dad figured that a sheila who'd grown up with half a footy team of brothers in the rough and tumble of the Richmond River prawn fleet would likely forgive him for not owning a complete suite of delicate fine manners.

Not that Joan Lowe didn't have high standards – far from it. Mum was a very observant Catholic who forgave a little colourful language and rough-housing in the men around her, but heaven bloody help you if you were blasphemous or disrespectful.

It took a lot of gumption for Dad to pursue Mum early in the piece. Ballina was a very difficult thirty-five kilometres up the coast from Evans Head on a very shitty road, for a start. Bull took to riding his old Ariel motorcycle up the long, straight beach instead, so he was a pretty sandblasted, dishevelled Romeo by the time he got to see his sweetheart. And Dad isn't the greatest talker at the best of times, let alone when you throw in a dose of romantic nerves.

Then there was Mum's dad, Ted. To say that Ted was tough is a bit like saying that a Bentley is a good car, or that Sunset Beach breaks nicely. Grandad Ted used to run a boat off the old Byron Bay jetty before the big cyclone in '54 shattered it and half the whaling station like toothpicks. He and his family lived behind the dunes at Belongil Beach, right near what is now the millionaire's row made famous by the likes of Paul Hogan.

It's folklore that Ted once had a trawler sink beneath his feet in massive pre-dawn seas some fifteen kilometres off Ballina. There was no GPS, EPIRB, radar, mobiles or even decent radio in Dad's time, let alone Ted's. Therefore the first anyone knew of his mishap was when he swam ashore in boots and overalls, eight hours later and twenty kilometres north at Lennox Head. The one great slice of good fortune he had going for him was that the pub stood all of a hundred metres from his landing spot. So, with profuse apologies for his 'damp' money, he was able to eulogise his trusty boat with a dozen beers before hitching a ride home for dinner.

Suffice to say that Dad's degree of difficulty in courting Mum was ratcheted up considerably by the dead certainty that Ted Lowe would rearrange his face (and probably a fair bit of the rest of him) if the boofy kid from Evans put a foot wrong with his Joany.

In the end, Bull needn't have worried. The official merging of the Elkerton and Lowe prawn-trawling clans on 9 April 1960 was as close to a royal wedding as northern New South Wales is ever likely to see, if a touch less posh.

Initially, Mum and Dad lived with either the Elkertons or the Lowes – at Evans Head or Ballina – depending on which river bar Dad was crossing on which boat. By '61, they had enough behind them to buy their own trawler, the first of many – *The Rhonda*.

ST BRENDAN WAS PRETTY HOPELESS

The way Dad and Mum lived was simplicity itself. They owned a Holden station wagon, a caravan and a trawler. Wherever the work was, wherever and whenever the prawns were 'on' in Queensland or New South Wales, from Cairns to Narooma, they were there. Sometimes Mum towed the caravan to a nearby camping park, but more often than not she was on the trawler with Dad. Birthdays and holidays were enjoyed inside four walls with relatives from Byron Bay down to Grafton.

Life changed but the lifestyle didn't when baby Gary Keith Elkerton took his first ever drop in the Ballina Base Hospital on 21 August 1964. Thus began a first decade of life that critics would've written off as far-fetched had it been the work of Mark Twain. Huck Finn had nothing on me, not that I realised my great good fortune until much later.

I was smoothly absorbed into the Elkerton routine of movement around the east coast of Australia, all the while surrounded by family, both of the genetic and of the fishing variety. My stand-out first memory is of sitting on the northern rock wall of the Richmond River with Mum, waving goodbye to Dad in the wheelhouse of his boat as it pitched and rolled through Ballina's treacherous river mouth. The smile on Mum's face was at odds with the nervous way she wound her rosary beads around in her hands. I'd come to know this routine of Mum's very well. Waving goodbye at the riverside while praying to St Brendan – the patron saint of seamen – for his protection of her loved ones. Soon enough I was to become accustomed to seeing Mum's routine from the deck rather than from her lap.

Unfortunately, St Brendan was off duty a bit more often than you'd imagine a saint should be. Actually, he's either quite a bludger or Mum's rosaries needed a grease and oil change, because the Bullfrog had more close shaves than a cyclist's scrotum.

Dad used to cross river bars to hunt down prawns when no-one else would attempt the task. The more cyclonic the seas, the more gigantic and chaotic the waves in the river mouths, the less competition there was 'outside' in the open ocean for the catch. He'd often get his best catches in the most dangerous conditions, when the other trawlers were hove to at the moorings.

Not that the Bull was reckless. He read the waves with Zen-like calm and accuracy. When things went off kilter, you'd never hear him use the old 'freak wave' excuse of the weekend recreational boatie. According to Dad, you either read the rhythms and cadence of the ocean properly, or you bugger it up. Funny how 'freak waves' so rarely strike ocean professionals! Putting himself through challenges of courage, patience and skill under pressure was what the old man did to earn a living, but there's no doubt that he enjoyed it immensely, despite the hardships.

Dad's no great yarn spinner, so it's fortunate that plenty of people who knew him in the early days are. Stories of his river-mouth crossings are still told by old-timers at pubs from the Tweed to the Clarence. Sometimes they're even told by his not-so-old son at the same pubs.

Like the time he'd got wind of the prawns being 'on' at Ballina when he was eighty kilometres away, up on the Tweed River. While leaving in the middle of the night gave him time to get a jump on the opposition, it also meant crossing the Tweed bar during a cyclone in pitch darkness. They'd nearly made open ocean when Bull saw a phosphorescent mountain of white water bearing down on the trawler from dead ahead. The wave must have been tremendously large to have already broken in such deep water. Dad and the boys had just enough time to throw themselves as flat as starfish on the deck and hang onto something – anything – bolted down.

BOOM! The wave came and went.

Dad stood up in the pouring rain and did a stocktake of life and limb for a few seconds. Beauty! All hands accounted for. Ripper! No major injuries. Then he realised that standing in the pouring rain *was* the problem.

Fuck! Where's me bloody wheelhouse?

The entire wheelhouse had been torn from the deck and was on its way up the Tweed and past the Twin Towns RSL Club. All that remained of the boat's control centre was Bull himself and the steering wheel and stem, which were squashed as flat as a pancake against the deck.

Bull burst into action, as you'd expect him to, considering the urgency, to nurse a partial wreck back to the dock. Except he wasn't on his way back to the dock. He bent the wheel back into vertical position, rigged up rope controls and took off for Ballina, where he filled the hold with prawns before steaming back to the Tweed. And that's the tale of 'The Air-Conditioned Trawler', as it became known in the region.

You might've guessed correctly that Dad is not one to abandon ship. The one and only time he did came to a thoroughly unintended conclusion.

While crossing the notoriously evil Jumpinpin Bar – which separates North and South Stradbroke islands off southern Brisbane – a random floating hazard split the hull. What it was didn't matter as much as it what it did, because seas were high on a dirty night and they were going down fast. Better to get in the drink now with South Straddie only a couple of hundred very sharky metres away than to get sucked through the bar on an outgoing tide and out to sea on a quick-sinking boat.

The deckhand was gone and halfway to shore by the time Bull took a big swan dive off the stern. He swam hard to clear himself of the boat as the raging current swept both skipper and trawler outward into the open Pacific and their unpalatable fate.

Before he had time to consider his chances of survival, Bull had the bizarre pleasure of seeing a huge, clean swell pick up the mostly submerged, stricken trawler and send it trimming daintily – all the way to the beach. It surfed along perfectly, just like a riderless longboard, according to the old man. Remarkable. Ten minutes after making a coffee on the boat and planning the night's trawling with the deckhand, the boat, the deckhand and the coffee were on dry sand, and old Keithy-boy was being swept out to the prawns.

At length, Dad managed to stay clear of the sharks and was knowledgeable enough to float through the bar and swim himself southward toward the open side of South Straddie. The big seas worked against the tide and washed him ever closer to the beach. He came ashore, walked a few kilometres across the island and declared himself alive to the deckhand, the boat and the cold coffee, just as first light was illuminating the scene.

Naturally, he wasn't too keen to leave a vessel which wasn't either at anchor or on the bottom after that.

My favourite Keith Elkerton story is the first-hand account of a five-year-old deckhand. It wasn't my first voyage with Dad, but it is one I can recall with perfect clarity from start to (very early) finish. There was a big swell running on the Evans Head bar and the rain was torrential enough to restrict Mum's usual interaction with St Brendan to the comfort of the caravan. Must've been why the slack bugger couldn't hear her prayers that day.

I was in the wheelhouse with Dad, loving the thrill of riding up the wave faces and the weightless feeling of descending their backs. Although I knew to keep out of the way, I was still close enough to be in a cloud of smoke, thanks to the ever-present Benson & Hedges Special Filter jammed into the corner of Bull's gob. He'd actually just lit up a new one when suddenly all hell broke loose.

Within the blink of an eye and a 'get the fuck out', my loving father had gripped me under the armpit and tossed me over the port gunwale. I was in the water before I had time to wonder what I'd done to make Dad so angry. In hindsight, it's nice to know that Bull had such faith in my five-year-old swimming ability. At the time, though, I was busy ducking white water and keeping one eye on the trawler.

The reason I got the heave-ho was because it had become apparent to Dad that the boat was most likely about to be crushed and sunk. So I got chucked out and he returned to the wheelhouse while a gigantic wave gathered its full height in preparation to break precisely in between the bow and the captain's seat.

As Dad had planned, I was swept away a considerable distance in those few seconds. I watched thunderstruck as our twenty-metre trawler was rolled like a toy in an explosion of foam and the crashing noises of gear below decks being cast around like lottery balls in a barrel. I saw Bull standing at the wheel, steering stoically as she went over. She didn't sink. The old boy had gotten just enough angle on her to get tubed rather than impacted mid-deck. I got my first look at the bottom of a trawler before she righted herself, a bit worse for wear, but generally shipshape.

And there was Bull – still at the wheel.

A good Samaritan rock fisherman helped me ashore while Dad signalled madly to make sure I was alright. I don't remember feeling fear when I recall that day – I remember the whole episode as an adventure. And I remember the pride I felt in Bull as he stood in the wheelhouse giving me the thumbs up, smiling as a dry Benson & Hedges replaced its drowned predecessor.

A bloke would have to be crazy to take a five-year-old on a trawler, right? It's a matter of perspective. By our standards, if you can walk and swim, there's no reason why you can't be included in life on board. I've never considered my oldies as irresponsible for this, or for any aspect of my childhood. Quite the opposite. Not only was I in a close, caring family environment, but I was given a life straight out of a *Boy's Own* adventure, albeit the MA15+ version.

PRAWNUCOPIA

Australia's Gulf of Carpentaria is to prawn fishing what Hawaii is to surfing or the Himalayas are to mountain climbing. It's as rugged and untamed a part of the world as can be imagined.

The Gulf is actually a sea at the top of the country, bordered by the isolated majesty of Cape York Peninsula in the east, the mystery of Arnhem Land in the west and the colossal vastness of the Gulf Country in the south. It opens north into the fickle Arafura Sea and Torres Strait. Huge swathes of the Gulf's 300,000 square kilometres remained largely unexplored by white men right up until World War 2. Today, while all of the Gulf's coastline can be observed from space, the task of reaching some parts by land is still beyond our technical ability.

The tropical perfection of its waters disguises lethal difficulties for even the most experienced seamen. An average depth of only fifty metres creates fearsome tidal movements, closely spaced cross swells and high surface temperatures conducive to the rapid formation of vicious localised storms. Its U-shaped coastline and hinterland is both beautiful and mind-blowingly inhospitable. Coastal terrain varies from the densest jungle to arid semi-desert to vast mangrove-covered flood plains; from horizon to horizon. Tiger sharks and terrifying Irukandji jellyfish are abundant, the world's biggest saltwater crocodiles even more so.

So the Gulf of Carpentaria is an epic, remote and pitiless wilderness, with one of the planet's most dynamic and diverse ecosystems.

About halfway between plankton and tiger sharks on the marine fauna side of things is *Fenneropenaeus merguiensis*, the Gulf banana prawn. While five magnificently healthy rivers pour their nutrients into the ocean in northern New South Wales, making the region a world-famous prawn nursery, all of sixteen pristine rivers empty into the confined, shallow waters of the Gulf. It was the allure of this miracle of nature that stimulated the northward predatory migration of *Elkertoneus bullfrogenus*.

In 1967, we were in Townsville when Dad made a decision that changed our family life forever. The Bull thought he'd have a crack at what was rumoured to be the thickest, richest prawn fishery on earth. He just had to steam the trawler halfway round Australia through the parts of the Great Barrier Reef that nearly killed Captain Cook. No worries! The Elkertons were going to Karumba, the little port in the Gulf's south-east corner.

Now, the Bullfrog was pretty bloody familiar with the ocean all the way from Newcastle to Cairns, and he generally got from A to B using nothing more than his eyes, experience and instincts. He had some charts once, according to Mum, but they were a bugger to read and he could have rewritten most of them, anyway, after his first ten years at the caper. The trawler's antique compass looked pretty impressive in its big teak box. Great as an ornament, but shithouse at telling directions since it had demagnetised sometime before Elvis released 'Blue Suede Shoes'.

Despite his proven self-sufficiency, heading into unknown and infamously tricky waters was a touch perilous even for Dad, who for once in his life allowed that he may need a little extra navigational assistance. Before we set off from Townsville, Mum was dispatched in the direction of the nearest petrol station to purchase the critical safety item. Yep, a Shell roadmap of Queensland was utilised by Bull to shepherd his family around Australia's northernmost point and down to the end of the prawn rainbow – by *boat*. Well, at least the radio worked sporadically.

For the next seven or so years, the family settled into trawler life spent between the frontier outpost of Karumba and the New South Wales mid North Coast, with a hell of a lot in the middle. It doesn't seem likely that a town of 500 people in the extreme south-east corner of the Gulf of Carpentaria – as close to Bali's Uluwatu as it is to Snapper Rocks – would form such an important part of a professional surfer's development. But Karumba certainly did, even though it's over a thousand kilometres from the nearest recognised Aussie surf break.

We spent the middle part of every year up north. Life seemed to be spent on the way to Karumba, in Karumba or on the way back down from Karumba. My love of the outdoors, of the ocean, of animals, of self-reliance, of almost anything I can point to that is intrinsically 'me' was formed during my first ten years when Karumba was a such a focal point of our lives.

PARADISE

Even though Mum and Dad busted a gut prawning on the northward voyage every year, we were never too busy to enjoy ourselves. I remember lots of adult laughter on board, since we'd always travel with a couple of relatives from one side of the family or the other.

Most of the now world-famous resort islands of the Barrier Reef were either uninhabited or the tiniest of fishing settlements in those days. The Whitsundays were all but empty, populated by the occasional tin-shed general store which catered for passing mariners and hardcore drop-out beachcombers.

While Bull would never drink grog 'on the job', it was definitely open season on XXXX Bitter Ale once the nets were emptied. Dad would anchor just about every day or night in a postcard tropical paradise and more often than not we'd have it all to ourselves. Many of the really small atolls weren't even on the map.

The adults would enjoy a few beers and an open-fire BBQ while I'd be off exploring and fishing. I'd catch giant trevally that were twice my weight on a handline. I'd jump from coconut palms into clear freshwater springs and swim underwater into brilliant coral caves just metres from the beach. From my very early years I was used to swimming with dolphins, reef sharks, turtles and even dugongs in the remote lagoons which hug the hundreds of tiny coral and sand islands all over the Coral and Arafura seas.

We had a minuscule dinghy that I was able to use from when I could first grip the oars. I could paddle it to get ashore from the trawler – all too often without Mum's knowledge. Poking into to every nook and cranny of every island was irresistible to me, and no doubt a big pain in the arse for Mum! If there was a rock cave on the island, I'd be in its deepest recess. But she'd only look there after she'd checked the top of the tallest palm tree. I was that kind of kid.

One time, as we were rounding Cape York, we slept under the stars on a classic 'one-palm' coral atoll with a beautiful little mooring lagoon. Under a bright moon, I crept away from the sleeping adults and was handline fishing up the beach when dozens and dozens of turtle hatchlings emerged from the sand and scurried past me into the shallows. It was awesome. To my little-kid logic they needed saving, as I'd heard Mum talking about how many of them were eaten up by just about everything that flew or swam and had a mouth.

Poor little things! I scooped up as many of them as I could and lovingly placed them into one of Dad's empty beer coolers before ferrying them out to the trawler. They were shivering, so I wrapped them all up in a deck tarp and put them beside the big vertical exhaust pipe, which was always nice and warm. They looked happy and I was very proud of myself.

Of course, the oldies were a bit shocked to find that a mini-turtle farm had sprung up on deck overnight. They humoured me by keeping the hatchlings moist and allowing me to cuddle and nurture them throughout the next day. But I've since been told that Dad tossed a handful of my 'babies' overboard every time he walked passed. Mongrel.

Eventually, Mum explained that the babies would miss their own mummy and that it was best they go into the water so she could find them. She said that the mummy turtle would be very grateful for my help and that the baby turtles would remember me for looking after them. They'd always be my friends. So, with much sadness and with appropriate ceremony, over the side went my turtles. 'See ya, everyone,' I said with a wave.

No doubt many of them were lunch within minutes, but I like to think that Mum was right and that there's a few old turtles floating around the Pacific that remember me. While my flippered friends would more likely recall the horrific postnatal experience of being stuffed in a smelly beer cooler then being half-cooked on an exhaust pipe, I remember it as a very tender couple of days ...

It's a bit of a paradox that in addition to being a junior greenie of sorts, I was also mad keen on shooting guns and riding my little motocross bike. My oldies were sensitive to my need for excitement, so a little 50cc Honda Monkey was always stuffed down the boat hold and ready to go whenever there was the time and space for me to open her up on one of our stops. It goes without saying that there was lots of time and space up at Karumba for me to tear around the bush for hours.

Motocross remains a great passion of mine to this day, and kickarse bikes are fixtures in my garage. In fact, had life's twists not led me to professional surfing, I'm sure I would have pursued motocross as a career.

Granddad Ted loved to shoot. Roos, wild boar – that kind of thing. A .303 rifle was standard as deck gear on the trawler, since it was common to hoist some big stowaways with big teeth on board along with the prawns. We always had several beautifully kept and maintained rifles which were used for targets and hunting in the bush on days off. I'd often ride into the scrub with a .22 slung jauntily across the handlebars and challenge myself to shoot beer bottles from what I thought were mighty distances. Those were different times. Imagine seeing a gun-wielding tot tear past you at fifty kilometres an hour during your morning bushwalk in this day and age!

Perhaps the greatest privilege of all the adventure and wonder of my early boyhood was the insight I gained into the world of the Anindilyakwa people of the Gulf and Groote Eylandt. Of course, at the time it was normal for me to hang out with the other children living around Karumba and Groote Eylandt, but it's taken the passage of time and adult perspective for me to realise how special it was to be a white kid with so many indigenous mates up in northern Australia. I've lost track of my friend Kenny from those days, but I'll never forget exploring and swimming and fishing with him and his cousins. I was even invited on a few dugong and kangaroo hunts.

I cannot remember a moment of upset or sadness in my earliest years. Mum and Dad were earning great money and they were fully 'lifestyle oriented', as demographers say these days. We'd get fantastic catches from New South Wales all the way up to the Gulf, and Bull would often haul in tonnes within minutes off Karumba or around Groote Eylandt. At season's end, we'd meander back down to Evans Head or Ballina, enjoying the voyage without the pressure of trawling, and spend the profits on holidaying. It wasn't unusual for Bull to moor the boat somewhere and fly the family to a place like New Zealand for a week or two in between seasons. The old man was no tight-arse that's for sure.

But all things must change.

For a start, there was the fact that new arrivals were on their way to join our family crew, in keeping with Mum's obligations as a good Catholic. Then, Mum got it into her head that Bull couldn't just buck the whole world and raise himself a ready-made child deckhand. The word 'school' became a disturbing new addition to the family vocabulary.

And something called 'surfing' would enter my life like an atom bomb.

BROTHER DAVID, SISTER BERNADETTE

I love my little brother David so very much. I wish I was better at expressing this fundamental though so infuriatingly complex truth to him. He'd be shocked to know that I also *admire* him.

We haven't always enjoyed the greatest relationship. He can be a difficult person to get along with, but no more difficult than I can be. We're more alike than we probably realise, which has been both a blessing and a curse. Many a time we've treated each other poorly. Many a time I've been an insensitive prick to David. Often inadvertently, but a prick nonetheless.

But I have so much to thank him for.

For all the difficulties we've had, for all the awful and unnecessary run-ins we've put ourselves through, there have been beautiful highs of the kind that can only be shared by brothers, both in blood and in spirit. I'm thankful for it all, because, of everyone I've ever known, nobody has ever held a mirror up to my own behaviour in the way that David has.

He's caused me to reflect on myself more than a thousand victories or defeats ever could, more than the most humbling of wipeouts, more than any accolades or criticisms from people who think they know me but don't. And in that reflection, I've not always liked what I've seen. What more could you ask for from a brother?

Everyone who isn't the youngest sibling in their family will recall the overwhelming sense of anticipation that comes with finding out that a new brother or sister is on the way. I was five years old when Mum sat me down and explained that a baby was growing in her tummy. I remember being confounded by the fact that she told me Dad had put it there.

'Why did he put it in there when he just could've handed it to you? I never even got a chance to see it first! Why do I have to wait eight months to see it?'

I was a bit pissed off that Bull hadn't just stuck the baby straight into a crib on the boat so that we could get on with the job of playing and being friends. Being a *very* good Catholic, Mum told me to shut up and stop being so silly. Bull laughed his head off and told me that it was just 'the way things were' – that I would have something good to look forward to.

And boy did I look forward to it.

I'm not a great one at delaying gratification, so waiting for my little brother (I was *certain* it would be a boy) was nothing short of excruciating. Mum helped by marking off the weeks on a calendar for me. As Mum got bigger, I got the hang of the idea that my brother was alive in there and would emerge at around about the day the big star was on the calendar. The bigger she got, the more worried I became. The stress got too much with about a month to go.

'Dad, how's he getting out?'

Bull's blunt, anatomical explanation made me pissed off at him all over again.

Poor Mum! I thought Bull should've done the right thing and stuck the baby in his own guts instead. What a bastard. It ought to be noted that this was one of the few times in my life that I could be accused of being a feminist.

When the time drew near, we returned to Ballina and the support of the whole extended family as we all waited for the new arrival. David finally arrived on 5 November 1969 in the Ballina Base Hospital. And he was gravely ill.

David was born with an extremely rare congenital condition which can most closely be described as situs heterotaxy. The mumbo-jumbo of medical Latin was lost on us, but the physical meaning certainly wasn't. My little brother had most of his internal organs positioned upside down and around the 'wrong' way.

To this day, I wish I understood it better. The layman's explanation is that his heart, liver, kidneys and intestines were not where they should have been. Expert opinion was that he would probably not survive his early infancy. At the very least, intensive surgery was required to give him a chance at survival. In all of Australia, only one specialist in Sydney had the expertise to offer hope. David would die for sure if he remained in small-town Ballina. That was the basic science of it, something I would not grasp for many years.

The emotional impact was something I did grasp to the full. In the days following David's birth, the pillars of my life – rock-hard men and solve-all women – were in tears, comforting each other. It was all so strange. I wanted to cling to Mum and Dad, but they were consumed by the necessities of saving their new little treasure. I remember aunties, uncles and older cousins rallying to me, but I couldn't comprehend the reasons why.

I just wanted to see my brother. I just wanted my Mum and Dad.

At length, Mum and Dad hugged me close as they showed me my little brother in intensive care. Bull was teary. That rattled me. They prepared me for the fact that David was very sick, but they reassured me soothingly that he'd be okay – not that they knew whether he'd live much longer at that stage.

I thought he looked like an octopus. He had a blue tinge and lots of tubes extending from his body, this way and that. But as weird as he looked, and as different as he was to what I'd expected (I envisaged a robust little toddler, ready to play with), I was overcome with a sense of pride and love.

'That's my little brother. That's my brother, Mum!'

The wait was worth it. Somehow, I just knew he'd be alright. Or maybe I simply hoped and hoped until it hurt.

Dozens of operations were ahead for my tiny, tough sibling. Lots of visits to Sydney and lots of Mum's prayers to every saint with a set of ears. Fortunately, there are saints up there with a bit more influence than old St Brendan because David pulled through, not just with a couple of pig's valves in his heart, but with a full life ahead of him. That life would be full of confronting issues that few people have to imagine coping with and also full of intense ups and downs, many of which have involved his ever-loving – but often immensely stupid, overbearing or absent – big brother.

* * *

I'm sure my friend and darling little sis, Bernadette, won't mind me saying that she was a slight disappointment to her arsehole of an oldest brother when she was born – also in Ballina – on 13 November 1972. Of course, I was assuming another brother would be duly delivered to the Elkerton rugby league team that I'd constructed in my weird imagination. The disappointment passed the second I set eyes on her. Actually, we were all thrilled to have a girl to dote on – especially Mum.

How is it that the baby of the family would prove so often to be the most sensible, reliable, dependable and wisest of us all? I admit that David and I haven't set the bar particularly high over the years, but Bernadette would be a champion source of constancy in families a lot less radical than the Elkertons, that's for sure.

At least Mum didn't have to grind her rosary beads to a pulp over *all* of her children. And I had one more Rock of Gibraltar who'd love me and care for me unconditionally … whether I deserved it or not. Love you, sis.

SCHOOL

Part of Mum's plans to civilise me included an attempt to augment our totally failed efforts at on-board remote schooling, by depositing me in a land-based classroom with four walls.

Mum insisted that she dropped me off at the primary school every day when we were in Karumba. It either didn't happen with anywhere near that regularity or I pissed off the second she was out of sight, because I have no memories of sitting in classes at Karumba. I remember what the school *looked* like though. From the outside.

I don't doubt that Mum tried real hard, but the fact remains that I didn't do too much school of any type up until 1973. That was the year Joan's foot was put *all* the way down about the stalled career of Gary Keith Elkerton, scholar extraordinaire. Despite Bull's scepticism, I was enrolled to start year four at a venerable old school in Queensland as a full boarder. Because I can't be bothered dealing with the inevitable legal shit fight that would accompany what I'm about to tell you, I won't name the place.

Poor Mum. She probably had visions of me turning into an academically gifted young gentleman and a prefect steeped in the traditions of the old school tie. This hellhole had traditions alright, but most of them were far from what well-intentioned parents would have expected.

I quietly cried my eyes out the first night after I was dropped off at school. The truth was that, as tough a little cookie as I was, I'd never spent a night out of earshot of Mum, Dad or my relatives. Strange to think, but the eerie silence of the dormitory at night unsettled me badly, so accustomed was I to the noise of the sea lulling me to sleep.

It doesn't take a genius to figure out that a kid who'd never even lived in a house would have adjustment problems being dropped into the highly regimented, draconian hierarchy of rules, regulations and conventions presented by a boarding school. Being stuck indoors with schedules, routines, uniforms, shoes, and seemingly hundreds of people angrily telling me what to do was a deep shock to my free spirit. It made me miserable. But the shock of having my freedom squashed was nothing compared to the stuff that terrified me.

For a start, there wasn't one scintilla of human empathy or kindness in the place or in any of its people. The adults and teachers were like robots. The older kids were just plain vicious. Little kids like me were beaten up for food, for pocket money and for the few personal treasures we were allowed. Mostly we were just beaten up for fun, because the older boarders *could* beat us up. Just like they were beaten up when they were the younger boarders. Some tradition.

I was bigger than the other kids my age, I fought back and I was new. Therefore I was targeted for special hidings from the word go. The teachers did nothing. Most of them were sadistic dickheads anyway, who clearly enjoyed the brutality and caned kids for minor transgressions whenever they could. I boisterously resisted being humiliated by the older boys and teachers alike in the daylight hours, which probably saved me from far worse at night.

I was aware that older boys would sneak around the younger boys' beds after lights out. This would leave the little kids sobbing and blubbering bitterly. Not knowing any better, I assumed it was just a case of more beatings and theft. Sometimes I'd hear the housemaster pad quietly around and murmur soothingly to this kid or that.

I'd lie awake – scared to death – waiting for my turn. Anticipating one of these night visits is the worst fear I've ever experienced, far worse than anything the ocean's ever sent my way. Every night I'd wish with all my might that they'd just get it over and done with so I wouldn't have to deal with the terrible waiting. And the terrible listening. Even now, I'm often woken in the dead of night by the same awful dread I felt as a little boy in that dorm.

The only ray of light in that forsaken place was that I got to play rugby league. I loved my footy boots. They were my one treasured personal possession, the only things that made me feel like a real person rather than like livestock. As silly as it seems, I took them into bed with me every night, because having my boots held tight gave me some small comfort and a tiny feeling of protection.

A boy I'd befriended was one of the victims and he eventually told me what happened at night. It wasn't a beating or theft as I'd thought. He'd been forced to masturbate and fellate his tormentors. Such perversities had never occurred to me. Why would anyone want to put their willy in your mouth? It didn't compute.

'They like it when the spoof comes out,' said the kid, who I'll call Sam.

I had no idea what he was talking about but I was paralysed by the idea that it would only be a matter of time before these unthinkable things happened to me. The intensity of my night horrors deepened.

When Sam eventually risked the promised repercussions by telling the housemaster, nothing happened. One night afterwards, he saw the same housemaster watching from a doorway as oral sex was again being forced on him by a senior kid. Sam told me it could be much worse, as he hadn't been 'bum-jacked' yet. Another torture I didn't understand and that I didn't *want* to understand.

The terror of the showers wasn't much better than the dorms at night. Standard nastiness about people's small penises or lack of pubes was one thing, but getting beaten up in the nude by nude older kids was plain sick. That the teachers overlooked it was even sicker, I reckon.

The last straw of my bleak few terms at this school came when Sam – the very kid who had poured his heart out to me about being assaulted and my one decent friend in the whole joint – asked if he could touch my dick when we were showering beside each other.

Well, at least he had the good manners to fucking ask, I suppose.

The next morning, I rang Bull – who was ashore in Karumba – and desperately begged him to come and get me.

I'd never gone into great detail with Dad about what was making me so miserable because I didn't want to talk about such embarrassing stuff. But he seemed to know that I wasn't just whining about the rigours of school discipline. He sensed that I *needed* to get the fuck out of there, so he said, 'Righto, son,' and left by light plane immediately. I was back in the Gulf within a few days.

Dad coming to get me literally felt like a rescue. I really felt as though I'd cheated death – if not physical death, then the death of who I was. The stress of feeling endangered every minute of every day in that school had just about caused me to give up, lose hope and let go of the idea of ever getting back to my normal life again. I felt like I was going crazy.

Bull was a bit taken aback when I hugged him. But the craggy bastard hugged me back just as hard. Turns out that Bull missed me, the big sook. I've never spoken to him about what went on at that school, but I reckon he had a fair idea that it was no place for his wild little deckhand.

Joan was probably disappointed that I didn't settle into life at such a prestigious institution, but my happiness superseded those concerns. Being such a loving mum, she never made me feel bad for failing to cope there, even though I never fully explained the horror of the place.

For the time being at least, I was back to non-attendance at Karumba Primary and very, very rare multiplication tables on the trawler. I'd had a gutful of school, that's for sure.

I NEED TO DO THAT

Once David and Bern came along, we spent less time up north and more time in northern New South Wales. When not at Karumba, Dad stayed put, trawling out of river ports that weren't protected by the Great Barrier Reef. This meant that we had longer periods staying in caravan parks which were usually positioned right nearby breaking waves. Surf breaks.

I'd seen decent waves before around my relatives' homes at Byron Bay, Ballina and Evans Head, but I was a bit young to imagine myself actually surfing, like I'd seen a few blokes doing. There weren't many little kids giving it a go in those places during my earliest years.

My perceptions changed one day not long after we'd taken up residence in the caravan park at Kingscliff, a beautiful seaside village just south of the Queensland border. Dad was working the nearby Tweed River and our caravan was only twenty metres from the high-tide mark.

Danny Watson was a kid who lived in the van next door. We'd only just settled in when I saw him walk past with a surfboard under his arm. I thought he was a bit bloody small to have one of those. My curiosity got the better of me and I followed close behind as he walked over the dune.

The next few minutes absolutely electrified me. I can access that exact feeling right now. It proved to be an emotion that would visit me almost every day from then to now. I can measure the progress of my whole life by the times when I've felt just as I did when I was that nine-year-old crossing the dune at Kingscliff.

Like the first time I rounded Pacific Parade at Kirra and saw its spitting sand barrels. The first time the curve of Oahu's Kamehameha Highway exposed the awesome sight of the North Pacific unloading its fury on reef after reef into the distance, as I drove through the Hawaiian island's fragrant pineapple fields. The first time the isolated, untouched perfection of Moreton Island's North Point came into focus from the deck of the trawler. The first time I explored my new home in southern France to see Guéthary breaking at fifteen feet beneath the cliffs of an ancient Côte Basque village. The first time I saw Grajagan. The time I walked to the water's edge with my daughter, Lunna, as we shared her very first surf.

The feeling I was awakened to after I followed Danny over the dune at Kingscliff was one that everyone who has ever surfed knows well: *intense anticipation followed by a supreme sense of discovery*. What will the waves be like today? I can't wait to find out and get wet!

When the weight of life's various responsibilities threatens to crush you, nothing is as uplifting as getting the 'feeling' back.

And that feeling coursed through me like a physical force when I saw Danny paddle out into perfect, gentle little beach breaks at Kingscliff to share waves with a handful of older locals. They took turns riding two-foot peelers to the beach, like an exclusive club. The hooting could be heard from the beach. And they were going so fast. I liked fast.

The whole scene caused me to look at waves differently. Before, waves had been things to negotiate, to burst through, to cope with, to survive. Almost to oppose, I guess. I now beheld the surf as some kind of inexhaustible playground. And the waves just kept on coming, each one different to the last, one after another after another. Wow!

I've made a lot of shitful decisions in my life. But right there and then, I made the best one ever.

'I need to do that.'

TRIPPY TINTS AND BLOODY SOULS

Danny lent me his board after a few days of pestering. To his surprise – but not mine – I paddled straight out the back at Kingscliff, stroked onto a fair size wave, got to my feet and rode it to the beach. I know it sounds unlikely, but that's exactly how my first wave happened. Having grown up at sea on the pitching deck of a boat, it never occurred to me that I *should* have any trouble surfing.

I'd never even seen anyone 'learning' to surf before I tried it, I'd only seen people who could already do it. Because I'd never given a thought to 'learning', I just skipped the process altogether.

Mum was assailed with continual, round-the-clock requests for a board from that afternoon onward.

'Ask your father when he gets home.'

Dad was at sea. I counted the seconds until he wobbled into the caravan annex a few days later, sozzled – as usual – after celebrating a good catch at the pub. Asking Dad for something when he was drunk was a high-risk/high-return exercise. Usually he was chock-full of love when he was chock-full of grog. Sometimes, though, he cut up a bit cranky. I threw caution to the wind.

'Christ, a man hasn't even got his boots off yet, son!' he laughed, giving me a playful headlock and hair rub combination. 'Sounds bloody fantastic! A surfer, hey? Ha ha – Joany, ya eldest is a fucken hippy, darlin'!'

Mum gave the Bull a severe dressing-down for using extreme profanity and blaspheming within five seconds of arriving home, but her knowing shake of the head indicated that she was mighty glad to see the big guy home safely. Dad's arrival after a session at the pub wasn't always as serenely received.

My gamble worked beautifully. Bull presented me with my very own fibreglass surfboard within a few days. One of his trawling mates knew a bloke who knew a bloke who could get one.

What a sight it was. No wonder Bull thought of surfers as hippies. This stumpy thing had a high-gloss purple-tint finish with a kaleidoscope of coloured resins smeared through the glass. Not that I knew it at the time, but my first board was perfect confirmation of my now long-held belief that breakfasting on hallucinogenic drugs is an entry criterion for the Surfboard Laminators Union. Trippy.

School-less days on end were spent getting cooked in the sun from early morning until twilight, riding what seemed to be a million waves. I'd sneak straight back home after Mum walked me to Kingscliff Primary School, slide the board out from under the caravan and off I'd go. Very fashionably attired in my grey school Stubbies for board shorts, I might add.

For the first time, I felt sad when we eventually had to leave for the waveless northern tropics and the Gulf prawning season. Of course, my motocross bike soon soothed my yearning for surfing. But it never *quite* made up for it.

During one stint down south at the Evans Head caravan park, my relationship with the 'purple flying machine' came to a halt, fickle mongrel that I am. Yes, another surfboard came into my life.

It was here that I formed one of my first lifelong friendships, with the son of one of Dad's fishing mates. Kevin Aleckson was my age and shared my complete obsession with surfing. We surfed from first light until hunger drove us ashore. A banana or two was gulped down at light speed, then back out in the water until nightfall.

Kev and I split the cost of buying *Tracks* magazine every month. We argued over who'd get ownership of which pictures once we'd finished reading it aloud to each other. Then we'd carefully cut the photographs out so we could sticky tape them onto our bedroom walls. For me, this meant a wallpaper of black and white surfing shots plastered onto the faux-wood veneer of the alcove in my cramped caravan bunk. Michael Peterson's cutback, Peter Drouyn's soul arch bottom turn and a kid called 'Rabbit' getting tubed at Kirra were the last things I saw before crashing off to sleep every night.

Kev's older brothers were like gods to me; they'd just returned from Hawaii – the North Shore of Oahu. Like everyone, I'd seen the photos and read the stories. To my mind, going all the way to Hawaii from little old Evans Head – and, what's more, returning alive – was at least as brave and adventurous as returning from a moon landing. People got killed 'all the time' in Hawaii. Cooool!

The Aleckson boys also explained that the traditional Hawaiian method of measuring a wave's size was the height of its *back*, not its *face*. The back of a wave is normally about half to a third of the height of its face, so there was something coolly understated about the quirky surfing custom of calling a wave as high as our caravan 'four feet'.

Just being within a couple of metres of the Aleckson lads gave me a sense of reflected glory. I felt like a matador just to *know* blokes who rode Pipeline, Sunset Beach and Waimea Bay. Of course, my heroes couldn't have treated us little grommets with more disdain. When we weren't ordered to retrieve something for them (wax, food, cigarettes, beer, etcetera), we were sent packing from their esteemed company with a clip around the ear and a 'Piss off, ya little bastards!'. It was fantastic to get this kind of attention though.

All of the Alecksons, including my mate Kev, rode sleek, pointy modern-looking boards. Real spear-like and futuristic-looking, they were made by Soul Surfboards of Ballina. Let me tell you, my purple pride and joy turned into an intolerable piece of pure shit overnight.

I can't even remember what happened to my first board. What a pity. From my late teens, I became reluctant to part with my favourites, and to this day I have a personal museum of surfboards accumulated throughout my career, all lovingly maintained. Which is why I still feel a bit guilty about how quickly I replaced Ol' Purple with a spanking new orange-railed diamond-tailed Soul.

The Soul copped an even heavier workload than Ol' Purple

with constant, marathon surfing sessions. In the days before leg-ropes, a wipeout always resulted in a long swim, and was often punished by damage to the board on rocks, other boards, people's heads. Even young kids like Kev and me had to become expert (or so we thought) ding repairers. At some stage on most weekends, the annex of our caravan was stunk out by toxic repair laminates and epoxies. We became so cocky about ding repairing that a truly stupid and ultimately painful project was undertaken after I'd had the Soul for a year or so.

Kev's oldest brother had bought himself a Soul swallowtail. Priding myself on an extensive pre-teen design knowledge, I informed him that his surfing would now certainly be 'looser, but with no less drive', thanks to changing from a pintail. Rather than receiving heartfelt gratitude for this astute observation, I was instead gifted with an agonising 'nipple gripple' and sent on my way amid uproarious laughter. The nipple pain quickly faded, but the appeal of the sleek swallowtail did not. Kev and I resolved to reshape the tail of my board asap.

We got a hacksaw, a school compass spiked thing that you drew circles with, and our trusty repair kit. A few hours later we furiously hand-sanded our masterpiece with old bits of sandpaper we'd found in Dad's toolkit. Ta-daaa! An original Soul-Elkerton-Aleckson swallowtail was born. It didn't look like a bought one but although the older blokes thought it was hilarious, Kev and I were bloody proud of our handiwork. Geez it was dangerously razor sharp where we'd sanded it back. I thought that made it even faster, so what was actually a disaster waiting to happen was a super-clever design attribute, according to Kev and me.

The inevitable transpired one day when Kev and I walked over five kilometres into a nearby national park to surf a 'secret' point break. Naturally, bad childhood accidents can't occur right next door to a hospital, or even at the very least somewhere handy to Mum.

The tail of my reshaped Soul speared deep into my thigh like the giant carving knife that it was. I exited the water bleeding profusely. Blood was pumping in spurts from the wound and I quickly lapsed into shock. Luckily, there were older blokes nearby who torniqueted my leg then helped Kev drag me all the way back to Evans. They got me to first aid before I was transferred up to Ballina hospital. Kev reckons I cried and screamed the whole way back. I vehemently dispute this. Regardless of who the bullshitter is (note: not me), we agree that I could quite well have bled to death without the quick thinking, strength and endurance of my friends.

The orange-railed Soul was thrown up into the scrub in the national park. I was not to retrieve it for weeks – until well after my leg had healed. Its tail was duly blunted down and I continued to ride it until it too lost its appeal to a sleek new design.

Occasionally, when I catch sight of the old scar on my thigh, I become sentimental about my first two boards and those innocent yet oh-so-important early years in which surfing dramatically gripped my life, never to let go.

SETTING ANCHOR

The year 1976 was a massively important one in the history of surfing. In that year the International Professional Surfers organisation was formed by Hawaii's Fred Hemmings, facilitating the first fully coordinated twelve-stop World Tour. The competition boasted a calibrated points system (lifted from Formula One!) and culminated in the crowning of the first professional World Champion. That first winner was the Gold Coast's Peter Townend, one of the 'wallpaper' surfers from my caravan. Today's Association of Surfing Professionals World Tour still operates on a largely unchanged basis.

Months later, one of my other heroes and a bloke who would become one of my very closest mentors and friends – Wayne 'Rabbit' Bartholomew – wrote a magazine article announcing that an emerging crew of Aussies and South Africans were the new young kings of surfing, leaving the traditional power structures of the Hawaiians and Californians in their wake. The unholy shit-storm this article unleashed turned what was already a challenging – and at times very dangerous – sport into a full-on gladiatorial battlefield.

This competitive cauldron awaited me. However, in '76, all I knew was that surfing got more fun the more I did it, and that every time I opened a *Tracks* magazine something new and radical was buzzing out of the pages. It was really exciting. Even though I was less than a total nobody, I felt part of something special.

Maybe it was portentous that a year of upheaval and change in surfing coincided with a year of upheaval and change for the Elkertons.

I was eavesdropping one night when Mum made a series of rather heavy suggestions to Bull. At eleven years old, I needed schooling in one spot. My inveterate truancy was a shocking example to David as he got older. Besides, it was best that we stay near larger communities in case David needed emergency care. All the dangerous river bar crossings in all the various ports we visited meant that our luck would run out sooner or later.

We were dropping anchor. It was perfect timing, because I was starting to wish that we'd never leave surf breaks again. The big question was, where would that be?

I threw in my two cents worth about settling near the Tweed River, picturing myself sharing Kirra's heaving barrels with my heroes on the bunk wall. Of course, I may as well have been talking *to* the bunk wall for all the effect my selfless suggestions had. Nope, Mum and Dad settled on Mooloolaba and it's safe, north-facing passages to open ocean. I knew nothing about Queensland's Sunshine Coast, other than having seen it go by from the deck of the trawler. I visited the Big Pineapple once with my cousins, then spewed up a lovely fresh cream, mango and deep-fried kabana combination all over the backseat of Dad's new Ford Falcon. Other than that, nothing.

Bull promised me that there were waves on the Sunshine Coast, but I was sceptical because no famous surfer ever said that he'd come from there in *Tracks*. According to Bull, there were waves at the top end of the Sunny Coast that peeled off for as far as he could see from the boat deck. Based on my 'long' experience, I knew for sure that he was trying to butter me up with bullshit.

ENTER THE BEAST

Mum chose the location of our new home base with more than a smidgen of evil genius. The pretty little thirty-site caravan park was a few metres from a secluded cove into which perfect peelers rolled almost to our doorstep. Yes, that was great. But the first day I saw it is tattooed in my brain because it marked the first occasion that I deployed the f-bomb in my mother's company.

You see, straight after I charged excitedly from the car and jumped down onto the sand to admire our stupendous access to a crowd-free private wave, Mum took me on a tour of the immediate neighbourhood. An immediate neighbourhood which featured the front gate of the local primary school about a hundred metres from our caravan, in direct line of sight.

'FUCK!'

I didn't mean to say it out loud. It just burst out spontaneously.

What Mum had given me by way of our new home and its impossibly perfect proximity to endless waves was instantly taken from me by way of our new home and its impossibly shitful proximity to compulsory education.

Our caravan stood exactly between heaven and hell. The irony was 'exquisite', as my classier French mates would say.

Before I even had time to consider what I'd just said, let alone calculate the savage new complexities attached to wagging school, Mum was unleashing an impressive combination of slaps to my thighs and ears.

'Gary Keith Elkerton, how dare you use that word to me! How DARE you!'

Naturally, Bull was also in the crosshairs for 'teaching' me foul language. To prove his complete innocence of the charge, he dutifully took over the slapping for a few minutes before he had to stop for a smoke break.

Dad and I sat there in silence looking out the beach while Mum was inside. He smoked and I fought back tears. It was an emotional day.

'You alright, mate?' asked the Bull.

'Yeah, Dad.'

'It's a big day for everyone, son.'

'Yeah, I know.'

More silence and smoking.

'You think you're gonna like it here, mate?' Bull directed the question to me, but I reckon he was asking himself.

'Yeah, Dad.'

'Good. Me too.' He sounded more hopeful than conclusive. 'Gary, don't use that fucken foul mouth of yours to your Mum, ya funny little bastard. Alright, mate?'

'Okay, Dad. Sorry.'

With that, he stubbed out his Benson & Hedges, flashed me a crooked grin and rubbed my head as he always did.

'Why don't you get out there for a surf, hey? Mum will be okay.'

'Yeah, Dad.'

So while Mum contemplated the idea that her oldest boy was nearly a teen, while Bull sat in his camp chair and contemplated the concept of a 'home', and while David pushed around his newest Matchbox car in the sand, I paddled out for my first surf at a break which would in time be known forever as Kong's Cove.

It was a big day alright. A bloody big day.

Later that week, Dad bought a new board to replace my battered Soul. I reckon that was his version of giving me a big girly hug. It was another orange-railed board, but this one was a very, very early channel bottom by Jim Pollard. The 'corrugated iron' shaped hull helped take my surfing to the next level and I give its unique characteristics no small credit for developing the lines I like to draw with my surfing. I've been a channel bottom aficionado ever since.

As she always did, Mum forgave me quickly. And, as I always did, scheming escape routes from Mooloolaba Primary commenced just as quickly. However, Mum was simply too good for me. There was no way I was going to walk out of the front gate at school, grab my board and surf when she could plainly see the school, my surfboard and the waves from her position in the van. Napoleon had nothing on Mum – it was strategic perfection. Surrender was a foregone conclusion.

In any case, having been comprehensively outsmarted by Mum, I found myself actually liking this school. Well, that's a bit strong – 'not hating' this school might be closer to the mark. Year Seven – the last year before high school in Queensland – would be the first and last time that I had an acceptable attendance record. This didn't reflect some sort of miraculous transformation of scholastic character, but it indicated that the kid who grew up in dozens of different towns and was raised on a boat deck had now finally been 'socialised'. Somewhat.

It took about a week for me to gravitate to the resident twelve-year-old surfers in the school. After the usual suspicion and discomfort of the first few days, my total lack of interest in learning and my casual disregard of authority stamped me as acceptable to the right people. After I'd mentioned that I surfed, the bonding process began in earnest. It helped no end that I personally knew people who'd ridden Sunset Beach in Hawaii.

The names Brett Jewry, Barney Smally, Mick Folker, Robert Mackie, Mark Pripic, Reid Pinder and my best mate, Alex Gray, would feature in my life for many years beyond my Year Seven school photo. What a gang of hyper-grommet surf rats we made! Here was a bunch of blokes who breathed, slept, ate and *lived* surfing, just like I did. We spoke of nothing else. Though he was a bit less fanatical about surfing in the early days, Peter Sutherland was also a close friend with whom I'd share the breakneck decade ahead.

Girls were a long way off as an item of serious interest, although they were annoyingly interested in us. One such person had as much effect on me as anyone has ever had; so it's odd that I cannot remember the name of the girl who changed my life so profoundly.

I was exceptionally large as a twelve-year-old. Not that I cared, but it was a matter of considerable jealousy amongst my new mates that I sported an imposing crop of hair in my armpits. And in all of the other appropriate places. It must be noted that the curse of the early developer means that this initial crop also often seeds itself in *inappropriate* locations well before it should, but that was a problem for later in life. Just ask my mate, Martin Potter.

Suffice to say that I was both uncommonly large and uncommonly hairy for a student of Mooloolaba Primary at the time. One day, a group of giggling girls approached us surfers at lunchtime.

'Hey, King Kong, show us your hairy balls!' shouted the girl whose name escapes me. I do remember that she had the kind of dental braces that had elastic bands between the top and bottom teeth. She also had black hair and always wore long socks. That's all I've got.

We were pretty shocked, but coolly displayed no surprise at the highly confronting sexual sort of taunt. The chicks were driven off with a torrent of verbal abuse.

Of course, all of the fellas looked at me for a response, being the pubeless whippets they were. Was that a *good* thing she just said, or a *bad* thing? Who knew? Whatever it was, it was definitely *fucking* funny to everyone but me. As soon as the girls were out of earshot, the boys fell around laughing.

As is so often the case with nicknames, it's the one you hate that sticks like a fresh turd to a woolly blanket. For a week or two my mates would continually ask for 'King Kong' to present his fuzzy nuts for inspection. I didn't oblige but I stopped being pissed off after a while and started laughing along.

Eventually the whole testicle thing faded out, as did the 'King'. In fact, so did the name 'Gary', which virtually ceased being used by almost everyone except Mum. Unbelievable. But my old mate 'Kong' has never, *ever* left me. Oh no ... he proved to be a very, very persistent bastard indeed.

I hope the girl who was my year seven classmate at Mooloolaba Primary reads this. Whoever you are, you've got a lot to answer for! Should I thank you, or curse you?

THE CLUB

As fate would have it, Mum's great victory in marshalling her wayward son into a school routine was also a victory for me. Every morning, when the very first crack of light partially illuminated the eastern horizon, I grabbed my board and surfed our little cove. It didn't matter what the waves or the weather were like, from first light until Mum waved me in at 8.30 am I was all over every moving ripple. No-one else surfed there, because you couldn't park a car in front of it and it couldn't be seen very well from anywhere but our caravan park.

Also, in all honesty, the cove wasn't anything compared to nearby waves, either. All of my mates surfed the superior beach breaks a short walk further south, in the main part of Mooloolaba. The really good older local guys surfed Alexandra Headland, which was not the place to go for little grommets in that era. There were very strict pecking orders in those days.

Nonetheless, the cove was my front yard and I loved it. Mum could keep an eye on me and would make sure – with considerable effort – that I was fed and shepherded to school on time. It worked for everyone.

Not that I admitted it but I actually couldn't wait to get to school so I could hear (and tell) traditional grommet bullshit tall tales of massive imagined tubes and deadly imagined wipeouts. I guess the guys thought I was a bit weird for enjoying my morning surfs by myself but, thanks to my many years at sea and my solo adventures as a little kid, I didn't think of them as unusual. If anything, the couple of years spent surfing the cove alone each morning probably helped shape the peculiar style which has served me so well. I was never consciously or unconsciously trying to emulate anyone. It was all instinct.

I love surfing with friends but I also treasure being alone with the ocean, then and now. After school was different.

While other kids went home to watch re-runs of *Happy Days* and do homework, Alex, Brett, Barney, Reid, Mick, Robert, Mark and I would sprint home for our surfboards and then charge the Mooloolaba beach breaks until dark. Every lifelong surfer remembers the feeling of sharing the wonder with their grommet gang. Unstoppable.

As adults, we do our best to recapture the magic, don't we? We get close but there's really nothing like it. Pure fun and raw camaraderie, totally untouched by the various pollutants of life which find every one of us sooner or later, once the teen years come.

One of the biggest influences my mates had on me was that they were cadet members of the North Shore Boardriders, so named for being the north coast relative to Brisbane and not in small part to honour the stature of Hawaii's famous wave mecca. It's a surfing club steeped in the tribal traditions and white-hot rivalries of Australia's legendary amateur competitive surfing culture.

The boys regarded me as a 'real good' surfer. Until then I'd never even thought about being good, let alone 'real' good. Of course, I knew that competitions existed, because my heroes on the wall beside my bunk had won a heap of them, though I didn't equate the whole competing thing to what I did every day. It never occurred to me that I would ever have anything to do with it. I'd grown up with the ocean as familiar to me as land, so surfing was a natural extension of daily life rather than a sport. Rugby league. Now *there's* a sport.

My mates enlightened me.

'Come down to our contests, Kong. We get to hang around all day with Jodie and Brett. Plus we get to eat at the barbie and drink everyone's dregs!' said Barney.

Little did I know that the irresistible allure of free burnt sausages and the drinking of putrid remnants from the bottom of used beer cans would be the genesis of my professional surfing career. How very fucking apt.

So every second Saturday I'd ride my crappy old pushbike around to Alex's place at Alexandra Headland where we'd wait for Jodie Perry to come and pick us up in his crappy old VW Type 3 station wagon. Along with Brett Peacock, Jodie was the best surfer in the club. These guys were the kings of the local area and it was awesome to have them take us little grommets under their wing.

Jodie and Brett were only in their late teens themselves and hardly qualified as 'mentors', but they were wise old men to the cadets of the North Shore Boardriders. If professional surfing in those formative years had the depth to support more than a handful of elites, I've no doubt that both Jodie and Brett would've been highly ranked pros who enjoyed long careers. As it was, they were a force to be reckoned with as amateurs and damn near impossible to beat in local club contests.

For us grommets, the club contests were fantastic fun. Actually, we'd probably have been satisfied with the traditional North Shore death race to the nominated contest beach. Jammed solidly into the cargo area of Jodie's Type 3, he drove from beach to beach like a fucking lunatic against a dozen other fucking lunatics from the club in equally overloaded jalopies. It was a lethal, rust-bucket demolition derby every time. What complete fucking imbeciles we were! Brainless but gut-bustingly funny all the same.

Basically, for us young ones club contests were our gang of mates all up against each other. We didn't know anything about tactics or techniques, we just got as many waves as possible and surfed as hard as we could. It was a great laugh and I can't remember anyone being too upset about who won – that was a couple of years away.

Back then, it was just as Barney had described it. Once we grommets had finished our heats we spent all day watching the older guys battle it out and did the million and one errands expected of those at the bottom of the pecking order. We got to see judging in action and we were able to admire all the fabulous boards being ridden by the best surfers: Haydens, Cowleys, Pascoe Hoppers. We were forever being clipped and earbashed for picking them up.

As an added bonus, there were flocks of older girls around wearing tiny crocheted bikinis.

The best part was hanging around with the club veterans at the end of day, listening to their expletive-filled yarns and conversations. And yes, we really did eat the blackened barbecued sausages that no-one else wanted and we actually did drink the froth out of discarded beer cans. The best meal we could imagine! Shared under the protection and sharp good humour of the North Shore brotherhood.

We kids may have been all but inconsequential, cursed for 'getting in the way', randomly spear-tackled for amusement, and used as gofers, but we were *in*. Brothers one and all.

It was the first time I'd experienced a sense of belonging to something much bigger than myself – of respecting an institution and a tradition. I'm sure this is what Mum expected I'd learn in that awful bloody boarding school.

THE END OF THE BEGINNING

My primary school years (or, to be more accurate, 'year') gave way to my teens in a blaze of changes. First and foremost was that I had to walk to the bus stop to get to Maroochydore High.

Most kids don't have to catch their school bus from right in front of the empty midweek waves of Alexandra Headland. It was recipe for a schooling catastrophe and a surfing bonanza.

Brett, Barney, Mick, Robert, Alex, Mark, Pete and I went through the motions of walking over the hill at Alexandra Headland in the general direction of the school bus stop every morning. I might add that we were also responsible enough to get on the bus ... when there were no surfable waves. Of course, it is a well-known fact that a thirteen-year-old interprets any moving lump of water in the ocean as surfable.

It goes without saying that the years 1977 and 1978 did not unfold as red-letter years in the development of Kong the mathematician, historian, geographer or scientist. Not that I lagged behind my immediate peer group in these disciplines, let me tell you. Still, our intellects were constantly tested. Every day presented a series of mental challenges.

Could we sprint across the road – exposed to the whole neighbourhood – and enter the surf without being busted by passing parents or teachers? Was it possible to exit the beach after a long morning session and sneak into afternoon classes undetected? Did we have the stamina to surf continually for a whole school day? How many consecutive days of non-attendance would break the record? What did it take to keep our parents from communicating with teachers and with each other?

The challenge of overcoming these obstacles added to the fun and the feeling of danger. Each day was a major surfing mission.

There was a flat grassed area where the beach met the headland that we dreamt of using as a hangout. All the older surfers used to congregate there, but we were roughly ejected every time we tried to enter. 'The Corner' remains a famous feature of local folklore. We'd get our chance to take up residence soon enough but, in our early teen grommet-hood, we could only envy our elders and their special outdoor 'clubhouse'. They were loud and they were always smoking what we assumed were cigarettes.

Even though the older blokes didn't want us at The Corner, out in the water we often heard them yelling for us to take waves. Our little group had become famous as fixtures in the 'Alex' line-up – the 'crazy little bastards'.

We built our own perfect hide-out high, high up on the headland, overlooking the line-up. It was a really exciting project. We scaled a steep north-facing section of the bluff and carved out a cave of vegetation in the thick lantana underbrush. It couldn't be seen from the street, the car park, the beach or anywhere other than the surf. Only a kid or a mountain goat would go to the bother of climbing to it. We furnished it with teenage essentials like big-tit magazines and smokes stolen from our oldies. 'The Den' was the first of several 'homes away from home' we enjoyed throughout our teens.

This period represented the high-water mark in my life of daily hours spent surfing. Considering that I'd go on to do it for a living, that amounts to a *lot* of surfing.

Imperceptibly to us, we started getting very, very good at this thing that consumed us so completely. The boys and I revved each other up to take ever more radical drops, to do ever more radical manoeuvres and to emulate what we saw our heroes at the club and in the magazines do. Through our sheer constant presence, we started working our way into the upper echelons of the Alexandra Headland pecking order. The blokes on The Corner began giving us a scrap of respect.

Older surfers, who were perhaps not quite so good, began giving way to us. Tourists and weekenders barely stood a chance on Saturdays and Sundays. Our annoying, buzzing little pack knew every nuance of every section of the line-up so well that we swarmed over every decent wave that wasn't occupied by our respected elders. And still we got better and better, and our love of surfing got stronger and stronger.

Nearly every Saturday night, surf movies played in the old cinema at Caloundra. We'd bum a ride the ten kilometres south and then sneak in the exit door to watch classics like *Tubular Swells* and *Free Ride*. In those days, people actually screamed and cheered for every wave on the big screen!

This time also heralded the commencement of real competitive spirit between us, both in club contests and in our free surfing. I became dead set on getting the best waves and ripping the hardest. Barney and Mick were the best amongst the group, but the rest of us were determined to push them and each other to our limits. Every mistake was jeered in black good humour. It may have been in fun, but fucking up or being called gutless for pulling back on a big wave still cut deep. It was best to take every kamikaze drop and make sure you never fell in front of anyone. Simple.

I became known as the 'mad' one – the kid who'd charge any wave, any size. Truthfully, it wasn't something I set out to do but more a function of my upbringing. There just wasn't anything that happened in the surf that frightened me at that stage. Growing up on the boat exposed me to such a variety of seriously violent ocean conditions that I didn't yet fear what was thrown at me on a surfboard. Respect, yes. Fear, no.

Concepts of 'bravado' or 'guts' didn't enter my mind. They still don't. I surf what's in front of me. If people admire that, then great, but it's not an accolade I put much personal store in. I'd be bullshitting to say that I've pushed myself through some mythical fear barrier thanks to the sheer force of my giant figs and mental toughness. I'll leave that crap to surf industry marketers. To me, surfing big waves has always been a completely natural feeling, right from grommet-hood.

By the start of 1978, aged thirteen, Brett, Barney, Mick, Robert, Alex and I were competing in club contests in both cadets (which was our age group) and juniors (which was up to eighteen- and nineteen-year-olds), and we were doing really well. We each had our successes and it was a matter of considerable pride to beat older guys on a regular basis. To add to our cockiness, there was also the novelty of younger grommets appearing on the scene who we could boss around and tell to 'fuck off' when we saw fit. We were really getting somewhere! Eventually, we were even allowed to hang out at The Corner, so long as the older blokes weren't there. It was a classic rite of passage.

I distinctly remember one crystal-clear winter evening, sitting up in The Den with Brett, Reid and Alex watching the sun set over the hinterland. A rare few moments of silence fell between us and I remember thinking, 'This is my future, this is how I'm going to live.' I didn't have a clue about what constituted surfing as a career, but I was damn sure that I wasn't going to do anything with my life that would separate me from what I loved. As irresponsible as the resolution was, it was probably the first genuinely adult thought I ever had.

I actually sensed childhood ending right then and there.

THE SEAWEED

Not long after I started high school, Mum and Bull bought our first house. I use 'house' rather than 'home' because we'd always had a home, be it the caravan or the trawler. A house, immobile and conformist, was a very big deal for our little tribe of seafaring gypsies.

Naturally, Mum was very excited and busied herself buying lots of stuff to fill the spacious two-storey brick house at 22 Tombarra Street, Alexandra Headland. It was a massively wonderful pleasure for a woman who'd spent her adulthood living in superb locations, but with few beautiful luxuries and decorative knick-knacks. Dad was happy for Mum, but I'm pretty sure he surveyed the lawns, gardens and backyard pool as a maintenance issue rather than a suburban sanctuary. It was maintenance work he would ruthlessly subcontract to his two extremely unwilling sons.

We kids each had a room, which was a bit of a freak-out. None of us had ever known much privacy, so it was a major upheaval to have a bit of personal space. I'd never have admitted so at the time, but it was slightly lonely not to have David and

Bernadette sleeping nearby. Bern had her totally pink, fluffy, doll-filled room, and David's Matchbox-car garage was the next room to mine. All my favourite surfers from the wall of my bunk followed me to Tombarra Street and were joined by hundreds of others, now that I had so much wall space.

You'd think I'd have been stoked to move into a big house, with my own room and a pool, but I took some time to settle in. Although Tombarra Street was less than a kilometre from the beach at the Headland, I felt like a 'westie'. After being a few metres from my own wave at Kong's Cove for so long, our new location seemed like the fucking outback. I missed the cove desperately and continued to ride my pushbike there for the dawn surf for a good while after our move.

In time, I came to appreciate the benefits of my new address. For a start, I was now way closer to where most of my mates lived. The Grays lived just up the block. Secondly, there were several acres of bushland behind the house, with a fantastic freshwater swimming billabong called 'The Blue Lagoon' in the middle. Perfect for getting up to mischief and for motocross on my thumping Yamaha IT 175. Above all else, I had to walk straight past the front door of the local surf shop to get to the beach or the bus stop.

Perched on Alexandra Parade overlooking the beach, Headland Surf became our unofficial headquarters, much to the stress of its owner. John 'Seaweed' Tragere was my first real mentor, a sort of uncle figure. His tolerance of half a dozen grommets invading his business and personal space every day was all but superhuman.

We surely must have been a huge pain in the arse, using his backyard to hide out during school days, storing our boards under the shop, constantly stealing wax and helping ourselves to the contents of his fridge. We'd smear our grubby hands all over his shiny new surfboards and use his inflatable surf mats as lounge chairs while we read his massive collection of *Tracks* magazines again and again. The showroom was polluted by our daily 'World Fart Championships', which were modelled upon professional wrestling with a 'stench pin-down' as the ultimate three-count. Cane toads would invade the shop's backyard in their hundreds at night, attracted by the bones we'd leave behind after pooling our money to buy a roast chook from the snack bar.

If a bunch of kids were under my feet in a similar fashion these days, they'd be slapped around and kicked out in thirty seconds flat. But John treated us like family. And, like family, he'd get cranky with us from time to time. In the mornings he was most concerned about being complicit in mass truancy.

We also cramped his style no end with the chicks. Seaweed had a veritable conga line of beautiful girls coming and going from the shop. The presence of us grommets like a chattering bunch of Balinese monkeys couldn't have done much for his backroom rooting schedule.

The tiny ding-repair area at the back of the building shared a wall with the fitting room. The fitting room walls were covered in surfing posters. We took a hand drill to the classic *Morning of the Earth*/Michael Peterson cutback poster. Each time a chick tried on a new bikini we'd bolt out to the ding bay and perve at them, right through MP's eye! Little sickos.

To make matters worse, I don't think any of us ever actually purchased anything from the shop.

In the afternoons, John was always more relaxed and he enjoyed our energy and exuberance permeating the shop. It became clear to me later that an enraged rogue elephant would be relaxed if it smoked as much dope as John did after lunch.

Anyone who's seen the movie *Big Wednesday* would understand when I describe Seaweed as our 'Bear' during those early teen years – a wise sage who protected us and got to know each of us like sons. Or maybe like scarcely controllable nephews. He cared about sharing his treasure trove of surfing knowledge with us. He spoke at our level about everything from board design, to tube-riding technique, to mystical waves in faraway places, to the history of our local surf breaks. I didn't listen enough when he was trying to pull us into line, but I was always mesmerised by John's ability to share his passion for the ocean through storytelling. Perhaps it was the seagoing fisherman in me.

I get really choked up when I think of John Tragere and Headland Surf. His attitudes and philosophies about surfing and surfers played a big part in forming the outlook that I have on the sport and the lifestyle. I'm still very attached to Seaweed and I look up to him just as much now as I did when I was thirteen years old.

Seaweed wasn't the only oldie who began taking an avid interest in our surfing. Much to my surprise and (private) delight, Mum and Dad were at first concerned, then curious, then genuinely proud of my involvement in surfing contests.

After we moved from the cove, Mum was highly suspicious of what I was up to when I left home at dawn every day, because she couldn't monitor me from the caravan window. She knew damn well that there was a lot of less-than-savoury shit going on around the place. 'Druggies' and 'surfers' were one and the same animal in the minds of all responsible, God-fearing people in that era. When he wasn't at sea, Mum pressed Bull relentlessly about her concerns. A couple of years ago I found out that he was eventually worn down into spying on me one morning.

Bull followed me as I checked the old cove and then rode to the Headland for a surf with the boys. The sneaky bugger watched from the beach until I returned home for breakfast.

'All he's doing is bloody surfing, love,' he reported to Mum. 'You know what? The little bastard's pretty bloody good too!'

Mum was satisfied about my moral safety and the episode actually led my parents to attend most of my contests from then on. The oldies were happy that their son was committed to his sport and proud of what he was achieving. I was very chuffed to please them. Mum meticulously kept records of my competition results and Bull added surfing to rugby league as his sport of choice.

But it is a fucking idiot who doubts a mother's instincts. Joan Elkerton was dead right. Before too long, drugs would find me and I would find them.

A SILVER LINING

A few months prior to commencing the charming daily routine of shoving a filthy homemade bong into my face for breakfast, one small and brainless event caused a very significant chain reaction.

It was a day in early '78, and Alex, Robert, Barney and I were slothing around in Seaweed's shop instead of learning the fundamentals of geometry when the subject of surfboard shaping arose among us. Since no normal person could reasonably aspire to simply surf for a living – as our heroes such as Mark Richards, Shaun Tomson or Rabbit Bartholomew did – we concluded that shaping surfboards was the only other logical way to earn a crust whilst remaining free to hit the waves whenever we wanted to.

We were completely obsessed with board design, but John said that we'd have to pay our dues by sweeping up foam dust and being gofers in a factory before any expert shaper would even think about showing us the ropes. 'Fuck that!' we agreed.

Some hippy from Byron Bay had written an article in *Tracks* magazine about peeling the glass from an old longboard, reshaping the foam as a shortboard, then relaminating the finished product. Something to do with recycling. More like something to do with Byron's tremendous natural abundance of hallucinogenic mushrooms, I reckon.

I had experience with altering the tail on my old Soul board and I was the best ding repairer amongst us, so it was decided that I would 'reshape' my beloved Jim Pollard channel bottom as the first foray into a future career for us all. In order to maintain group morale, I didn't divulge the trifling fact that my last efforts as a surfboard craftsman nearly killed me.

We pressed on with a plan to strip the Pollard of its glass, reshape the rails, shorten the nose by an inch or two, then relaminate the whole thing – better than new. I took to the task under the supervision of Alex and Robert while Mum was volunteering at church one Saturday morning and Bull was at sea.

Dickheads. The hippy was a dickhead. We were dickheads to believe the hippy.

What an utter catastrophe. Bull's neatly kept garage ended up looking like a cross between a demolition site and a gigantic piece of wanky, abstract sculpture. My left thumb and forefinger got stuck together. Carelessly mixed laminating accelerant was spilled onto Dad's lawnmower and melted one of its tyres into the concrete. I used Dad's grinder on a piece of glass matting and covered a basket of Mum's unwashed laundry in superfine, super-sharp crystals. Stalactites and stalagmites of semi-dried polymer resin were all over the floor and even made it to the ceiling. Don't ask me which was which – I told you I never made it to science class. David, who was hanging around trying to help, was bleeding from behind his ear. Why, I don't know.

My Jim Pollard was totalled.

Fucked.

The more I fucked things up, the more desperate I became with my solutions to save the board and the hence the more thoroughly I fucked things up. It was a vicious cycle of overconfidence, panic and imbecility. By the time I admitted defeat, my poor old board wouldn't have even floated. It looked like it had been run over by a bus. I was heartbroken. I loved that board so much. What was I thinking? The boys left solemnly, knowing that the disaster was no laughing matter.

Unsurprisingly, Mum also failed to find the funny side of my morning's efforts. She took pity on me when I burst into tears after about five minutes of her verbal tirade. I wasn't a great one for crying, so she knew that I was taking the loss of my board pretty hard. Dad would not be informed, but I had three days to rehabilitate the garage before he got home. I worked like a dog and managed to fix everything up with barely an hour to spare. Penance complete.

Although I escaped Bull's wrath, I was still miserable to be without a board. I'd have to make up a story and beg him to buy me another one. That was going to be tricky, because even though Dad was generous, he couldn't tolerate people who didn't look after their things properly, a legacy of being a boat skipper.

Enter John Tragere.

Once he'd finished pissing himself laughing, Seaweed threw a fatherly arm around my shoulders and led me into the surfboard showroom.

'I've been wanting you to ride one of these anyway, mate. Here, it's free.'

With that, he pulled a spanking new Headland Surf pintail from the rack and handed it to me. I could've kissed him. It was shaped by Paul Pascoe of the local board company Pascoe Hopper Surfboards. I was so grateful that I could barely speak.

We never really called it a sponsorship. It was more like John helping me out and having a hot local grommet seen on one of his boards as a side effect. Today's grommets wouldn't comprehend how big a deal this act of kindness was to me. These days, every teenager who can wobble through a cutback marches to his local shaper and demands free boards like they're doing him some kind of idiotic favour.

I consider a surfboard to be a lovingly handmade treasure, not a throwaway tool. John not only gave me a fabulous new board but his unexpected, personal act of kindness set in train events that would lead me to global notoriety with an emerging giant of the new surf-clothing industry. In time.

IN FRONT OF A FACTORY, UNDER A POOL TABLE

I continued to do well in contests. Barney held his mantle as the best kid around, but my enjoyment of competing intensified. I won a few Sunshine Coast regional events and victory in North Shore contests became very regular as 1978 began.

The Pascoe Hopper surfboard factory became a new hangout. It was different to Headland Surf though. While Seaweed showed us parental-style patience, Paul Pascoe and Mick Hopper were hard, hard men. They were as much into their martial arts as they were into surfing. Both men were qualified with several degrees in Zen Do Kai karate. It was well known that they loved to fight.

No smart-arsing, disrespect or general grommet annoying shit were allowed in the slightest. We were tolerated because Paul and Mick appreciated our curiosity about surfboard craftsmanship and because we were known to be insanely keen surfers. If we shut up and kept out of the way, the guys were okay with us moving around the shaping, glassing, laminating and polishing bays.

They used to sit in front of the factory on their breaks and we were welcome to join them there and listen in, provided we didn't act up like dickheads. It took some mighty self-control, but we complied because it was such an honour just to be there. These guys surfed hard, trained hard and worked hard. If a grommet couldn't admire them, he'd never admire anyone.

Frequently we'd be told to stay in front of the factory while all the adults left to go inside. Once the door was shut, we were told we'd be killed if we came in. We had no idea what mysterious, secret stuff was happening in there. Our exclusion was intimidating in itself. Whatever was going on, it was way too cool for little shitcan grommets.

Of course, they were doing no more than smoking dope. Like John and all the other elders we knew, they didn't want to expose us to it. Plenty of time for that later.

And like Bull and John, Paul and Mick became the teachers I missed out on at school.

Amid all the surfing stuff in those frenetic couple of years, the incredible power of the female of the species also smashed into my consciousness like a two-tonne truck.

The sexuality of girls wasn't unknown to me beforehand. In fact, during my final few weeks at Mooloolaba Primary, a girl called Becky became disturbingly enamoured of my penis. She asked to see it in class. I pulled it out beneath the desk to show her and was amazed when she took it in hand and began doodling on it with a ballpoint pen. No shit. It fucking hurt, but I figured it would be the height of rudeness to tell her to stop. My dick ended up with several love hearts inscribed on it. I didn't show my mates, but she told all of her girlfriends. Weird.

I'd done a fair bit of fingering too. That was the thing to do. Finger. It's embarrassingly crude to mention but there you have it. Naturally, everyone told everyone else who they'd fingered and who they'd been fingered by. Actual feelings of sexual pleasure didn't have much to do with it. You were sexually advanced as either a boy or a girl in Mooloolaba Primary if you'd participated in the rather surgical activity of digital penetration.

A group of boys and girls would walk down to the back of the oval at lunchtime and pair off, A quick, awkward tongue kiss would precede a quicker plunge down the panties. A couple of minutes later, the boys would run off in one direction and the girls would run off in another. Names were carved into the big pine tree near the back gate and that was that.

I became much more curious about real sex once I started hearing the older guys talking about it. I figured there must have been something pretty amazing about an activity that got an (almost) equal billing to surfing in so many conversations. The smorgasbord of delights ogled at through Michael Peterson's eye at Seaweed's shop added to the appeal, and finally my chance to find out what all the fuss was about came during year nine at high school.

Suzy (not her real name) was a year ahead of me at school and lived just up the hill from my joint. Her house had a fantastic pool room, complete with an excellent stereo and full-size billiard table.

Suzy loved David Bowie's *Ziggy Stardust* album, just like I did. Normally when I was visiting, there were heaps of other kids around, shooting pool, the stereo blaring. One rainy Saturday afternoon when the surf was crappy, I headed up to Suzy's, expecting to find a few of the gang. I was keen on a quick game of eight ball before going down to loiter at the surfboard factory. Instead I found Suzy at home alone, lying under the pool table and chilling to the Spiders From Mars.

I joined her. Ten minutes later I was reflecting on losing my virginity.

There must have been some kind of previous sexual tension that escaped me, because three seconds after saying 'Hi' we were pulling each other's clothes off and going for it. Such as 'going for it' was.

I spent the first few minutes in awe of seeing Suzy naked, trying hard not to lose my cool. Then we mucked around for a couple of minutes getting some workable form of entry happening. Then I pumped madly before being completely overwhelmed by a shattering, blinding orgasm. It felt as though the end of my knob had been blown clean off. In a good way.

Bloody Suzy. I've been chasing that precise sensation ever since.

We lay there panting and giggling. Although it was a bit like patting your head and rubbing your belly, we both got through it and agreed it was very nice. In fact, it was a sweet, innocent, spontaneous experience. There was a tenderness of union which was every bit as enlightening and memorable as the physical sensation.

Suzy and I never became girlfriend and boyfriend. We stayed mates and kept our secret together, always sharing a cheeky grin every time *Ziggy Stardust* played on the radio or stereo. In any case, I suspected that I wasn't the only member of our group to enjoy Suzy's ball work on the wrong side of the pool table.

Still, I couldn't get the wonder of her soft, reddish pubic hair out of my mind. Every girl had one of these things! I made it my business to see as many of them as I could. Provided the surf was no good, of course.

As with all worthwhile quests, this one led me to both danger and romance. One particularly ill-tempered neighbour had a very lovely daughter with whom I shared a mutual attraction. In a textbook cliché, I used to sneak in and out of her bedroom window with cavalier frequency, knowing that death was a certainty if we were busted. It was a sick kind of adrenalin rush, I must admit. It was also only one of several night-time ports-of-call I'd established for the gratification of my penis, which had begun to operate as a separate – and almost uncontrollable – entity. The fucking thing (pardon the pun) was like an escaped evil genie which was never going back in its bottle.

Then there was Peta. Lovely Peta Tacey, by far the hottest girl our age in the district. Like every other bloke around, I had a huge crush on her. I was shocked that she responded favourably to a clumsy advance I made towards her at a party in year nine. I was so convinced she'd reject me that complete paralysis froze my best moves after our initial kiss. She interpreted my inability to continue our foreplay as being 'gentlemanly'. Wow … what incredible luck.

Did I plummet or soar into love with gorgeous Peta? It was a bit of both. And as with all first loves, it was a high-intensity exercise from the outset. We'd go out together on and off for the remainder of our teens, as beautiful, patient Peta persisted with her fawning yet shamefully immature and unfaithful boyfriend.

My list of lifelong passions and obsessions had begun to take shape in earnest.

THE FIEND

There exists a rather quaint fantasy that law-abiding, *decent* people cling to about drug use. They comfort themselves with the myth of 'The Pusher'.

Otherwise pristine young souls – moral blank canvases – are set upon by gaunt career criminals whose life work is to entrap, addict and attempt to kill their prey with illicit chemicals, all for cynical commercial gain. They exist in society's peripheral vision, scurrying in from the shadows to claim the young, the weak and the poorly parented.

Anyone who has ever taken drugs will tell you that it just ain't so neat.

I'm not minimising the despicability of the drug trade. It is the business of human misery. Fat cats who enrich themselves at the top of the hard narcotics tree are A-grade cunts. However, it's my experience that most people don't initially get forced into their habits. In fact, the vast majority of us actually want to sign up for the ride.

Peer pressure? I suppose it's a factor, based on the research. In surfing, the idea of peer pressure is a pretty difficult concept to nail down. You see, the sport and culture of surfing is awash with illegal drugs. This isn't a palatable fact, but it's a fact all the same. Yesterday, today and probably tomorrow.

I'm no academic on the subject, but years of field work tells me that surfers experience highs that are simply not available to people who don't ride waves. It could be that the euphoria is hard to leave behind in the water. Perhaps there's an element of counter-culture too, similar to the experiences of rock musicians, for example. Whatever the reasons, show me a genuine surfer from any generation who tells you that drugs aren't enmeshed in the culture and I'll show you a bullshit artist.

Of course, this doesn't mean that everyone who surfs or who is involved with surfing is *necessarily* a drug user. But every surfer who doesn't partake in something probably knows plenty of surfers who do.

Mind you, the average surfer isn't bolting from the beach desperate to inject heroin into his eyeballs. Many blokes just smoke dope and enjoy the occasional stimulant or hallucinogen. Of these people, a fair percentage will have dabbled in heavier narcotics when available or affordable. It's ingrained in the freedom, individualism and 'open-mindedness' of surfing mentality that drugs aren't frowned upon. I'm *not* saying that this is a good or desirable. I *am* saying that it's reality. More on this later.

My introduction to marijuana seemed as natural a part of my development in the surfing community as learning to ride tubes or winning heats. And I promise you that no seedy criminal jumped out from a darkened alleyway and forced a joint into my gob at knifepoint.

I forget who first cottoned onto the idea that we should give pot a try. Even at our age, we'd all heard of it and knew from *Tracks* magazine and conversations with the older kids that smoking 'mull' enhanced the experience of surfing. This wasn't some drug-pushing tactic but a universal and accepted reality in surfing. Acid and mushrooms were also recognised in the same way.

Acid sounded pretty painful and we didn't even consider it. Mushrooms were obviously overrated because Robert's mum fed them to him twice a week and he didn't surf any differently than after she'd forced him to eat peas. We discussed this at length, actually.

Mull (so nicknamed after the world-famous quality of the cannabis harvest from Mullumbimby, in Byron Bay's beautiful hinterland) was a drug we'd come to comprehend. We may have been sadly slow on the uptake, but we eventually figured out that the reason we were evicted from Seaweed's shop, banned from entering the surfboard factory, and ejected from The Corner by our elders so often was that they were doing something that was not meant for kids. Surely this was mull.

God knows, every adult we knew under thirty (and a good few older) reeked of the same sweet, sickly pungent stench. We knew what they were up to but – to the great credit of the older mentors who watched over us – we were steadfastly refused even the slightest taste, despite the Chinese water torture of constant pestering.

As usual, it was someone who knew someone who knew someone who knew someone else who eventually came up with the goods. Hilarious to think that we found getting dope so difficult since it could have been obtained from almost everyone in the entire district! I guess this in itself blows apart the notion of the lone, evil pusher.

It was like Christmas morning when we convened in the bush behind my place. Barney produced two matchboxes full of strong-smelling buds, the results of our meagre pooled finances. No leaf at all, not that we knew any different. Alex and I brought a few large bottles of beer that we pinched from our fathers. Time to party!

I can't remember by whom but a dirty, disgusting old plastic orange juice bottle converted into a water pipe with a cut-off garden hose was produced. The homemade bong is a very traditional, primitive device well known though little beloved throughout the world of dope smoking.

After a full half an hour of debate about its correct usage, a bud was placed into the little brass cone at the end of the hose and Barney wrapped his mouth around the open bottle top for the first puff. He choked and coughed and spluttered and ultimately gave everyone a big thumbs up. Seeing that Barne had survived, I volunteered to go next.

I can only assume that everyone else had a turn, because I immediately started getting dizzy and nauseous. After that, I remember nothing. I'm told I collapsed and the boys couldn't stir me, despite taking turns at poking me with sticks and farting in my face. They knew I was alive thanks to my loud snoring. Apparently this was the funniest thing any of them had ever experienced in their short lives.

Eventually, I crawled home and up to my bedroom. Poor Mum just thought I'd come down with a virus. I had the next three days off school and I scarcely moved from my bed.

If only I was bit smarter or a bit less stubborn, that may well have been the start and finish of my career in drugs. But a week later, I was back up for the challenge. This time it was a mellower weed and I enjoyed the warm buzz that would become a familiar, reassuring pleasure to me for the next thirty years.

As much as I fell in love with Peta, I fell in love with mull. Almost overnight I went from never having seen the stuff to choofing dope a dozen times a day. I had homemade plastic bongs stashed all over the neighbourhood and mull was cheap and plentiful. The feeling was great. I was always laughing my guts out on the land. In the water, I felt I had acquired a special focus and instinct.

As good as the feelings are, the laughter, focus and instinct are perfectly possible without marijuana. We addictive types tend to excuse our seedy habits by claiming 'special' side effects which help us in our creative or physical pursuits – like surfing. Such hippy crap. Why hide behind silly justifications? The truth is that getting stoned is a pursuit in itself, drug use for the sheer nefarious pleasure of drug use.

I'd volunteered to become a mull fiend and I was loving every second of it.

THE RECKONING

Dodging school every day wasn't all smooth sailing. By mid-1978 we'd honed our truancy routines and subterfuge to a fine art. I'd even developed into a formidable forgery expert, having copied the handwriting styles of everyone's mums with devious determination. Absent notes were not a problem.

Occasionally we were confronted by a teacher out in the surf during a weekday.

'What the hell are you doing out here, Elkerton? Get your arse to school immediately!'

'Ahhh, excuse me, sir, but what the hell are *you* doing out here?'

Touché. Several teachers who bludged off work when the waves were good were snookered by this vexing Mexican stand-off. The prospect of mutually assured destruction at the hands of Mr Law, their hard-arsed boss and our hard-arsed principal at Maroochydore High, served us well.

However, there was another difficulty which was bloody hard to counter. The troubling, lurking presence of Peter Weir.

Peter and his brother Brian were superb local surfers. Peter was quite a maverick, by local surfing standards, in that he was very smart and also had a responsible job. Unfortunately for the Alexandra Headland grommet crew, Peter's occupation was science teacher at our high school. Even more unfortunate was that he set himself apart from many of his colleagues by being admirably dedicated to his career. The bastard.

We'd see him surfing the dawn session. He'd see us surfing the dawn session. We'd see him in the car park, waiting for us to leave and get ready for school. He'd see us leave the water and go our separate ways. We'd see him drive off in the direction of school.

Then we'd reconvene at the surf shop and return to the waves. Since our little gang was known to be inseparable, one of us always returned to the school grounds at lunchtime where a big deal was made of casually walking past Peter and saying, 'Hello, sir. Good surf this morning, hey?' Ipso facto *all* of us were at school.

Geez, we were clever. By our standards, but not by Peter's. Peter had graduated from university. None of us had passed primary school. This major discrepancy in mental capability proved the undoing of my extremely comfortable teenage existence.

Good old Mr Weir was just biding his time.

The inevitable day of reckoning came when an early springtime northerly wind sprang up and spoiled our morning session at the Headland. With nothing left to occupy us for the rest of the day, we decided to catch up on our socialising by sneaking into school. Weir read the onshore wind – and us –

like an open book. Rob Mackie and I vaulted the back fence where we were greeted with unrestrained glee by our nemesis.

'G'day, Kong. G'day, Mackie. Too bad about that northerly, hey? Let's go and have a chat to Mr Law about your bad luck, shall we?'

Game, set, match.

We were marched into the office, where all of our attendance records were laid out on Law's desk. Parents were called. The whole gig was up. Maroochydore High School was officially finished with our contempt for it. Students Elkerton and Mackie were suspended for two weeks (which, when you think about it, is pretty fucking funny).

Mal Meninga: captain of the Queensland and Australian rugby league teams.

Benny Pike: Commonwealth boxing champion.

Grant Kenny: all-time Ironman legend (and terrific Alexandra Headland surfer, I might add).

Venerated names amongst the notable alumni of Maroochydore High.

Gary Elkerton: wagging, fornicating pothead. Not so much.

Mum and Bull knew that I wagged school 'a bit', but the extent of the problem made them extremely angry. They were great parents but my behaviour made them seem like shitty ones. I felt suitably guilty. That night, David and Bernadette were sent to their rooms as I was sat down at the dinner table. Mum was in tears. Bull looked relaxed, which really unsettled me.

'Gary, your mother and I are very worried about you, son.'

He didn't look too bloody worried. In fact, he looked vaguely smug.

'Just because you don't give a shit about your future doesn't mean that we don't.'

On the contrary. I gave a shit about my future. I cared very much about it. I wanted to surf and smoke mull and drink beer and have sex. Given the circumstances, I thought the better of pointing this out.

'If you think we're just going to sit back and let you waste your life away, wagging school to go surfing, you've got another fuc ... you've got another thing coming, my boy.'

Fair enough.

'So ... *we've decided that you're coming to work with me on the boat.*'

Arma-fucking-geddon.

BAD NEWS, GOOD NEWS

The sham that was my schooling was finally at an end.

While he wasn't exactly punching the air with parental pride, Bull was actually pleased that the useless efforts of others to tame his eldest son were over. That was his job. He was finally free to get on with preparing me to take my place in the family business. Sure, he went through the motions of lamenting that I was too young – at age fourteen – to dispense with school, but at the end of the day, the Bullfrog was stoked.

Whatever the exact opposite of 'stoked' is, that was me.

It wasn't fear of the unknown. I knew very well that the 'romance of the sea' had nothing whatsoever to do with what lay ahead of me as a deckhand for Dad aboard a working prawn trawler. Long, long days of hard work for a hardened skipper was what it was. Worse than anything, I'd be separated from my mates, my surfing, contests, Peta and my precious mull by hundreds of kilometres of open ocean for days or even weeks at a time. My prospects for teen happiness could hardly have been worse.

Paradoxically, the commencement of one unwelcomed career coincided precisely with the commencement of an altogether different pathway. Actually, one clashed quite violently with the other.

In the months leading up to getting kicked out of school, my competition results started to stack up impressively. I'd placed in enough local junior events to get a bit of a write-up in the local papers. I wasn't the best kid on the Sunshine Coast, but I was doing enough with my competing and my free surfing to make an impression on at least one important person.

In addition to being the owner/shaper at Pascoe Hopper, Paul Pascoe was the local agent for Quiksilver. Paul had observed my surfing and monitored my progress. I guess he was impressed, because he was happy to place me on a new-for-old swap-over arrangement for my surfboards. I was flabbergasted by my good fortune.

A bigger shock was to follow. Not long after I was pressed into servitude on the trawler, Mum casually mentioned that Paul Pascoe had called and wanted to have a chat with her and Bull about me. He was going to pop around that afternoon.

'What's it about, Mum?' I asked, concealing my nerves.

'I don't know, son. Be home at four-thirty.'

I was shitting myself. Paul was a friend to me, but a friend in the way that a football coach is. He was an authority figure, someone I respected and even feared in the way that teenagers fear their god-like idols. What the hell did he want to see my oldies about? He didn't strike me as a dobber, but had he got wind of my pot smoking? Was he going to tell my parents 'for my own good'? Was he sick of me getting under everyone's feet at the surfboard factory? I spent the day processing all of the possibilities until I couldn't wrap my head around anything but a bad outcome.

Finally, we were all seated around our dinner table. Dad cracked two beers and the adults exchanged chitchat for a few minutes. It was agony.

'Keith, Kong ... er ... Gary is an exceptional surfer,' Paul eventually announced.

'Yeah, I bloody know!' replied the Bull with a rueful laugh.

'I think he could be anything he wants to be as a professional surfer.'

'Deadset?'

'Deadset.'

'So what do you mean, mate – like making a bit of a crust at the caper?'

'One day, mate, yeah, definitely. I wanted to get the okay by you and Joan to give him a sponsorship from Quiksilver.'

You could have told me that St Brendan and Pope John Paul were going to help me set the nets on the trawler and it would've had less impact.

Fuck. With my recent record of being in the deepest of shit whenever a group of adults used me as a topic of conversation, I'd expected the worst of proceedings. This was unbelievable. Paul was not a bloke to hand out praise. He'd certainly never told me about any of this before. As far as I knew, I was just another kooky kid whom he tolerated. *His* approval struck me way before I allowed myself to think about sponsorship.

'Ohhh, that's good, isn't it, love?' Mum said, looking into my dumfounded face.

Dad and Paul finished another couple of beers as the details of representing Quiksilver were explained to my oldies. It wasn't complicated. I'd get some logos for my board and some free t-shirts and board shorts. The company would also pay my entry fees into contests and a few travelling expenses.

Bull was reassured that the arrangement wouldn't interfere with my work. After all, I still had to keep my head screwed on and prepare myself to make a proper living on the trawler. He was also concerned that I didn't get full of myself.

'No worries with that, Keith. We'll pop the little prick's head if it gets too bloody big.' They clinked their beers together with a knowing chuckle.

Time would prove that this would be a harder task than they thought, but it was nice to sense that Bull and Joan were proud of me after what I'd put them through in the weeks before.

We waved goodbye to Paul then sat down to steak and three veg for dinner. Mum and Dad sternly reminded me that this Quiksilver thing was good but not something to get carried away by. Dad went to the pub. Mum, David and Bern settled down in front of the TV.

In what would typify my reaction to good news for many years to come, I took off into the bush behind our place and celebrated by getting stoned.

I can't overstate the effect that Paul Pascoe's belief in me and the initial sponsorship by Quiksilver had. Not only on my surfing, but on my entire sense of identity and confidence.

Sponsorship was very uncommon in the late seventies, and not all good surfers enjoy the attention. Everyone responds differently. I'd never thought about the scenario beforehand, but I quickly found that instead of manifesting itself as pressure, the expectation and the attention brought out the showman in me. I felt a new freedom to express myself on each wave. I guess you could call it pride; you could also call it ego.

For the first time in my life, I put my head down and worked bloody hard at practising. There is such a thing as practising your instincts, as unlikely as it sounds. With my big stumpy legs, naturally low centre of gravity and an innate sense of balance from growing up on the boat, I found that I could actually work on being radical in the most critical sections of a wave.

There were no formal coaches when I was a kid as there are today for talented kids. If there were, chances are that I would have had the rough edges of my technique 'smoothed' out, which probably would have destroyed my pro career. Low body torque along with building then releasing energy through a heavy reliance on bottom turns characterised my every wave. It didn't always present as the most elegant or balletic of styles, but it was getting the job done.

BACK ON THE BOAT

Of course, my version of getting the job done and Bull's were far from being one and the same thing. I had what seemed like five minutes to bask in my new-found glory as a sponsored surfer before the *Miss Bernadette* replaced Alexandra Headland as my standard habitat. My maths wasn't so hot but I knew that Dad was at work a lot more than he was at home, which meant I was going to be chasing prawns way more often than I was going to be chasing waves or pussy.

In all my previous years aboard I had been more of a mascot, helping enthusiastically in an effort to please the old man, though most often being told to stand clear when the hectic, dangerous action was on. I was stoked to contribute and even more satisfied to receive a 'Well done, mate' and a slap on the back from Bull. Ah, for the days of volunteering!

My job specification would now be described in the corporate world as 'Tasks As Directed'. Which at sea on a commercial fishing boat is described as 'General Shitkicker'. Thanks to my extensive experience on board over the years,

I had a fucking lot of shit to kick for a fourteen-year-old. Complete expertise was expected of me from the first second I set foot on deck. 'Come on, boofhead, get the fuck on with it!' amounted to my orientation course.

While Bull was awake, my time was occupied by maintenance, cleaning, gear preparation, coffee brewing and cooking, without a scintilla of space to think for myself. And that was the down time.

In the midst of a catch, the frenzy of activity is almost impossible to describe. As much as it's work, it is also a high adrenalin rush of finely drilled activity, which sees all hands combine to execute dozens of simultaneous tasks on a pitching deck.

It's certainly not a warship during a naval engagement, but the sense of reliance on each other is probably a mini-version. There's a thousand kinetic factors that can go dangerously wrong, both mechanical and natural. It's not exaggerating to say that a single mistake – particularly in rough seas – can kill one or maybe all aboard.

Trifling concerns about safety during a hunt and haul are back of mind. Deeply ingrained, but not the primary, conscious motivation to get things right. A major fuck-up could jeopardise the whole catch and therefore thousands and thousands of hard-earned dollars. *That* was the main game. *Do not fuck up.*

Once the exhausting mechanics of emptying the net into the bins is complete, the job has only just begun. Nets, jigs, booms and pulleys need to be cleared, stowed or reset immediately. As lovely as it would be, the catch never comprises 100 per cent commercially saleable prawns. Sorting must commence immediately. Prawns are deposited into a slide that goes below decks. Everything else needs to go overboard.

A lot of these things aren't the kind of critters one relishes picking up.

There are hundreds of thrashing, toothy species that need to be repatriated to the deep. No fun for them. No fun for us. But both parties want the same outcome, so generally things work out.

Notwithstanding our usual teen–parent fighting, Bull would often put to sea with just me as support. He must have been confident in his son getting the job done, despite the complaining and adolescent resistance. He shouldn't have been so confident, because every time he slept below deck when I was on watch, with the nets stowed and the engines on idle, I'd sneak back to the little aft hold where I'd grease the steering bearings. That was where I hid my bong.

While the skipper slept, I'd choof mull and enjoy the sublime solitude of the deep, black, open ocean. Hanging my legs off the stern, I'd spend hours under the stars, feeling the swell lift and pitch the boat, picturing what each wave would look like when it hit the sandbanks and reefs of my favourite surf breaks far away, back inshore. I'd climb on top of the wheelhouse and sit there scanning the moonlit 360-degree curve of the horizon, with no land in sight.

Life on the trawler was bloody busy, but it could also be magically contemplative at times.

FRINGE BENEFITS

I was at home often enough to keep my surfing fairly sharp. Still, I became justifiably concerned that I'd lose my edge. I couldn't have conceived that my untimely enslavement would accidentally transport me into a new realm of mind-blowing possibilities.

Bull ranged from North Stradbroke Island all the way up to the southernmost fingers of the Great Barrier Reef. The 'Prawn Highway' we traversed day in and day out just happened to be chock-full of world-class waves which were totally and utterly invisible on the world's surfing radar.

While North Stradbroke Island sits just off Brisbane and its superb variety of points, reefs and beach breaks are populated by a small but hardcore band of local chargers, the northward locations of Moreton Island, Fraser Island, Double Island Point and the Tewantin coast provided vast, remote and uninhabited surfing potential accessible only by boat.

Further north still, the Great Barrier Reef commences its protective vigil over the Queensland coast a couple of hundred kilometres out to sea from Gladstone and the townships of

Seventeen Seventy and Agnes Water. Out there, in the middle of nowhere, a huge south-easterly dogleg in the coral system produces rideable waves which loom out of black water and unload onto thousands of technicolour reef passes and lonely mint-blue lagoons. They're fickle and dependent on wind and tide variables that are completely unaffected by land, but they're numerous beyond belief. The waves out there are often very large. And being in mid-ocean, they're always extremely powerful. Like tiny pinheads on a football field, Lady Elliot and Lady Musgrave islands pop up from nowhere, each providing anchorage and totally untouched surfing potential.

I'd seen these areas before, but not with the surfer's eye I had at age fourteen. It only took me one voyage – my first as a 'deckie' – to realise what a dickhead I was for leaving my board at home. I would never make the same mistake again. I raved on and on and on to Dad about the waves we were passing by until he blew his stack and told me to 'shut the fucking fuck up'.

Since so much of the frenetic work action happened at night, it was important for us to rest up in shifts during the day. From the get-go, this arrangement created a heavy struggle between the Bull and me. I just couldn't stop reading the swells, looking inshore for the breaks and generally behaving like a standard surf-nut during daylight. I had the binoculars out ogling insane barrels winding down the point at 'Boulders' on Moreton Island in sets of six or seven. I was spellbound at the A-frame beach breaks pounding tens of kilometres of Fraser Island's coast, one after the other after the other.

All without a single soul to be seen. Not a building, not a vehicle. Nothing. A dinosaur could have appeared from behind the dunes and it wouldn't have looked out of place. It was torture ... and it was really only the tip of the iceberg.

We filled the hold with prawns and returned to port in quick time on that miserable, boardless first trip. Since Bull would usually anchor for a day or so at one port or another while we were away, he relented to my pestering and allowed me to stow my board below in future. Provided I only used it on lay days and strictly on the condition it never interfered with work.

Yeah, right!

As a matter of fact, I was a pretty good deckhand. I could do everything expected of an experienced trawlerman, not to mention handle working the wheelhouse when it was required.

As a matter of further fact, I would also have been fired and thrown overboard by any other skipper, thanks to my chronic insubordination and my habit of diving off the boat with my surfboard.

Poor Bull. He was the fiercest of trawlermen, as rock-hard as any crusty sea-dog invented in fiction. Hemingway or Melville could've used him as a consultant. But here I was – an idiot kid – driving him out of his mind.

I scarcely slept when we were in wave zones. I'd often advise Dad that he needed to anchor because I was going surfing while I was in mid-air, launching from the stern. He'd curse the bejesus out of me from behind a Benson & Hedges as I shouted over my shoulder that I'd be back in 'half an hour'.

I put him in a terrible position, little shithead that I was. The loving father had no choice but to watch over me as I paddled across hundreds of metres of deep, sharky water to where the waves were. The commercial skipper had no choice but to interrupt his daily schedule while a junior crewman went AWOL.

Eventually we settled into an acceptable routine which grew from argumentative forbearance into an unlikely kind of mutual enjoyment. He accepted that I'd be no good to him or the future of the family business if I didn't surf the fabulous waves which so often presented themselves on each voyage. In turn, I accepted that I had to be 100 per cent focused and energetic when the catch was 'on'.

So, we gave a little ground to each other. I grew to enjoy the intense bonding experience and shared sense of victory that came with filling our hold with prawns. Dad – bless him – would brew a coffee and sit in a deckchair on the roof of the wheelhouse, watching me surf through the binoculars.

How lovely. If only things were always so Hallmark-card perfect.

FROM THE SUBLIME ...

I'd forgive anyone for doubting the truth of the surfing experiences I had during this time on the trawler because they do seem too good to be true. A kid spends his mid-teen years surfing maximum quality waves that aren't on the map. Alone? It's really hard to swallow, I know. If I hadn't done it myself, I'd have trouble believing it too.

There are waves way out there on the Great Barrier Reef which are every bit as good as Fiji's Cloudbreak. There are right-hand points on Queensland's offshore sand islands which look for all the world like Burleigh Heads or South Africa's Jeffreys Bay, except that they are totally untouched by people. A week would hardly go by when I wasn't able to surf myself to exhaustion in surreal, primordial isolation. It was just the way life was for me. If I didn't surf off the boat, I didn't surf at all for long periods.

As much as I was stoked to surf off the boat and as much as I found a way to like the work and enjoy the solitude, I missed being at home every day with my mates, my girl, my club and my unfettered access to mull. At home I could have a laugh with my friends, hang at the factory or the shop, ride my skateboard, dominate the local breaks, win contests, fuck and smoke dope at will. Such is the mind of a teenager.

At sea I had the Bull for company, my prawny fist for sex, no skateboard, a limited supply of high-risk pot and no-one at all to share my surfing with. I simply surfed what was available to me, without an adult's perspective on the insane enormity of my blessings.

I liked surfing alone but it's nice for a grommet to have his comrades actually *see* him on *real* hell waves, rather than just regale them with scarcely credible tales. There was a bittersweet quality to the adventure I was living. It was like the philosophical question of a mighty tree crashing to earth in a remote forest: if nobody saw it or heard it fall, did it really happen?

It wasn't big business back then, but these days surfers pay thousands of dollars to go on boat trips such as I was gifted with every day.

Dad used to gesticulate madly and yell at the top of his lungs for me to return to the boat after I'd been out surfing for hours and he wanted to hoist anchor. Sometimes I obeyed. Mostly I didn't – claiming deafness and blindness. Every so often, when we were way outside on the Barrier Reef, Dad would row our little tin boat in through a coral pass and watch me surf from a lagoon. He'd have a snooze and a maybe a swim too. Then we'd share the oars back to the trawler.

Still, I was so keen to get off the boat on homeward courses that I'd often wave down passing trawlers or charter boats when Bull was below deck, asleep. They'd cruise to within a few hundred metres and I'd paddle over to them and beg a passage back to port. Brisbane, Redcliffe – any place on the mainland from where I could hitch a ride back home. Bull would wake to find a note from me. Once, I forgot to leave a note and he thought I was overboard, dead. Great son, hey?

... TO THE RIDICULOUS

To be even-handed about our relationship at the time, I must say that Dad also betrayed some faults in his duty of care to my physical and mental health.

All recreational fishermen know that tangled gear and rigs are a giant pain in the arse. Tangles in the massive, mechanised gear and riggings on a prawn trawler at night in rough seas can be such a pain in the arse as to cause death to all concerned. Fouling of the equipment is an occupational norm for professional trawlermen. Fouling could be defined as the nets or other rigging being caught in the keel or the propeller while the trawler was making way dead ahead into the swell.

An office clerk gets pissed off when his computer locks up. A carpenter spews when his nail gun seizes. Bar staff spit chips when beer plumbing clogs up. Prawners face drowning when booms, ropes, pulleys, guides or nets fail under pressure in any way, shape or form. Think about that next time you're tucking into a shrimp cocktail.

Because Bull was gung-ho enough, experienced enough and

competitive enough to put the nets out in even the roughest of seas, 'fouling' was always on the cards.

Usually twenty metres long or less, a prawn trawler can easily be drawn down and sunk sideways by its booms, or rendered powerless by fouling, causing it to drift fatally abeam of the swells. Any gear that fouls the boat below the waterline has to be cleared immediately. Even in a well-run boat, veteran trawlermen know that at some stage they will need to go overboard to clear obstructions, tangles and impediments.

Which is all well and good without the existence of sharks. Even without the nets down, a trawler is normally shadowed by dozens of predators of various species and sizes. When the nets are down, there's always hundreds of them trailing near the surface. When the nets are full, there can be literally *thousands* of sharks around the boat. At night during a haul, the deck lights throw out an illuminated circle of about fifty metres around the boat. Within that circle you could step off the aft transom and literally walk across the sharks, they're that thick.

This doesn't raise an eyebrow on board until there's a fouled propeller or keel to deal with.

I recall at least a dozen occasions when Dad had to roll the dice. I knew the fun had begun when he'd march towards me wearing nothing but his Y-front underpants and an old-school sixties-era dive mask. He held the .22 Winchester in one hand and a torch in the other. This in itself was a frightening sight.

'Shoot the first fucker that gets too close. Don't fuck up.'

With that, he'd shove the Winchester into my hands, unsheath the gigantic knife we stowed near the prawn bins and lop the head off a big mackerel or tuna that we had in a cooler. He'd toss the carcass as far out into the sharks as possible, then *splash* – he was gone. Never a second of hesitation or sentimental bullshit reassurances. On with the job.

I – on the other hand – shat myself every time without fail. These particular circumstances had a way of cutting through the morass of adolescent drivel that usually cluttered my mind. The father is going overboard, untethered, with a torch and a knife, into pitch-black water, under a twenty-metre boat, which is adrift and pitching violently in large seas.

Check.

There are so many sharks surrounding the boat that you can hear their jaws snapping as they beach themselves on top of each other to get to the diversionary bait. They thrash away at the bait and they thrash away at each other, though this exercise only occupies a small percentage of the swarm.

Check.

The teenage son, who is stoned and sleep-deprived, aims a rifle from the rolling deck at a small underwater disc of light from the father's torch. Sharks are everywhere. A shot is as likely to kill the father as it is to kill anything else.

Check.

It occurs to the son that the father could be killed in about ten different ways here, none of them pleasant.

Check.

The son contemplates being left alone on a helpless boat, horizons from land, as he mourns the father and his own lonely predicament.

Check.

The son begins to cry like a baby.

Check.

'Are you up there, St Brendan?'

I never once fired the rifle. Dad always made it back on deck. Then I'd knock off the blubbering and get busy stowing the rifle. The old boy would just breeze past me, barking orders and proceeding as if the whole thing was nothing. Which, to him, it was.

One night, when we went through this procedure some thirty kilometres off Fraser Island in rough seas, he stormed back up topside and launched a tirade at me. 'You're not holding that fucken thing for fucken show, boy! Fire the fucken thing for Christ's sake!' He stood there raging at me, looking like some kind of disgusting alien.

A huge abrasion scored him from armpit to ankle on his right side, his saggy, tissue-thin underpants had become transparent and his voice sounded comically nasal from beneath his decrepit face mask. What a sight. I laughed through the tension. He started to laugh too, despite himself. He was probably in shock.

'Where's the knife, Dad?'

'In that bastard,' he said, pointing at a two-and-a-half-metre bronze whaler that was being torn to bits by dozens of its mates. It had the handle of our trusty knife sticking out from the top of its head.

'Shit,' I said.

'Yeah, shit,' said Dad.

'Sorry, Dad.'

'Nah, to tell you the truth, I was worried you'd shoot me. Now put a coffee on, will ya, son.' He was shaking just a little as he lit his cig.

* * *

We often anchored off North Stradbroke Island as a last port of call before heading back to Mooloolaba. At other times we stopped offshore for a lay day to replenish supplies and service our gear before continuing a hunt. It suited all aboard: one day of surfing for me, one day of drinking at the magnificent Straddie Pub for Bull.

Dad never drank while we were at sea working. Never. There was no grog on board at all. But by God almighty did the old man enjoy a drink when the work was done. It was celebratory. He used to admonish me that 'every prawn is a dollar bill, son'. When he had a boat full of dollars, he was inclined to raise a glass to every single one of them.

The only time the presence of my surfboard really sat well with Bull was when we steamed into Straddie. There's no formal moorings on the ocean side of the island. A twenty-metre trawler like the *Miss Bernadette* has to drop anchor well offshore, safe from quickly developing onshore winds that could blow her onto the rocky reefs of Frenchmans Beach, or push her high and dry onto the shifting sandbanks beneath Point Lookout. Therefore, Bull would usually anchor a kilometre or so off the rocky inlet of Frenchmans or off Point Lookout at Cylinder Beach, depending on the wind. So it was then that my surfboard and I came in handy.

'You want to go surfing, son?'

'Bloody oath, Dad.'

Thus entrapping his son by the promise of a day off, he'd fill an old hessian onion bag full of prawns and dispatch me to shore. The idea was for me to paddle a mile to the beach, scale the cliffs, exchange the prawns at the general store for coffee, bacon, eggs and cigarettes, then store the supplies in a bag of ice at an agreed place on the beach. I would then be free to surf all day.

Later, after he'd had a snooze and made shipshape what wasn't shipshape on board, Bull would row ashore in the little tin boat. He'd stow the supplies in the tinny and then go to the pub for a big drink. I'd paddle back to the trawler after my surf and settle down for bong smoking and sleep for the night. Dad would row the supplies and himself back in the morning, having made the tinny his bed for the night ashore.

In the context of my daily long, lonely paddles through shark-infested waters, these Straddie missions didn't seem overly dramatic as a price to pay for a day of surfing. In reality, paddling across a kilometre of open water on a small surfboard with a bag full of raw prawns jammed under my guts in one of the world's recognised magnets for alpha great white and tiger sharks was taking a pretty big risk. The prawns would spike and stab me, causing a blood trail to mix with the delectably smelly bag contents. I was stalked to the beach as a matter of course.

It *was* overly risky and locals came to know me as the 'temporary' grommet from Bullfrog Elkerton's boat. I was lucky. Dad and I now recognise that we were too desensitised to the dangers, thanks to our unusual exposure to them.

An interesting footnote to my prawn trading was that Nell Durbidge ran the general store at Straddie and her husband, 'Durbo' Durbidge, was a drinking partner of Dad's at the pub. Both are local generational legends of the island and parents of Bede, my dear friend and current ASP World Title contender. A small world indeed.

Bull and I had one particularly memorable day on North Stradbroke Island. I'd paddled ashore with the prawns and left Dad's luxuries on the beach in the tin boat while he spent the day at the pub, which overlooks the long point break at Cylinder Beach. In fact, the *Miss Bernadette* could be seen bobbing offshore from both the main bar and from the waves I was surfing. I paddled back to the boat after an incoming tide disrupted my session mid-afternoon.

I was enjoying my post-surf bong as the setting sun turned the shoreline of Straddie soft pink when a tiny familiar figure rolled down the extreme slope in front of the distant pub and staggered up the beach. I didn't need the binoculars to know it was Bull. I laughed to myself and waited for him to stumble his way over to our tinny, where he'd no doubt sleep off his day on the grog. Amusement turned to concern as he bypassed the tin boat and ploughed directly into the shore break.

'Maybe he's just cooling off before calling it a night,' I thought.

'Oh fuck! Maybe the silly old prick's blind drunk and thinks he's Aquaman,' I corrected myself seconds later.

Bull battled to swim through the head-high surf fully clothed, work boots and all. A strong rip was pulling him down the point and inexorably out into the expanse of South Passage Bar, the shark autobahn that separates Straddie and Moreton islands.

Bull's intention was to swim a mile to the boat, then clinically shoot up the pub with the .303 like some special forces sniper. He was irate at being refused service for being too drunk. Given the Straddie was one of Australia's roughest pubs, he must have been spectacularly inebriated. Too blotto to swim and shoot like John fucking Rambo, that's for sure.

I put the binoculars on him, which confirmed that he was struggling to stay afloat and in deep, deep trouble. My heart sank, because experience told me that his chances of survival were very low. With the little tinny ashore and the impossibility of piloting the *Miss Bernadette*'s bulk into the pounding surf, there was nothing else to do but grab my surfboard and go after Dad as hard as I could. Twilight began to give way to night as I went over the side.

At great length and with amazing good fortune, I located Bull wallowing on his back in the impact zone and wheezing the word 'cunts'. His boots were dragging him down and his arms were limp. I manhandled him onto my board, dropped into the water and began the long, exhausting task of kicking us back to the boat. It was safer than trying to take him through the shore break. Dad was snoring by the time I dragged him aboard. So much for the great Elkerton naval bombardment of North Stradbroke Island.

Dad returned to the pub a few weeks later, the death grudge either forgiven or not remembered. He never spoke one word of it to me again.

THE LAST PRAWN

Obviously, something had to give on the good ship *Miss Bernadette*. My surfing was going from strength to strength. Whether it was jumping from the boat or ranging around home, my confidence and skills grew by the week. Unbeknown to me, the common knowledge that I was surfing remote and uncharted waves off the trawler was doing wonders for my reputation. Combined with a growing list of contest successes, I had very happy sponsors in Quiksilver and Pascoe Hopper.

Seafaring matters came to a head when I won both the junior and senior Sunshine Coast titles in 1980, just before my sixteenth birthday. This made me the champion junior and senior competitive surfer on the entire Sunshine Coast. An expectation grew in the community and in the media that I would expand my contest schedule with a view to turning professional. But no other expectation was as strong as the one I carried in my own mind.

I needed to get off the boat and get started on fulfilling my potential and meeting my destiny. I still couldn't define what that was; I just sure as shit knew I wouldn't find it a million miles from anywhere, prawning with Bull.

Deep down, Dad knew it too, but he satisfied himself by having a few massive arguments with me before we parted company as shipmates. My head was in the clouds, I needed a profession to fall back on, that kind of thing. It must have been a big disappointment for Dad that I didn't aspire to participate in – and one day own – the traditional family business, as he had done. After all, it *was* a good life. Hard work, but also exciting, interesting, adventurous and very lucrative when you knew what you were doing. In all honesty, had I not had the talent and the opportunities I'd been blessed with as a surfer, I would've been a very happy and fortunate man to have taken over at the wheelhouse from Bull.

Dad and Mum reminded me that I wasn't yet an adult, so while they gave in to my demands to exit the boat, they insisted that I find work to occupy me between surfing contests. I'd planned at least a year or two of sporadic amateur and pro-am contests before hitting the ASP Pro Tour full-time. If I was to remain under their roof, they wouldn't tolerate the kind of laziness that characterised my school years.

After finishing my two-year stint as a deckhand, I got a labouring job on a building site opposite Alexandra Headland. It lasted one very lethargic week before a big swell lit up the whole Sunshine Coast. By lunchtime on the first day of the swell I'd had enough of looking at the waves roll in while I sweated it out like a maximum-security prisoner. Down went the shovel.

I walked off that building site and straight into a warts 'n' all professional surfing apprenticeship. In short order I placed second in two contests with very high profiles on the Australian scene – the Brothers Neilsen Open and the Cue Cola Pro Junior.

To my surprise and immense enjoyment, I discovered that my recent contest record, a few photos in *Tracks* and a blurb in the local papers had given me *minor* celebrity status around the Sunshine Coast. Bouncers and bar staff overlooked my well-known age as I was welcomed into hotels and nightclubs all over the place. Chicks actually competed with Peta for my attention, which was a shock. Beer was bought for me inside the pub. Cannabis was given to me in the car park by anyone and everyone. It was a surfing town and I was a surfer who had grown to become a less than microscopic fish in a small pond. I embraced it all, full steam ahead.

The fish and the pond grew a little bigger after the famous 1980 Queensland Titles.

ALL THAT GLITTERS

The 1980 Queensland Surfing Titles were famous because the waves were ten feet and perfect throughout. To my great good fortune the event was held at Cylinders, the right-hand point break at North Stradbroke Island where Dad had nearly drowned a few months before. It had become a favourite stomping ground of mine and I knew it well. Mind you, I'd never surfed it at such an imposing size. Huge, clean barrels thundered down the length of Point Lookout for the whole contest.

It wasn't only the surf that had me awestruck. The island had turned into a full-on madhouse, a veritable Woodstock of Queensland surfing. In the era before there were thousands of people who described themselves as professional surfers, the state and national amateur titles were very important events. Big-name star surfers were everywhere I looked, in and out of the water. The campground and surrounding village echoed to the noises of debauched drinking, drugging and partying all night, a very traditional way of preparing for a day of elite surfing competition. Actually, it was a very traditional way of preparing for a day of doing anything for most of these blokes.

That week was a severe physical endurance test. It felt like a year of partying had been compacted into five days, while in every heat I surfed against guys who absolutely shredded. There were no let-ups. I'd need to get used to these dual challenges in the years ahead.

My two main rivals in the juniors became friends of mine and would influence me greatly. Craig Walgers and David McDougall were Gold Coasters with huge talent. Craig and I hit it off right from the outset. He was the first bloke who really opened my eyes to the Gold Coast.

During the 1980 Queensland Titles, I surfed a week of roaring, giant point surf with equally roaring hangovers. For the most part, I was stoned off my brain on mull.

At week's end, I was sixteen years old and crowned the best surfer nineteen years or younger in Queensland. The Queensland Junior Title had been won previously by living legends such as Peter Townend and Rabbit Bartholomew. I knew it was a big achievement, but it took a while to sink completely into my thick skull.

I received a hero's welcome when I got home to Mooloolaba. Which meant being showered in alcohol and mull, not ticker tape. More exposure in mainstream local media followed, along with some more coverage in *Tracks*. 'Kong is King' and similar pithy headlines were cut out lovingly by Mum and kept for posterity. Even the old man gave me a big pat on the back and a 'Good onya, son'.

Kids these days think it bizarre that Quiksilver didn't always make wetsuits and Rip Curl didn't always make clothing. After my Queensland Title, it wasn't long before I had endorsement arrangements with Rip Curl for wetsuits to go with my sponsorhip deal with Quiksilver for clothing and apparel. My mug had begun to show up in the occasional advertisement for both companies. Appearing in *Tracks,* as small as the references were, increased my self-belief and the inner drive to keep proving myself.

After I became mates with Craig Walgers, I began viewing the Gold Coast as integral to my future. Everyone knew how good the waves could be down there, and Craig also opened my eyes to how much I could gain by surfing incredibly consistent waves, surrounded by such an excellent general standard of surfers, under the gaze of influential people in the sport's growing media and business sectors. The first weekend I stayed down at Craig's place turned into a fortnight of surfing my guts out all over the Goldie. I made a habit of getting down there as often as I could.

In my eyes, it was a big town. Bigger in every respect than the life I was used to at home. More quality waves, located much closer together, and everywhere you looked, guys were ripping. The standard in the water was like our North Shore club contests but every session of every day at every break. The vibe was super-aggressive and made the Sunny Coast seem relaxed by comparison. Everyone was pushing each other to the max. People would paddle over the top of their best mate, competing for position. A smartarse, chunky kid from the Sunshine Coast with a bombastic nickname was given no favours, let me tell you.

Breaks like Burleigh and Kirra were overflowing with people who'd won big contests. Having a Queensland junior champion from out of town in the line-up simply presented the local hard bastards with another fuckwit whose big head needed deflating. Fair enough too. I actually enjoyed being kicked down the pecking order – this stone-cold natural selection process really fired me up.

The girl situation was outrageous. It may have been my grommet enthusiasm, but it appeared as if every gorgeous chick in Australia had converged upon the Gold Coast intent on meeting 'surfies'. The night-life on the glitter strip made the little old Sunshine Coast seem like a bingo convention.

While the boozing and dope smoking was nothing I didn't expect, I was taken aback by the sheer amount of heroin, cocaine and other exotic narcotics that were being offered and used by so many people. It made me feel like a naive little boy. This part of the scene scared me, I have to admit. Not that I shied away from it. I'm curious by nature.

From the very outset, heroin didn't appeal to my personality. Blokes would swear by how fantastically mellow it made them feel, but I'm one for being 'up', not going 'on the nod'. Thank goodness, because I could very easily have become one of the many outstanding surfers from Queensland who dropped off the radar and sometimes, tragically, out of life itself under the seductive curse of 'hammer'.

Cocaine was different. I got my first taste sometime on the Gold Coast during the first hectic year after I won my inaugural State Junior Title. I formed a lifelong love/hate relationship with coke immediately. During those late teen years it was good that I hardly had a cent to my name because, believe me, if I'd had the money, my burgeoning career would have disappeared up my nose before you could say 'another wasted surf champ'.

As financial matters stood, it would be another few years before I could subsist on anything other than the generosity of precious benefactors like Paul Pascoe and the meagre savings Mum had put aside from my years on the boat. I was your classic scab, getting a lot of stuff for free but thankfully never enough to form a fully developed coke habit. That was a joy for later.

Early in this awakening to the Gold Coast, the extent of what surfing had become for me sank in. Craig and I were walking beneath the Norfolk pines on Goodwin Terrace at Burleigh Heads late one afternoon after clocking up a full day at the point. I clearly recall admiring a girl who was sunbaking in the park, not looking where I was going. The hypnosis that all men suffer while they're perving was broken by Craig's voice.

'Oi, wake up, idiot! I want you to meet someone.'

There in front of me stood Wayne 'Rabbit' Bartholomew, hand extended. 1978 World Professional Champion. My number-one hero. The bloke who watched me sleep from his posters and photos for so many years.

'How ya goin', mate? I've heard a lot about you! We should catch up sometime. Let's go for a surf together soon, hey?'

I mumbled something I can't remember and shook his hand. Then he was off, sprinting up the cove for his evening surf.

Another of my rare revelations struck.

You ain't flapping around at Kong's Cove any more, dickhead. Rabbit wants to surf with you. You belong here. With these guys. Doing this. And you'd better be fucking up to it.

While these profound thoughts stirred in my subconscious, the best I could produce on the surface was to say to Craig,

'He's way fucking shorter than I thought he'd be.' True! I swear I really said that the first time I met the man who'd become my biggest inspiration, mentor and supporter. A lifetime friend through thick and thin. How lucky am I to be able to count my childhood hero as one of my best mates? It's been one of the most special, sentimental outcomes of my entire chaotic journey through life to date. Love you, Rabs.

HOT STUFF

The more I split my time between the Sunshine Coast and the Gold Coast, the more time rocketed by in a continual torrent of changes and major events. So much so that in the years between leaving Dad's boat just before my sixteenth birthday and turning twenty, I usually felt like an observer of my own life.

'Kong' had well and truly begun his reign over Gary.

I did have that surf with Rabbit in 1980. It was the first of many and it very quickly established us as kindred spirits. He never treated me as the relative nobody that I was. I was privileged to be taken under his wing, not that he ever made me feel like he did. He just looked out for me without being preachy or overbearing.

One of the things that struck me about Rabbit was the beautiful surfboards he rode. They had the coolest airbrush sprays and featured his famous Warner Bros 'WB' Bugs Bunny logos. I'd met several guys from Burleigh who rode the same sleek looking craft, including local legend Peter Lawrence. Many of the best Gold Coast surfers I encountered rode these pieces of art. As a confirmed surfboard nut, I became obsessed with them.

I can't remember whether it was Rabbit or Peter or even Craig who first introduced me to the guys from Hot Stuff Surfboards. What I do remember is that the owner, Paul Hallas, or 'H', wasted no time in telling me to pick out any board I wanted from his Burleigh Heads showroom and take it for free. Hot Stuff's shapers were like a list of the hottest craftsmen around: Al Byrne, Gil Glover, Neal Purchase Snr, and many other legendary Gold Coast shapers such as Peter Drouyn and Nick Anagnostou had all made boards under the label.

With supreme adolescent insensitivity, I didn't think twice about taking 'H' up on his offer. There was a definite sense of glamour involved with being on the Hot Stuff team at the time. I put my Quiksilver and Rip Curl stickers onto that first Neal Purchase Hot Stuff and – just like that – had unthinkingly spat in the face of the man who had been the first person to believe in my surfing.

To his enormous credit, Paul Pascoe never made me feel bad about my actions. As my Quiksilver sponsor, he was happy for me to keep growing my profile. As my original surfboard sponsor, he must have been shitty at my unannounced change of equipment.

There was never anything wrong with my Pascoe Hopper boards. They were superb. I was simply an easily influenced grommet who had stars in his eyes and a childlike love of Hot Stuff's impossibly cool 'devil' logo and 'flaming' word mark. It was the hippest surfboard company in Australia, as rock 'n' roll and high-profile as any surf hardware brand has ever been. The allure was irresistible.

I wasn't completely forgiven by many North Shore stalwarts for my thoughtless betrayal of my Sunshine Coast roots. I understand why many Sunny Coast locals judged me as being an ungrateful bighead. I can only defend myself by saying that I wasn't the first young man who has ever failed to engage his brain before making important decisions.

The Neal Purchase Snr flat bottom and subsequent Al Byrne flying six-channel-bottom Hot Stuff boards were under my feet during a dizzying run of contests that propelled me headlong into the spotlight of the surfing world.

During 1981, the mental clouds created by non-stop partying were parted by contest wins in the Tony Biltoft Memorial, North Coast Open and Juniors, and another triumph in the Queensland Junior Titles.

I started 1982 with a funky new promotional logo that Paul Hallas had organised for 'Kong Model' Hot Stuff surfboards. A guy we knew from the Sunny Coast had come up with a gorilla holding a surfboard, not unlike, but *enough* unlike, King Kong swishing around a hapless fighter plane in his big fist.

A third consecutive Queensland Junior came in 1982 along with the rare double of winning my first Queensland Open at the same event. Victory in the Cue Cola Pro Junior at Sydney's North Narrabeen later in the same year was by far my biggest win to date and put me centre stage in the surfing world. The likes of veteran professionals Peter Townend, Mark Warren and Cheyne Horan described me as a future World Champion in the mainstream daily newspapers. I was in every surf magazine from Australia to the USA, from France to Japan to Brazil.

Actually, Mark Warren was a Narrabeen local and nice enough to allow a skinny kid from Tweed Heads and me to pitch a tent in his backyard during the Pro Junior. We drank and ate the poor bugger out of house and home, not to mention littering his lawn with empty beer bottles, joint butts and piss stains. It must have been great preparation, because I beat the skinny kid in the final: Gary 'Kong' Elkerton first, James 'Chappy' Jennings second. Our names were to be inseparable in the coming years. Kong and Chappy.

Paul Pascoe visited Mum and Dad again. Quiksilver would pay me $750 a month for 'incidental expenses' (rather than 'wages'). My oldies finally started to see a viable future for me and my amateur status was still protected. I wasn't a pro but I was all but there.

Life was moving super-fast for the kid who'd lazed around off a trawler and out of a caravan for most of his life. And every step closer to surfing stardom was outpacing my ability to make adult sense of the attention I was receiving. It was a never-ending party in which Kong was central.

Kong. The relentlessly hard-charging, surfing, drinking, drugging, womanising force of nature. I was completely absorbed in the life I was leading, even though I had already begun to recognise that that life was leading me.

In the world of surfing, then and now, barely anyone pulls a seventeen-year-old kid aside to tell him that there are dangers attached to moving so fast. Rather than advising me to locate the brake, people lined up to help me press the accelerator.

ROAD TRIPPERS

I'd love to have kept my 1982 Pro Junior trophy. Pro Junior trophies are true collector's items. As well as being a physical reminder of the first flushes of professional success, they're also really cool clay sculptures – Mickey Mouse riding a big tube, handpainted in great detail.

Mine was smashed to bits four hours after I won it when Mark Warren's cat bumped it off the top of his refrigerator. To be fair, the poor feline was only trying to find a safe haven from the orgy of alcohol and other miscellaneous abuse that was raging throughout its usually peaceful home. Poor old Mark had just cause to doubt the wisdom of his hospitality.

Around midday the next day, Bruce Channon and Hugh McLeod from *Surfing World* magazine waded through the party detritus and sprawled bodies, eventually digging me from the wreckage. Al Green, the founder of Quiksilver, had engaged *Surfing World* to produce a feature piece about a surfing road trip featuring me and Chappy.

'Great ... let me know when you need us,' I croaked, feeling as though I had a fur coat for a tongue and sandpaper for lips.

My hangover was so acute that I had to physically press my fists to my temples to stop the terrible pulsating of my swollen brain.

'Okay. Get your shit together. We're leaving now,' said Bruce sadistically.

It was 37 degrees Celsius. I had just enough time to throw our boards on the roof of Hugh's Saab, take a two-minute drink of solar-heated water from Mark's garden hose and fireman-lift Chappy into the back seat. We had two days to travel the thousand kilometres to Torquay in Victoria, where we'd meet Al Green and start one of the industry's earliest fully funded 'promotional photo trips'.

Al turned out to be a top bloke, a down-to-earth character who had a slow and considered way of talking but the sharpest mind I've ever encountered. We hit it off straight away. I've been through a lot of ups and downs with Quiksilver, but I've never exchanged a harsh word with its founder and original owner, Al Green.

Like our friendship, Al has never changed a bit. Whether it was 1982 or 2012, you'd never know that he was any wealthier than anyone else at the pub. From our first meeting on I've been welcomed to stay with his family at Jan Juc, near Bells Beach, whenever I've been in town. And it's been my honour to take the Greens up on their offer.

Chappy and I also linked up with Al's mates from Torquay Doug 'Claw' Warbrick and Brian Singer, our other sponsors and owners of Rip Curl. I also developed great respect and personal fondness for both guys.

In the early days of the industry, companies like Rip Curl and Quiksilver weren't yet giant multinationals. There were no middlemen, hangers-on, team managers or try-hards buzzing around in their hundreds. We hung out directly with the owners and tapped into the genuine surfer's energy behind these great characters.

Al hosted me, Chappy and the *Surfing World* boys on a crazy couple of weeks around the wild coastline of Port Campbell and the Twelve Apostles. The waves were awesome, the company was fantastic, the beer was cold, and I found plenty of mull and hash for myself. It was a binge of surfing and partying that hadn't stopped since the day we pitched our tent in Sydney.

At one point, I was exhorting my fellow travellers to find a second wind as we entered the pub at Apollo Bay: 'If ya can't rock 'n' roll, don't fucken come!' With that rather childish statement, *Surfing World* had the title for their feature story and the public persona of Kong was set in stone.

'If You Can't Rock 'n' Roll, Don't Fucken Come' also became a marquee advertising campaign for Quiksilver. It was one of the first surfing ads which didn't depict a surfer on a wave. I stood drunkenly atop an old station wagon in my Quiksilver shorts, letting out a big yell, looking like I was enjoying myself. The quintessential party animal and centrepiece of Quik's highly successful 'Echo Beach' promotions.

Al was nothing if not well ahead of his time. He had some unusual and groundbreaking plans in mind for Kong. Gary was hitching a ride too!

HOME AND AWAY

My return to the Sunshine Coast after the Pro Junior win and Victorian road trip set up a tiring cycle. I'd be away for months at a time, competing, promoting and generally running amok, before returning home for a few weeks of catching up with mates and generally running even more amok.

During these times, I wasn't the best brother or son. Tombarra Street was still my nominal 'home', but I'd fly in and fly out without paying much attention to my family. I still loved them but I was just so bloody busy. Places to go, people to see – that shit.

I believe I was becoming psychologically, if not physically, addicted to the ongoing rush of surfing to near exhaustion, then drinking and taking whatever drugs were on offer at night. Everywhere I went both at home and on the road, my social circle had expanded hugely. I loved meeting as many new people as I could, and nearly every night had the feel of a celebration to it.

The years before I turned fully professional were as hard on my brother, David, as they were a repeating loop of fun for me.

In his mid-teens by then, David had developed a drinking and dope habit of his own. It didn't help that almost everyone who crossed his path wanted to talk about 'Kong', not about him. David was left in Mooloolaba, trying to grow up and form his own identity between the shadow of a self-absorbed big brother and the growing weight of Bull's expectations of him as the torchbearer for our prawning business. David needed Gary. Gary was too fucking busy being Kong. I just wasn't there when he needed me.

I didn't have the sensitivity or wisdom to understand that a fourteen-year-old boy would naturally look up to an eighteen-year-old brother, especially if that brother was in *Tracks* all the bloody time. I thought we were both kids. It didn't occur to me that I should show him any special leadership or consideration, like I'd received from Seaweed or Paul. I'd swing in and out of his life for years, like an arrogant dickbrain.

'G'day, mate, how's it goin'? Let's surf, hey?'

The surfing was okay. The problem was that I never bothered paying attention to 'how it was goin' '.

Mum, Dad and Bern showed their customary forbearance of me, but David and I have had never quite solved the dynamics that were put in place during the early eighties. We still love each other deep down; however, there's usually been some kind of obstacle that stops us being as close as we both recognise we should be.

We've had our good times, for sure. In fact, we share some of the same difficulties that come with an addictive personality. If we'd been able to connect throughout the years, I think the relationship would have been extremely valuable for both of us during some dark times we've each been through. I take my fair share of the blame for that.

During my late teens and early pro career, I was in a kind of 'maturity suspended animation'. By the time I recognised the need to repair things with David, it may well have been too late. I hope not.

My surfing plans were set. I was intent on an Australian Amateur Title in what remained of 1982. A top-eight finish in the Aussie Opens would guarantee me a crack at the World Amateur Title. I'd do some pro-ams (stand-alone events, separate to the pro Tour, in which both professionals and amateurs could compete) and selected contests in between, but I was determined to win a World Amateur Title before turning fully professional. I believed this was the correct way to approach my career and such a path was conventional wisdom at the time.

There was an American kid called Curren who I badly wanted to knock off before we inevitably hit the Pro Tour together. The '82 World Amateur Titles would be held on the Gold Coast. Home-ground advantage. I could *smell* victory.

Alas, my nose turned out to be too close to my arse.

During a warm-up surf at the Australian Titles at Curl Curl in Sydney, an innocuous-looking wave speared my board into my leg. It was punctured rather than sliced, and a dozen stitches in my thigh and calf put me out of action. No World Amateur Title for me.

A few months later, I watched from the beach at Duranbah as my future sparring partner, the great Tom Curren, beat my mate Wayne 'Wickers' McKewen in the world final.

I became obsessed with winning a World Amateur Title before I turned professional. Unfortunately, they were only held every second year, which meant my entry onto the ASP World Tour would be delayed much longer than planned. I figured this would disappoint Al Green, so I didn't look forward to breaking the news to him.

'No sweat, big fella,' came his surprising reply. 'I don't *want* you to compete, anyhow. I don't want you flapping around in shit waves, copping shit judging for a living. You're way better value to me charging great waves and cutting loose. Just be yourself, mate – don't worry, we'll look after you.'

Fucking *hell*. To my mind, the boss of Quiksilver was telling me that all I had to do to earn my keep with him was to go find good waves, get messed up as often as possible and cause havoc. Provided it was all recorded for publicity purposes.

This was innovative. Al pegged me as someone who epitomised the new post-hippy, post-seventies generation. I wasn't a clean-cut athlete, nor was I a long-haired, mellowed-out throwback. I had an unusual, powerful, eye-catching surfing style. I drank beer and consumed drugs like a submariner on shore leave with five minutes to live. I even had a skinny sidekick. Or did Chappy have a big fat sidekick? Something of interest was always bound to happen around me.

These days, the industry abounds with full-time 'soul' surfers. Guys who ham up the new-age spiritualism and esoteric wisdom bullshit without having to go through the irritating process of defeating their peers in competition. Don't get me wrong – it's a top way to make money if you can swing it. Good for them.

Back then, Al wanted to prototype me in a similar 'promotions only' role. Except soul had nothing to do with it.

He wanted Kong straight up, the antithesis of both hippies and the letterman-sweater college surfers who'd begun to emerge from the USA's National Collegiate Athletics Association (NCAA) programs.

The only thing 'soulful' about me is the bottom of my thongs. And my scholarship was to the school of hard knocks. As tempting as the easy life of getting sponsored to go on surfing trips and benders was, the concept just didn't sit well with my competitive spirit and the goals I'd set myself. I wanted a career, like Rabbit or Mark Richards. In fact, I wanted to prove myself against exactly those competitive legends.

The one consistent driving force within me since I decided that surfing would be my life was the drive to be World Champion – World Amateur Champion, then World Professional Champion. It's what 'surfing for a living' meant to me. The whole process was defined by becoming World Champion, then and always.

So the uncomfortable conversation with Al that I thought I'd have about not going straight onto the Tour the next year in '83 turned into a discussion about how we'd fit Quiksilver's promotional plans around my firm World Title ambitions. It was quite a relief to say the least.

Al was very good about it and we continued with the same handshake arrangement that was originally put in place around Mum's dinner table with Paul Pascoe.

Time would prove that Al really knew what he was talking about. With my style and bulk, I would indeed always struggle to showcase my best surfing in the crap waves that the ASP Tour was held in throughout the majority of my career. And I certainly suffered well more than my fair share of heartbreak at the hands of the judges. Still, I've never regretted my decision to test myself against the best. I won't die wondering if I was good enough, that's for sure.

Al also introduced me to Hawaiian filmmaker Jack McCoy, the genius behind the landmark film *Tubular Swells*. Jack had recently finished shooting now historic footage of two of my local idols, Joe Engel and Thornton Fallander, at Lagundri Bay in Nias, Indonesia. *Storm Riders* was an instant classic.

Jack impressed me mightily. He thought there may be a 'project' ahead between us. I was stoked, but my short attention span moved to other matters.

Matters such as my first trip overseas.

GRAJAGAN

Chappy and I departed Brisbane International Airport in mid-'82 for six weeks of roughing it out on Bali's Bukit Peninsula. Quiksilver planned for us to surf Uluwatu, Padang Padang and Bingin, and even sneak into Kuta for the occasional night out. Chappy had been frothing about his previous trips to these perfect waves in such vivid detail that I could picture each of them clearly in my mind's eye.

We didn't present as an archetypical pro surfing entourage. I had one small duffle bag, four meticulously packed surfboards and 250 bucks. Aside from his boards, all of Chap's possessions were carried into the airplane cabin in a plastic garbage bag. Classy. We were so classy that Qantas stopped serving us alcohol after about six hours.

My first experience on foreign soil was being nudged awake by a steward. 'You're in Denpasar. Get the fuck off. And you've got two minutes to remove your mate or we'll get the cops to do it for you.'

Chappy was collapsed in first class, wearing a snazzy coat of his own vomit. Though he was still clutching his plastic bag.

Passing through customs in Bali was a *lot* more casual back then. I dragged my little mate through the thirty-second stamping process and had begun to search for our boards when a stranger with a beaming smile strode up and shook both my hands. He was Made Kasim, local surfing royalty and all-round nicest bloke you could ever meet. Quiksilver had sent him to greet us.

'We go to Java now, okay, Kong?'

So much for kicking back at Ulus. Twenty minutes later the three of us were sardined into an ancient public bus and embarking on a jarring 21-hour road and ferry trip to Java. Chappy was lucky to remain unconscious for most of it.

The Javanese fishing village of Grajagan feels like it's perched upon the edge of the civilised world, because it is. Its shallow harbour and rickety shacks are bordered by Alas Purwo National Park, which is an imposing expanse of untouched, impenetrable and unknowable jungle.

The poetic name Grajagan was familiar to me as a whispered place amongst surfers. In the early eighties it had the mythical aura of an El Dorado, the Indonesian jungle break of scarcely believable perfection, spied from passing aircraft by US servicemen in the early seventies. Years later, American surfer Mike Boyum set up a rudimentary camp there, which was subsequently taken over by Balinese surfer Bobby Radiasa. 'G-land' had only recently received wide publicity after being surfed by the great Gerry Lopez and Australia's Peter McCabe. There'd been photos, but consensus was still that its legend may well be exaggerated or even an outright invention. We were about to find out.

'The gorilla off my back.' The exact moment of my emotional
collapse on the beach at Lafitenia, France,
after finally claiming a World Title in 2000.

A rare photo indoors at Grandma Lowe's place. Proof that I was always keen on high-speed bikes.

Little Gary Keith Elkerton, all shined up for a day at Karumba Primary. I'd be stripped to the waist and off for a day of beachcombing with my Aboriginal mates as soon as Mum turned her back.

With brother, David, and sister, Bernadette, at 'Kong's Cove' in '76. Though I've often been far from the ideal brother, I love my siblings dearly. We all seem to have survived the mental torture of Mum's groovy dress sense!

David and I sorting prawns in the early seventies.
The task became a lot less fun when we stopped
being volunteers and started being deckhands.

'Every prawn's like a dollar bill, son.' Bull (on the right) working the Gulf
of Carpentaria around 1970. This is a haul of over two and half tonnes of
banana prawns, taken aboard in only five minutes. Trawler life is magically
adventurous and rewarding. But it's also dangerous and bloody hard work.

The Maroochydore Grommet Crew. What a bunch of high-
energy little delinquents we were. Spot the gorilla!

Some photos from early advertisements and magazine articles ... No more
trawling for me! Exciting times, though it wouldn't be long before I'd miss
the empty perfection of the Great Barrier Reef.

No other sixteen-year-old was burying the rail on single fins quite like this. Putting a Pascoe Hopper through its paces '79–'80.

My transition to Hot Stuff surfboards marked a change in focus from the Sunshine Coast to the Gold Coast and the Pro Tour. I was in for a crash course on the seedier, tragic aspects to the lifestyle.

The original 'Kong' promotional logo, circa 1982. It's changed little over the years, though my feelings towards my alter ego have travelled through a full gamut of extremes. Today, I'm perfectly comfortable with the hairy bastard.

Grajagan, as seen from our jungle treehouse in '83. Note the drums of drinking water in the foreground. Out to sea at the far left is the reef outcrop called 'Kong's'. Not long after this photo was taken, the camp was saddened by a tragic death and a hair-raising tiger attack.

joliphotos.com

The perfection of the Quiksilver Pro Grajagan '96. I'm on the wave in the centre of the shot, surfing in my famous semifinal against Kelly. Contest surfing just does not get any more enjoyable than this!

IF YOU CAN'T ROCK 'N' ROLL

DON'T FUCKEN COME

The ad campaign that gave birth to the legend of 'Kong' the unstoppable party machine. 'Gary' managed to do some surfing in between times.

Kong & Chappy. After our 1–2 finish in the JJJ Pro Junior, James 'Chappy' Jennings (right) and I were inseparable for years. We became a promotional double act as famous for our antics on land as we were for our surfing. Underneath it all, we're genuinely the closest of mates. This photo was taken by Made Kasim at Grajagan, Java, Indonesia, in '83.

Mark Occhilupo and I in '84, just after I'd arrived in France. Days later, we were debating the quality of the Cronulla Sharks when I met Pascale.

Pascale and I made a great team for many years. It was love at first sight for us both.

Wayne 'Rabbit' Bartholomew went from being a hero whose photo was plastered to my bedroom wall to mentor and lifelong best friend. I credit his guidance, support and advice with saving my career and my health in the mid-eighties.

A bloke whose friendship I've treasured since the day I set foot on the Pro Tour. Tom Carroll probably saved my life in '85, and in '93 he sacrificed a shot at his fourth Pipeline Masters to help me win a World Title.

Tom Curren and I shadowed each other from Amateurs to Pros to Masters to retirement and beyond. It's an honour to have had so many epic battles with the great Californian.

Aaron Chang

Ultimate proving ground. Sunset Beach's shifting, surging West Peak hunts down even the best surfers like a remorseless predator. A foot or two of poor positioning on acres of Sunset's huge reef system can have lethal consequences. Falling in love with the beast in '83.

Jeff Hornbaker

Learning the ropes, Waimea Bay, Oahu, Hawaii, '84. Every wave I surfed at 'The Bay' helped keep me alive during the historically colossal swell at the '86 Billabong Pro.

Simon 'Swilly' Williams. Inset: Peter Simons, courtesy *Tracks*

Power surfing defined. Then (inset) and now (above). Aside from getting tubed, my aim was always to build maximum speed before carving as much of the surfboard into the pitching wave surface as possible. With my large build, hopping into the air was never going to define my style.

Aaron Chang

Winning the '87 Billabong Pro at Sunset Beach. One of two consecutive victories in as many weeks at my favourite wave.

With sixty-eight stitches freshly removed and parading a gut earned by a month of ice-cream and painkillers, could it have been my own extra blubber and not Sunset that snapped my board? Filming *The Performers I* with Jack McCoy.

With Ol' Yellow. This unique Brewer/Chapman super-gun was under my feet on some of the biggest paddle-in waves ever ridden. After pinching it from Mike Miller during the '86 Billabong Pro, I risked my life saving it from destruction at maxing Waimea Bay. It is now stored under the steely eye of Ray Street. If only Ol' Yellow could talk. PS: Ross Clarke-Jones (to my right) looks like he's got severe board envy!

Hawaiian Triple Crown Champion, '87. My two wins in two weeks at the cauldron of Sunset Beach made me the first non-Hawaiian to claim the prestigious title.

Paul 'Gordhino' Cohen

Pipeline Masters Champion '89. It was a week of theatrical, gruesome surf. This dramatic victory formed the centrepiece of my second Hawaiian Triple Crown title.

Brian Bielmann

You're out, *fucker*! Michael Ho's infamous deliberate interference cost me my shot at Curren for the '90 World Title. Michael and his brother Derek are wonderful guys who – these days – are two of my closest mates in surfing.

My final win on the ASP Pro Tour in Durban, South Africa in '93. Derek Ho and I traded blows for the World Championship right down to the last day of the last event of the year. By '93, I was well used to the circumstances.

High emotions. With Kelly Slater minutes after my first World Masters Title victory in 2000. The champ and I shared a very heated but immensely enjoyable rivalry at the end of my career and the start of his.

Simon 'Swilly' Williams

Indonesia, 2011. It's a fantastic pleasure to ride terrific waves and meet new friends from all walks of life on my hosted surf tours.

Neca and Lunna. The love of my beautiful girls is the greatest joy in my life.

Keith 'Bullfrog' Elkerton sporting a lovely coat of propellor shaft grease. I reckon the people who invented 'Bring Your Child To Work Day' might think we took the concept a tad too far.

Mum and Dad – Bull and Joan Elkerton. Inspirations, friends and parents, who gave me the most wonderful childhood imaginable. We all miss Mum terribly.

Chappy, Made and I rode a disintegrating, underpowered fishing boat out over the gigantic rolling swells of the bay and into open water. Our Quiksilver connections – Garth Murphy, John 'Spider' Adrian and filmmaker Jack McCoy – would be joining us later.

Chappy and I stood speechless as the wave became visible towards the end of a slow voyage. It was a left-hander as long as any of the right-hand points at home. The waves were square, airbrushed tubes reeling off with mechanical perfection in sets of ten or more at a time. Eight feet and as smooth as glass, without a soul to be seen in any direction. A razor-sharp live reef, fringed by deep jade-coloured jungle right up to the water's edge, framed the scene.

The 'camp' wasn't as it is today. There were four bamboo sleeping platforms built about four metres up in the canopy. That was it. Not a TV or a refrigerator to be seen. There was no clearing, just the reef, the beach and the tree houses. The rainforest was so thick that it was physically impossible to walk into. Just as well.

As the local fishermen were unloading our supplies of rice and water, I asked Made why we had to sleep in the trees. I thought that it was because the high tide may have washed us into the jungle.

'No, brother,' he said, pointing at a huge paw print in the sand. 'She likes to visit at night.'

Fuck.

I'd heard that this mythological perfect wave was protected by mythological tigers and panthers. In the parlance of the famous TV show, both myths had been 'proven' within minutes of each other.

The boat guys departed leaving Chappy, Made and me alone. I felt totally intimidated. The sense of solitude was familiar, but there was an abiding undertone of danger that went with the isolation. It put a lump in my throat. We surfed overhead perfection until sunset then huddled together up our tree.

That first sleepless, moonless night was spent trying to block out the deafening sounds of an ecosystem alive with predators and the predated. From monkeys fighting, to bugs eating bugs, to reptiles eating reptiles, to bugs eating reptiles, to reptiles eating bugs. All the while Chappy and I listened intently through the cacophony, waiting for a feline roar. Or even a purr.

Made laughed. 'Don't worry, bros. She hunts in silence. If she takes you, best to be dreaming of barrels than to be waiting in terror! Sleep! Ha ha!'

Fuck.

'Besides,' he chuckled, 'Chappy and me are small, no good feed. Blessed to sleep beside a big man. Goodnight.'

Fuckity fuck. A funny man is my great friend Made Kasim.

G-land's a wave which, at maximum size, has all the venom of Teahupoo or Pipeline. But it maintains that intensity for hundreds and hundreds of metres. Having made the drop, it isn't just a matter of riding a tube to the channel. You cannot kick out. You *have* to ride tube after tube in section after section before safety is reached. Which is usually terrific. But above a certain size, G-land can't be ridden without inevitable severe injury.

Garth, Spider and Jack arrived as the height of an unrideable pulse in the swell passed. While Jack filmed, the five of us surfed ten-foot perfection for days. We spent four weeks existing to the beat of the tides, six people living on the edge of our abilities, on the edge of the earth, enjoying the largest, longest, most perfect combination of conditions in the known world of surfing.

One day we hiked past the outermost take-off spot – Money Trees – and into the remote foreshore beyond, sensing that there may be waves further around the peninsula. You could almost feel the beating heart of the jungle. After a few hours, it was obvious that we could go no further. On the way back we spotted a peak breaking outside of Money Trees. Its surfability was debated on the way back to camp. Nobody had ridden it before.

Suitably challenged, I hurried to get a board and returned to make the long paddle out to what is now known as Kong's, the second – and somewhat more substantial – wave to be named after me. Funny to think many more thousands of visitors to the modern surf camps at G-land have ridden Kong's than have ever ridden little Kong's Cove on the heavily populated Sunshine Coast!

Mike Miller, a Hawaiian resident and major Quiksilver investor, sailed his catamaran into the camp about halfway through our stay. On the biggest rideable swell of our trip, Mike and I shared a radical session during which he blew my mind with his positioning and bravery. Our connection would prove to be an important one in the years to come.

Not long after Mike's arrival, the camp was hit by a terrible tragedy when one of the supply boats was capsized on its way into camp. A local fisherman was drowned despite everyone's best efforts to save him. The poor fellow's body was placed beneath rocks and banana leaves under our tree house. On the next calm day he would be transported back to the village. We were all tremendously saddened and agreed that we'd also return, as a mark of respect to him and his family.

That last night, Chappy, Made and I were awakened by a terrifying roar and commotion beneath our platform. We looked down to see a huge tiger attempting to drag away the boatman's corpse. The man's friends who had stayed behind circled the big cat and drove it away with sticks and palm leaves. As disturbing as the scene was, it was also an unforgettable display of love and courage.

I've returned to Grajagan many times since. The wave remains a unique miracle of nature, though the camp and immediate surrounds are now downright opulent in comparison to the early days. The reef may not crawl with giant lobsters and the jungle may not seethe with quite so many panthers and tigers as it once did, but it's still an untamed, wild environment that should top any surfer's 'must-do' list. My first ever surf trip outside of Australia is also the best surf trip I've ever had.

You often hear people say that a particular wave is 'just like Grajagan'. That's bullshit, I'm afraid. There are only two waves I've ever seen that aren't 'like' anywhere else. Waves which can't be defined by any other location, and Grajagan is one of them.

The other was coming my way in short order.

THE MAIN GAME

From my earliest interest in surfing I've always considered any achievement at all as secondary to performances in Hawaii. Every surfer I've looked up to has mastered the North Shore of Oahu's 'Big Three': Pipeline, Waimea Bay and Sunset Beach. Having surfed Tahiti's colossal behemoth Teahupoo at its best, there's no doubt it should join this esteemed triumvirate.

I'm of the old-school (and these days unfashionable) opinion that Sunset Beach is the ultimate test of any surfer. It's one thing to be towed into gigantic swells at high speed; I do it regularly and there are few thrills to match it. It's quite another thing to paddle under your own steam around several shifting, heaving acres of terrifying ocean variables in a chaotic line-up in which the difference between the greatest wave you could ever imagine and a pounding of lethal, biblical savagery is a few centimetres of positioning and judgment.

Sunset Beach at anything over ten feet resembles a moving mountain range. It doesn't have an easily defined take-off area. There's a unique, almost proactive malevolence to it. You feel like you're being 'hunted'. Each set can impact in a subtly different part of the expansive reef system. Each individual wave has lumps, tricks, bends and backwash that are completely different to any wave before. Evil currents conspire to move you into the worst possible areas, even as your cumulative experience tells you that you're safe. The wave itself invites you to believe that you're better than you are. It often offers you a seemingly perfect curve upon which to carve or a perfect tube to pull into, only to change shape in an instant, casting tonnes and tonnes of steel-hard water onto your unworthy head.

The best way I can describe the challenge of riding Sunset effectively is to say that I've seen pretty average surfers with very big balls get epic rides at 'readable' waves such as Pipeline and Teahupoo. But I've never seen anyone but elite surfers get epic rides at Sunset. I know plenty of veteran expert pro surfers who readily admit that they simply don't enjoy the place, because it's too difficult and too scary.

Unlike any other wave, Sunset Beach at its maximum size demands more than supreme courage and supreme skill. It demands calmness, fitness and clarity of thought while it does its best to deceive the instincts you usually trust. It demands an intimacy with the ocean of the kind that only begins with your quality as a surfer.

If you take your ego into the line-up at Sunset without also taking your patience, humility and utmost respect, *it will fuck you up*. It will fuck you up so bad, you'd wish you'd never seen your first surfboard.

If you're prepared for all of the above, it will reward you like no other wave. But it's fucking tight-fisted with its blessings. Sunset Beach is not a perfect wave. In fact, it is an imperfect wave. It *is* a perfect challenge.

It is the best.

Frankly, it's ludicrous that fans around the world never get to see much of Sunset Beach in photos, movies or articles any more. The line-up is just too hard for most travelling professionals to come to grips with in the usual two weeks they spend on 'fly-in/fly-out' stopovers. It's also very difficult to film or photograph from the beach. With its fickle collecting-points, take-off spots and whirlpools, and with its lack of a dependable safe channel, Sunset is also Russian roulette for water photographers.

The ASP don't even have a top-ranked World Tour contest at Sunset Beach any more. Incredible. World Champions are crowned year after year without even needing to paddle out at the world's most challenging surf break. I'm certain that they'd want to.

Despite falling from favour with marketers and administrators, Sunset has never lost its place at the summit of all proving grounds. Top surfers know. You need to pass the exam unassisted by towing or ski backup at Sunset. Cameras or no cameras, contest or no contest, or else all of the chest-beating in the world doesn't add up to a fart in a tornado.

My years of Sunset Beach experiences were all ahead of me. As I sat on a plane bound for Oahu in November 1982 with four whole months on the North Shore ahead, life was about nothing else. No future beyond my immediate future in Hawaii existed.

I cleared customs and sat nervously in the Honolulu arrivals area with my one small backpack. I stupidly assumed that some surfboards were being sent ahead for me without confirming or organising the process.

Al Green had assured me that someone would come to pick me up. I had no phone number to ring, no contacts to call on. Nothing. I knew that Chappy and Rabbit were already over on the North Shore, but I had no way to get there and no idea how to find them. I waited forlornly like the kid I was for three hours until a very familiar face threaded its way through the crowded terminal and headed straight for me.

'How's it going, man?'

My belated welcoming party was none other than 'Mr Sunset', Hawaiian icon Jeff Hakman.

I sat in the car on the drive out to the North Shore in total awe of being in the company of Jeff Hakman, immortal master of Sunset Beach. He chatted warmly about surfing and life, like we were old mates. I was so starstruck that I could barely converse with him.

I let out a spontaneous gasp as we rounded the famous curve on the Kamehameha Highway, which first exposes travellers to a sweeping view of the best surfing coastline on earth. The North Shore was pumping. Remarkable. The most well known and violent waves in the world, all lined up consecutively on a lush, otherwise placid little stretch of coast less than half the length of Australia's Gold Coast and much smaller than LA's bay area.

'Ha ha. You don't get sick of that, man. Unbelievable, huh?' he said before the road dipped back into the pineapple fields. 'You'll be okay here, Kong. I've heard a lot about you, man. You'll be fine.'

His confidence in me was a surprise. Aussies were known to Hawaiians as fantastic surfers, but they had also developed a reputation in the islands as cocky interlopers, ignorant of ancient Polynesian cultural sensibilities and blind to the nuanced obligations of mutual respect that come with the beautiful traditions of Hawaiian 'aloha' spirit. We aren't bad or disrespectful people in general. We simply have a massively different, highly competitive, super-aggressive undertone to our surfing traditions. Even the more laidback amongst us.

Understandably, this irks Hawaiians for sensitive reasons that are best understood in the context of the islands' history since colonisation. Aussies need to take a deep breath, contain their excitement and think about what they're doing when they visit. This doesn't always happen. Considering that I'd rarely used rational thought in my life to that point, I'd be on a steep learning curve.

Jeff is a *haole*, which means white or American Hawaiian. He knew better than anyone how important respect was. I'd learn much from him and many others during my first journey to surfing's holy ground.

I found out that Al Green and Mike Miller had assured their numerous Hawaiian contacts that I came from a 'salt of the earth' fishing family and that I grew up at sea. Thank God. Because I arrived, to all intents and purposes, as yet another 'next big thing' who had a brash reputation. I even had a personalised marketing logo, for fuck's sake.

Being befriended by Jeff Hakman was the first of many lucky breaks I got on my initial trip to Hawaii.

PISS OFF, YOU LITTLE PRICKS

Jeff dropped me at David Kahanamoku's place behind Foodland at Waimea. The area is so revered amongst surfers that even the local grocery stores are part of folklore.

David was named after the brother of the legendary 'Duke' and is a member of the world famous Kahanamoku clan. To be guided from the outset by so gracious a man, so steeped in Hawaiian spirit, not to mention a terrific surfer, was fortuitous beyond description.

The next day, Mickey Nielsen swung by to pick me up. Mickey is a North Shore local whose house is situated right in front of Sunset Beach. Needless to say, he could surf the place, just a little. No offence to people who are covered in ink, wear funny caps and get all frothed up about being surfing tough guys, but you are modelling yourself on Mickey. I reckon Mickey wakes up in the morning and enjoys a nice refreshing glass of concrete for breakfast.

Another reason to thank Al Green and Mike Miller. Al actually paid Mickey to 'keep an eye on me' for as long as I stayed. Soon enough we became close mates. Having Mickey as a shadow (and vice versa) was like winning Lotto. Thankfully Mickey was on my side because, believe me, if he had told me to fuck off out at Sunset, I would most certainly have obeyed him by fucking off instantly – I'd have paddled all the way back to Mooloolaba!

On the subject of friends old and new, I wasted no time in finding Chappy. The stupidity of arriving in Hawaii without the trifling detail of surfboards was quickly fixed by Jack McCoy, who generously loaned me his three spanking new Hot Stuffs.

Chappy and I were walking down the beach to Pipeline for our first surf when we spied Rabbit walking toward us. We hurried over to him, eager to hang out. The tender feelings were not reciprocated.

'Ohhhh no. I knew I'd see you two together before too long. Piss off, ya little pricks.'

'Ha, ha, yeah sure, mate. What do ya reckon, are we surfin' Backdoor?' I replied, enjoying the familiarity of good-natured banter.

'Nah, I'm serious. Look, I've been punched in the head quite enough for one lifetime, thanks very much. You smartarses are trouble waiting to happen and I'm *not* going to be in the vicinity when it does. So when you see me anywhere, fuck off in the opposite direction.'

Chappy and I killed ourselves laughing, but we could see the 'elder statesman' was dead serious. We couldn't blame him. He was damn near murdered in Hawaii during 1977 thanks to writing an article in *Surfer* magazine about the rising superiority of Aussie surfers.

Rabbit was no longer beaten up on sight and he had learnt his lesson well. Still, the locals weren't exactly throwing frangipanis at his feet, and a couple of green, wave-hogging hellraisers hanging around may not be good for his health. Let alone his wave count. He fully expected that we would learn our Hawaiian lessons the hard way, just as he had.

From then onward we surfed Log Cabins a lot and mostly hung out at David or Mickey's places. Consequently, we weren't hanging around with any Australians or other foreigners. It wasn't that we deliberately ignored our countrymen, more like we were making lots of friends amongst Mickey and David's friends. In deference to Rabbit, we became occupied enjoying the company of new friends and a new culture.

Once the local crew figured out that we weren't on the North Shore to compete or to 'prove superiority' and that we simply wanted to surf and have a good time, we were accepted with tremendous 'aloha'. It was very humbling.

Chappy and I weren't making a pit stop in Hawaii to win contests and get photographed before hurrying away to the next Tour stop. We were there to *learn*, and we were supported by our Hawaiian friends in a way which totally contradicted their recent reputation for ill temper and violence. It helped that we'd be quick to share a sixpack or a joint as we sat in front of Mickey's place, which was a local gathering point. We were even invited to Eddie Rothman's New Year's Eve barbecue. That really put a full stop to Rabbit's fears that we'd be run out of town!

I studied Sunset fanatically. I watched it for hours on end, even sitting on the beach at night to observe the way surges hit the inside reef. Mickey, David and Jeff allowed me to follow them around the huge, intimidating line-up, as did many others, including lifeguard legend Darrick Doerner.

I absorbed every morsel of advice and information like a sponge, while I paid my dues day in, day out for four months. I often hit Sunset well before daybreak in an effort to challenge my memory and 'feel' the water beneath me. The chaotic environment felt familiar, not unlike being on the trawler during cyclonic storm seas. I was intensely curious. Very gradually, I became able to position myself safely during big, broiling west swells.

I grew to understand that nothing can be assumed or expected of Hawaii, and that confidence can only come from as many hours as humanly possible spent making big mistakes and small steps forward. If you stop wanting to learn in Hawaii, you will never, ever be in the right place at the right time often enough to truly test yourself on her majestic waves.

Before Rabbit left in January he rocked up at Steamers night club in Haleiwa. Chappy and I were there with a few of the guys. We hadn't spoken to Rab for weeks, so it was great to catch up and the three of us set about our usual play-fighting and rough-housing. He was in a relaxed frame of mind and stoked for us that we had fitted in and avoided getting ourselves murdered. He was in the middle of applying a jokey headlock to Chappy when a bear-like set of paws gripped him around the neck.

Bird Mahelona was a man mountain. He back-slammed Rabbit against the wall. The '78 World Champ's face turned blue as Bird informed Rabbit in plain terms that, while his insults of yesteryear were partially forgiven, he would be dispatched for a long rest in the hospital or maybe the cemetery should a hair ever be touched upon Chappy's head again. Good old Bird!

The big guy was reassured that it was all fun, and beers were shared in peace for the remainder of the night.

'Fuck me dead,' squeaked Rabbit through his bruised voice box. 'And here I was thinking I'd be killed because the locals would *hate* you!'

Chappy and I stayed on the North Shore long after the pros left town for the Tour and continued to enjoy phenomenal late-season surf and hospitality.

Al Green could not have done me a bigger favour than to think ahead by hooking me up with my new Hawaiian friends. Had I hung exclusively with the Aussie crew, the story of that North Shore winter and the shape of my whole future career could have been very different. And in hindsight, perhaps my friend Rabbit deliberately separated himself from us for our benefit, not his. He's never admitted as much though – the big softie.

It was a sad day when Mickey dropped me back at the airport. Four months is a long time, but I never once felt homesick. Lifelong friends were made and lifelong relationships begun with the very best waves on earth. I returned home a vastly better surfer and a more aware, more insightful person than I'd been when I'd left.

HELL AND HEAVEN
(IN THAT ORDER)

I was mildly shocked and surprised by the surf media's level of interest in my and Chappy's long stint in Oahu. On our return to Australia in early '83 after the Hawaiian winter, we found that all the major magazines in both the US and Australia had given coverage to the efforts of two Aussie youngsters who were yet to join the World Tour, but who had surfed with bravado during one of the most memorable seasons for waves.

It gave me pause to consider the hype.

I thought that Chappy was way more impressive than me. The bloke was so skinny back then that he deadset had to run around in the shower to get wet. He had no right to charge Sunset, Pipe and Waimea like he did. There's no way Chappy was some kind of support act. His surfing in Hawaii that year – especially backside at Sunset – was awesome.

Mind you, it didn't stop me enjoying the approval of my Hawaiian mates and others as 'the real deal at Sunset Beach'. I enjoyed the crucible of the North Shore's biggest, best waves and I wasn't backward in telling anyone who asked that I didn't think too many of my teenaged American rivals shared my enthusiasm.

I had my potential competitors in the far off 1984 World Amateur Championships firmly in mind when I made these comments. They were tactless, arrogant remarks, but they psyched me up. Although I believed them at the time, my remarks were also more than a little tongue in cheek.

Perhaps the American boys didn't enjoy the same warm welcome that was extended my way at places like Sunset Beach? That perfectly reasonable excuse didn't enter my mind when the media pressed me for an opinion. Kong was always good for a quote. Did I *really* have to call them 'soft cocks' though?

It's the Aussie way to stir the pot with some good-natured jabs. We do it to each other mercilessly ... water off a duck's back. I was to discover that such stirring wasn't received in the best humour on the other side of the Pacific.

The Jesus Classic Pro-Am was a big contest at the time. It was a well-run and highly publicised event, as well as having terrific charitable connections via the large Christian surfing community in Australia. In '83, I was probably not the ideal person to be charging through the contest in the unstoppable form I'd brought back from Hawaii.

The point at Burleigh Heads was breaking in all its regal glory at six feet. Before the final, I used Wayne McKewen and Ian 'Ern' Byrne's place at Burleigh for a quick choof to 'calm the nerves'. Truthfully, I wasn't nervous at all, but I *was* a mull fiend. I must say that both guys went on to great success as master shapers at Mt Woodgee Surfboards. I must also say that I got as stoned as I've ever been.

I walked through the crowd on the grassy point in a complete daze, oblivious to the cheering and wellwishers. I was suppressing laughter at jokes that I couldn't remember. I must have somehow negotiated the infamously dangerous boulders to jump into the surf because the next thing I remember is floating around the line-up on my belly, marvelling at the assembled spectators and the muffled commentary that was blasting through the PA system.

I recall being bemused that a concert or a circus must have come to Burleigh while perfect waves at the point were completely uncrowded. It must have been some fucking concert, I thought. Maybe I should paddle back in, so I don't miss out on it?

I discovered that I didn't have the energy to return to shore, so I stayed put, motionless on my board as wave after wave rolled past. For the first time in my life, I was actually too fucked up to surf. And of all times to find my outer limits, it was during the final of a massive pro-am event!

I just laid there beyond the break, doing nothing for a full fifteen minutes. Wayne and Ian had got over their convulsions of laughter and were considering a rescue mission when a huge set loomed out wide and threatened to break on top of my inert, empty cranium. Amazingly, my mind cleared as a wave crested above me. I swung around and freefell into a stand-up tube from which I emerged before shredding a combination of acute re-entries and cutbacks to the beach. Something clicked. The clarity remained for three more excellent waves before the final siren sounded.

I'd won with a blistering charge in the final fifteen minutes.

I was still groggy and numb when the microphone and trophy were thrust into my shaky hands at the presentation. I concentrated very hard on not blaspheming, but the effort caused me to lose focus on avoiding other bad words that shouldn't be said in public, let alone at a Christian gathering.

It was not a great speech. I may have done myself no favours, but I definitely enhanced Kong's irreverence credentials. I'm ashamed to say that I can't even remember who my opponent was in that final. Whoever you are, mate, I am truly sorry.

The postscript was worse.

The win was celebrated with my Gold Coast friends and Hot Stuff connections with customary vigour. Amidst the madness, the huge crucifix trophy I'd won was accidentally broken in half.

Later that week, I returned home to Tombarra Street needing a decent sleep. I walked through the lounge room past Mum, smelling of stale beer and holding the halves of the crucifix in each hand. Joan flew into an ecstatic rage of – literally – biblical proportions. She recited Hail Marys as she sprinted for her rosaries. Without so much as a 'hello' she swung a clinched fist into my earhole, wrenched the broken cross from my hands and left me on the floor with my head ringing. After decking me she scurried downstairs and superglued the trophy back together. It's never been returned to me.

I'm told I'm going to hell. Fair enough, I can't argue with that assessment. At least I'll spend eternity surfing six-inch Venice Beach, drinking hot English beer and watching New Zealand beat Australia at rugby league with a heap of my good mates.

Jack McCoy had arrived back in Australia from Hawaii before I did, preparing to shoot a project with Chappy, Rabbit and me. Thanks to his experiences with us on the 'Don't Fucken Come' road trip, Al Green was convinced that the fun, mayhem and high-performance surfing should be translated onto film.

Jack originally thought that we should travel back to Java, or maybe even up to my old happy hunting grounds on the Barrier Reef. Quiksilver was providing the budget, so potential locations were restricted to planet Earth. Anything beyond that could not be done.

The four of us talked over our options long into the night at the SurfAir Hotel at Marcoola on the Sunshine Coast. Eventually all the resort's bars closed for the evening. We got some takeaway beers and walked down to the beach, waiting for sun-up. A good swell was predicted.

Jack squinted at the silver lines of foam that were appearing out of the black ocean to our south. 'Man … there's some serious shit going down on that reef out there. What the fuck *is* that, man?'

'Oh, that's the Old Woman,' I explained. 'Mudjimba Island. Local Aborigines say that a long time ago, a lady got swept away from the mainland and was stranded out there. She lived all alone for a long, long time. Her spirit's still there … you know, all that kinda stuff.'

'Waves?' enquired Jack.

'Fuck yeah! The waves pump. Heavy as buggery, peeling rock platform. I paddle over there heaps.'

'Anchorage?'

'Yep. Fisherman and divers are there all the time.'

'Right,' announced Jack, throwing his foaming half-full beer at me, 'get me a fucking boat!'

Jack was pretty drunk, but his renowned creative vision was perfectly unimpaired. Mudjimba or 'Old Woman' Island, only a few football fields in size and barely two kilometres off the Maroochy coast, was perfect for the project. No-one but a Sunshine Coast local would know where the hell it was, for a start.

Secondly, we could spend more time shooting because we could start immediately. No travel, transit or even accommodation plans were necessary.

The next few weeks were superb. We scored top waves out on Mudjimba and Jack secured excellent footage from the boat, the water and the island. A road trip was made a few hours down into New South Wales and some great action was also shot at Lennox Head and Spooky Point.

The end product was very pleasing for all concerned. Especially Al Green, who got great exposure for Quiksilver. When *Kong's Island* opened at the Sydney Opera House in 1983, it was received with universal approval. 'Where *is* Kong's Island?' asked the promotional collateral, in which Mudjimba was billed as 'Incredible and Perfect Tropical Paradise Surf'.

Some mystery! The secret location was positioned about three kilometres from my bedroom and anyone can see Mudjimba Island simply by looking out to sea from almost anywhere on the Sunshine Coast!

BELONGING

The 1983 Bells Beach Easter Classic was a golden opportunity to measure myself as an amateur against the world's best professional surfers. There was a lot of hype surrounding me by this stage but, despite my many successes, I'd yet to prove that I could match it with the best of the best. To date, it was all anticipation. Had my sponsors – Quiksilver, Rip Curl and now Oakley – created a 'legend' of nothing? Why hadn't I already turned pro if I was as good as they said I was? After all, I hadn't won an Australian or World Amateur Title.

There was no doubt in my mind that I was good enough, but I had to admit that hard questions were understandable, especially given the unprecedented publicity and promotion I'd received as an amateur. Was I really the best non-ASP touring professional in the world? Did I have legitimate claim to being regarded as amongst the world's best?

I'd had a taste of large events at pro junior and pro-am contests, but being accepted into the Bells Easter Classic as a 'triallist' was something *completely* different. I imagine it would be like the first time a pro footballer runs into a stadium full of 60,000 fans. Except, unlike football, we surfers all share the same locker rooms, physios, masseuses and VIP areas. Actually, the VIP area was the thing that blew me away.

As is the case in all pro contests, competitors lounged in comfort, enjoying the best views of the contest site. All the food and drink anyone could ever eat were available from an inexhaustible buffet. Pro surfing legends chatted amongst themselves while eating, sipping a favourite drink and enjoying a rub-down between heats. Wives, girlfriends and other close relatives milled around, while sponsors' employees tried their hardest to appear busy and sound important.

Also, as in most pro contests, the judges were accommodated nearby, thanks to the high-viewing position. Their numbers have changed over the years but it's always an odd number, usually five. These days there are judges from many countries, though in the past there were often more judges from the host country than from elsewhere.

Surfers are judged using a maximum score of ten out of ten for every wave ridden during each thirty-minute heat. Each surfer's best two waves are counted towards a total heat score, the perfect score being twenty. Throughout pro surfing history there's been variations on the way total heat scores are expressed, but every wave has always been measured out of ten.

During most of my career, points were earned by the number of manoeuvres a surfer performed on each wave, with each manoeuvre given a weighting for difficulty. This protocol often led to success for slightly built surfers capable of deploying zillions of frenetic, small, flicking turns.

My heavy physique and natural instincts led me to do fewer but bigger turns at the sharpest angles, and I concentrated on executing them in the steepest parts of the wave. My focus was on degree of difficulty and on explosively slicing large volumes of water from the moving wave face with thick spray detonated high into the air by the gouging arc of the board. It looked spectacular and it felt great.

This was 'power surfing'. While universally regarded as the most respected style of wave riding, the method wasn't always easily rewarded under the prevailing judging guidelines. But the bigger the waves, the more effective it became. Tommy Carroll and Mark Occhilupo were also notable 'power surfers' during my career.

Judging criteria nowadays focus on the variety and 'radicalness' of manoeuvres, which is an improvement. Either way – no matter what criteria are in vogue – the judging of surfing is highly subjective, and an ever-contentious topic.

ASP pro events, like this one at Bells, had a static top flight of surfers, who were seeded directly into every main event. This top flight made up approximately half of the total field (of, most often, thirty-two surfers) in the main contest. Everyone apart from the top seeds had to battle it out through several four-man cut-throat 'trial' rounds, which involved up to a hundred guys who'd successfully applied to the ASP for a spot as a 'triallist' and a precious long shot at pro surfing glory. The top triallists made up the bottom of the main event draw.

Two-man – or 'man on man' – thirty-minute elimination heats are usually conducted in four rounds until the whole draw is reduced to eight men in the quarterfinals, then four men in the semifinals, then the two finalists (Hawaiian contests operated on a four-man format right through, for many years). 'Tour' points are awarded from first to last place in each main event. The person with the most Tour points at the end of each year is the ASP World Champion.

At season's end, the bottom few seeds from the top flight were replaced by the triallists from around the world who'd accumulated the most Tour points, or surfers who'd achieved the best non-pro-sanctioned contest record. In the late stages of my career, a two-tiered system evolved to replace the manic desperation of pro trials. To this day, top finishers in a parallel 'qualifying' tour replace the bottom-ranked pros in an annual promotion/relegation process.

Though all pro Tour contests are fought out for equal points, not all contests are equal in the eyes of the surfing world. Due to their history and the danger or quality of their waves, some contests are considered much more prestigious than others. All contests in Hawaii carry increased status, for example. The Bells Beach Easter Classic in Victoria – the oldest annual surfing event in the world – is also such a contest.

In '83, I'd have to surf my way through the sudden-death Pro Class Trials at Bells before I even got a crack at the main event and the big time.

I won the Pro Class Trials. I continued my form in the main event and made it through to the semifinals ahead of a draw that included nearly a dozen past and future professional World Champions.

Surfing before tens of thousands of cheering spectators and dozens of evening news cameras was a nerve-jangling buzz, though something I knew I'd need to get used to as part and parcel of every event, all over the world.

In time I'd forgo the luxury, lofty company and distractions of the VIP area for the privacy of rented apartments near the contest site, and I'd avoid becoming immersed in the massive crowd atmosphere before each heat. But in my first big-time contest and in the immediate years after it, mixing with the sport's elite and soaking up the public adulation was a rush that compared with surfing itself.

The semis were contested between the long, tall Texan Wes Laine and me on one side, with Joe Engel and Tom Curren on the other. Wes ended my giant-killing run and Smokin' Joe proved the enormity of his talent by winning the battle of the freaks against Curren. Joe then dispensed with Wes to 'ring the bell' and take the Easter Classic Title. I was shattered not to get a crack at the final, but as the obligatory piss-up ground on that night, the importance of my accomplishment gradually took hold.

I'd come third in the Bells Easter Classic. As an amateur, via the trials.

I looked around the after party and basked in being surrounded by blokes who ruled the world of professional surfing, many of whom still resided in posters on my bedroom wall at Tombarra Street.

Maybe some kid, somewhere, would have me on their wall soon.

I belonged with these guys.

The day after the Bells final, Chappy and I hitched a ride to Geelong where we hired an Avis rental car for a week. I was lucky to have Mum organise this for me on her credit card.

We planned a road trip over to Chappy's home state of South Australia. He was keen to show me the great variety and power of his home state's surf. The local SA crew are notoriously protective of the secrecy of their best waves and they are on the record as being delighted to break heads as part of the process. My little mate was my ticket to sampling some supreme Southern Ocean offerings that would otherwise be unavailable.

Potent South Australian desert cannabis would also have been unavailable to me without inside knowledge.

What a great couple of weeks we had in South Oz, featuring dozens of waves I can't breathe a word about. Chappy and I were in a self-congratulatory and reflective mood as we approached the Queensland border. The reflection suddenly reflected all the way back to Geelong.

'Oh shit! The CAR!'

A one-week rental had turned into a cross-continent jaunt of massive proportions. We were supposed to return our ride to Geelong seven days after we rented it.

Since we were so close to Coolangatta Airport, the filthy, mull-infused Commodore was parked at Avis's offices. We figured all would be okay since we'd actually brought it back, albeit after putting nearly 3000 kilometres on the clock, 2000 kilometres away from where it should be and three weeks overdue.

Idiots. Avis were not impressed. Neither was Mum. No-one was charged, but we were bloody lucky. The shit-storm got Mum in undeserved trouble and put me in debt to her for ages.

Our rental car debacle was the product of Gary's puerile oversight, not planning. But once word got out, the surfing media erroneously gave Kong more misplaced 'wild bastard' credit. My sponsors were stoked by my wild ways. I became loud and animated on the grog or drugs, which meant I was loud and animated a lot. When someone heckled me at the pub or in the surf, I'd enjoy shutting them up with my fists. If I didn't have many societal limiters as a kid, then I had even fewer as a young adult. The big, spontaneous, unpredictable guy had a big, spontaneous, unpredictable surfing style and a big, spontaneous, unpredictable life.

Wildness helped my profile, but the kudos didn't exactly encourage me to think through my actions in an adult fashion. I was a nineteen-year-old on the cusp of a meaningful career in professional sport. In most other sports, this would be a period in which I'd be getting deadly serious about preparation. Rather, I was becoming increasingly strung out by constant partying and improved access to illegal drugs, a fact that was no secret to anyone on earth but Mum and Dad.

But this was pro surfing, not pro anything else. My drinking and drug habits didn't worry me and they didn't worry anybody else. As far as everyone was concerned – including me – I was on the right path.

DEMONS

'Home' for the rest of 1983 was usually someone's sofa, since – despite all the recent successes and publicity – my $750 per month for expenses was still my only income. Not that I was complaining! That much per month kept me in a basic amount of mull and beer, with a little remaining to put fuel in the Chrysler Sigma that Bull was nice enough to buy me. Nothing was left for hotels or campsites. Cocaine and various other luxuries were usually free, which was just as well, because I discovered that I missed 'decent' drugs if I went without for too long.

I spent a lot of time in a farmhouse on top the Gold Coast's Mt Woodgee. Rabbit had introduced me to Nick Anagnostou a few years previously. Nick and his partner, Kaye, along with a few local fixtures such as Peter 'Mini' Munro and Peter 'Mont' Bryan, had been squatting in a century-old abandoned farmhouse on top of the little mountain behind Coolangatta Airport for many years.

A disused tropical fruit farm, overgrown by natural rainforest, Mt Woodgee was the happiest, most idyllic surfer's hangout I've ever known. From a hammock in front of the house you could see right down the barrel of waves breaking at Kirra, Greenmount, Rainbow Bay and Snapper Rocks. It was trippy to watch jets land beneath us and the world's best points reel away in the background.

Few people knew the way up to the mountain top, which was a kind of surfers' Batcave. Invited guests from Australia and all over the world were guided up to share the rainforest ambience, the panorama of the Goldie's famous points and the 'good times' camaraderie. Nick and the boys made their legendary local surfboards right there under the old shack. I'd ride many Mt Woodgee boards to victory in the years ahead.

These days, you can catch a glimpse of the old mountain top by looking up to the west before you pass the John Flynn Hospital southbound on the new motorway behind Tugun. You won't see the dilapidated farmhouse though. Billabong's Gordon Merchant bought the property in 1993 and has been enjoying the isolation and the view from his mansion up there ever since.

One of the beauties of Mt Woodgee was that there were no hard narcotics there. It was an oasis of tranquillity, perched high above the seediness that lay below the shiny surface of the tourist strip. Demons were tearing at the surfing world – and especially the Gold Coast – during 1983 and 1984.

The cops had done an excellent job of curtailing the trade in cannabis. Too bad they weren't so effective with heroin, which became cheaper and more broadly used as demand strengthened in the absence of mull. While the first wave of 'hammer' cut through the Gold Coast like a plague in the seventies, the early eighties surge was just as destructive.

As much as I liked chilling out on Mt Woodgee, I was just as often night-clubbing, pub-hopping, fighting and womanising from Coolangatta to Surfers Paradise. I used cocaine and LSD wherever I could get them, which was everywhere. The careers of so many promising Gold Coast surfers were in ruins. More importantly, their lives were in deadly jeopardy. I was lucky to navigate through it. A saving grace was that I kept clear of heroin, which continued to scare me. More off-putting than my distaste for being sedated was its visibly destructive side effects. My old junior rival and friend Craig Walgers had gone from a bone fide surfing champion to a physically tortured addict within three years.

I lost a true comrade and brother – as did hundreds of people – when Craig was hit and killed by a car as he crossed the Gold Coast Highway under the influence of heroin in 1984. The manner of his passing has never lost its rawness for me. I can't think of Craig without being consumed with grief and the searing frustration of immense waste.

Ridiculous to think that we surfers – myself foremost – are quick to blame heroin, as if the drug itself is a murderer. We sit lamenting how fucked heroin is, while we smash ourselves with alcohol, marijuana, cocaine, LSD, speed, ecstasy and whatever else comes our way.

Surfers never, ever judge. We allow people the 'freedom' of their habits. This is either enlightened or contemptibly immature. After many years, I'm now leaning towards the second perspective.

Odd contradictions are the norm. The act of surfing itself could hardly be any healthier for body or mind. Yet many seemingly transcendent surfers who espouse pure living through stuff like yoga and vegetarianism ingest filthy chemical concoctions when the mood takes them. A pro surfer may train his body to near perfection but thinks nothing of polluting his innards with all manner of mind- or mood-altering sludge.

I'm as much to blame as anyone for falling in with the pervasive culture of drug and alcohol abuse. No-one told Craig how much they were worried about him because it is simply not done to question someone's ability to handle their habits. It's stupid, but any honest surfer will tell you that it's the height of bad manners and general uncoolness to question someone's drug or alcohol use. People very rarely say anything of the sort.

Side effects are a strictly personal matter. In the hustle bustle of partying and surfing, too few of us stop to consider the health of our friends. We're all bulletproof. Charge in the water, charge on land.

The world of surfing brims with people coping privately with a multitude of emotional, mental, physical and financial miseries caused by the sport's entwinement with drugs. From the old shaper so beset by paranoia that he can barely function without a morning joint, to the clothing-company executive with a $100K cocaine habit, to the pro surfer who rewards himself with oxycodone binges, to the kid who takes pills before waxing up his board. To the semi-retired champion who still struggles to contain his compulsions. Like me.

Who tells them, who tells *us*, to stop? Besides, what surfer doesn't flip the bird to *anyone* who tells them how to behave?

If the cultural conundrum remains unsolved today, what hope did Craig have of counselling or intervention in 1984?

The surfing community, me included, did not look after Craig as much as we might have.

Few lessons have been learnt over the years. As surfers, our collective minds are blocked to the reality that we have created a self-protecting, self-perpetuating culture of drug use. The drugs are to blame when things go wrong. Our surfing 'brotherhood of freedom' has nothing to do with it. Live and let live. Don't step on anyone's choices, man!

There have been some superficial efforts at testing randomly for recreational drugs in pro surfing over the years, but nothing that was legally compelling. I refused all such tests. Had compulsory WADA – World Anti-Doping Agency – testing in line with global benchmarking been enforced when I entered the sport of surfing I would have *had* to choose between a drug-addled lifestyle and a professional career; an easy combination of both wouldn't have been possible. I'm sure I'd have chosen surfing. I'm also sure I would've made mistakes and caved into bad habits along the way. But they wouldn't have been ignored or – worse – celebrated.

I want to make it clear that I take full personal responsibility for all of my choices, good and bad. My point is that it would have been easier for me to make good choices had my professional sport made it impossible to make bad ones and still enjoy success. As it was, it took the uncommon intervention of surfing mates to save me from myself a few years into my pro career. More on that later.

Then there's the issue of performance enhancers such as steroids, hormones, EPO and others. You know, the kind of substances used by cycling and athletics cheats over the years. In the absence of rigorous 'world's best practice' testing, how can we be sure no pro surfer uses them? Believe me, being fucked up on mull, cocaine, heroin, acid, meth or any number of other recreational drugs generally does the *exact opposite* of 'enhancement', despite what your hijacked mind may be telling you.

You generally won't hear candid facts about drugs from anyone who's reliant on trickle down from the billions of dollars currently generated by the business of surfing. This is unfortunate but completely understandable, given the commercial realities. The industry has to project surfing and surfers into the hyper-competitive global recreation-wear market in a controlled fashion. After all, if Mum is buying a hoodie for little Johnny, does she buy the sports label as used by the world's best footballer, or does she buy the surfing label as endorsed by athletes who are culturally renowned for their driving passion to get high? There's a lot at stake.

Sure, you'll hear about celebrity surfers drinking and 'partying'. That's actually good for business. What we do is fun, which is an integral part of all youth brand strategies. It's the details of the 'partying' that don't get too much scrutiny.

Consideration of revamped drug testing by the ASP is welcome news, although far from the first time such grand pronouncements have been made. Based on my direct experience, unless such testing has the full range, independence and legal 'teeth' of the WADA, it will be ineffectual. Mainstream sports media and 'non-insider' sponsors will be monitoring developments with interest.

I may well be cast as a Hall of Fame surfer hypocritically spitting into the hand that fed him for many years. Again, I understand the viewpoint, but it would be impossible to be honest about my life without addressing this issue. I'll be damned if I'll put a halo on myself or on the sport I love just to make sure I don't run out of free sunglasses and board shorts.

Surfing has endemic and enduring issues with illegal drugs, which are out of proportion with community norms. Since I doubt that there's a surfer on the planet who isn't aware of this abiding drug culture, and since surfing's governing bodies and giant companies are well populated with surfers, it's logical to assume that the controlling upper echelons of the sport are at least partially as aware of the penetration of drugs in surfing as I am.

I don't think the status quo is planned. It's just the way things have panned out over the decades. The industry, the media, the sport and surfers in general are certainly not liable, complicit, evil or ill-intentioned. Far from it. It's just that no-one has seriously taken the bull by the horns on the issue. After all, whose job is it to do so? Is anyone actually *responsible* for someone else's personal choices? Do we accept drug use as part of 'the life', in a similar way to the rock music industry? Do we seek to quietly separate the professional sport from this part of the broader surfing culture? Do we combine the resources of surfing corporations and pro celebrities to educate future generations of surfers as to the dangers of drugs?

The simple truth is that surfing just isn't the kind of lifestyle that invites or tolerates lecturing, nannying and regulation. I know I don't, and that's not the fault of surf corporations, organising bodies, the specialty media or any other collective.

I don't propose to have a neat solution to this – or know whether the situation even needs 'solving'. But I do know that collectively denying the bleedingly fucking obvious is an insult to intelligence. Acknowledging surfing's foibles is not the same thing as condoning or encouraging them. We don't *have* to look the other way.

Denial also clouds the passing of many fantastic people and brilliant surfers like Craig who have lost their personal battles with addiction. Denial turns them into rogues rather than tragically unfortunate, though not atypical, representatives of the wider surfing family.

Enough bullshitting. *Please.*

THE HOTTEST SURFER YOU'VE NEVER SEEN

I won the Queensland Open Title again in 1983, though a feature article written for American *Surfing Magazine* by sage Aussie surf journalist Nick Carroll boosted me as much as any contest win that year.

'The Hottest Surfer You've Never Seen' was my breakthrough introduction to millions of American surfers and to the massive American corporate surfing market. Sure enough, 'Kong' was familiar to Americans as a rising Aussie who'd made an impression in Hawaii, but the eight-page feature in *Surfing* put detail on my competition pedigree, my hard-partying ways and my plans to win the 1984 World Amateur Title. Carroll concluded that I surfed 'every bit as brilliantly as many professionals on the circuit'. If the American amateurs with their prissy academic structure weren't already aware that an animal from Australia's grungy, unforgiving club contest warzone had them in his crosshairs, they were now.

The issue was released in high summer, perfectly timed to

bookend my charge at Bells, the pending release of *Kong's Island* and the upcoming Hawaiian season.

I started nearly five months in Hawaii from late October. Unlike the year before, I didn't slide into the North Shore unnoticed. I also had my own surfboards, which was very professional of me. The reunion with my Hawaiian mates was touching. I was welcomed – if not like one of their own then maybe like a distant cousin twice removed.

In my second season, the older guys even allowed me to surf at places like Makaha and Velzyland, breaks haoles are normally forbidden access to. I think it was Mickey and Bird who first playfully jabbed me about being 'Mr Sunset'. I laughed, but inside I couldn't have been happier had I won the professional World Title. If I live to be 200 years old I wouldn't have enough time to repay the generosity of spirit extended my way during my first visits to Oahu.

Rabbit must've decided that I wasn't a health risk after all, because he shared a house with Chappy and me when he arrived.

The Hawaiian season of '83 was another in a long series of consecutive epic winters of sustained gigantic swells in the blessed islands. As always, I was focused on Sunset Beach and it didn't disappoint my expectations. There were several out-of-control days shortly after I arrived when she was in a dirty and violent mood, strong crosswinds and twenty feet. Initially I surfed Waimea because most other places were unsurfable and out of action. But the line-up at Sunset was so windblown and surging, yet so empty of challengers, that I knew the time had come to take my relationship with her to the next level.

The west peak had huge slabs of chop blowing up the face, conspiring with the wind to suspend me in the pitching lip. 'No wonder no-one's fucken out here!' I said to myself belatedly. It took every atom of skill and experience I had to make these drops and turn my way safely into deep water.

Some waves were like two ten-foot waves sitting on top of each other, with big shifting steps separating the levels. Instincts commanding me to bottom turn had to be ignored until I could clear my vision, because the feel of the board levelling out was not indicating that the base of the wave had been reached but that the drop had just begun. Driving turns were necessary to complete the descent and bottom turns were a function of survival, not of technique. The tubes were cavernous and imperfect, yet it was utterly impossible to reach safety without riding through one. Every wave required a degree of calmness and commitment to every second that I'd never been called upon to find before. I'd reached a new level.

During these few sessions, I noticed that crowds had gathered to watch me. For the first time in my life, I wasn't deriving any affirmation or pleasure from entertaining people with my surfing. I was pleased to have survived, because it was the first time that it occurred to me – genuinely – that death was a realistic, possible consequence of what I was doing. People watched because it's perfectly natural to be fascinated by someone who could die at any minute. Even so, death didn't dominate my thoughts – totally the opposite. All I could think about was life. Wave after wave of peak experiences that resonated like the culmination of my life to date, from getting chucked overboard by Bull as a tiny kid, right up to the moment of pushing myself over the edge of these mammoth swells. Yet in each instant, there was no thought at all. Just 'doing'. Pure consciousness.

I was changed by those few sessions. I'd triumphed, if you could call it that, but there was more to it. I'd learnt that my skill set may very well lead me to surf waves that could actually kill me. I'd figured out that I surf these waves because I profoundly love the personal process of riding them. I acknowledged that bravery is necessary, but it wasn't – and still isn't – the point.

Having recognised that I was surfing at a level that could expose me to death, I came to appreciate big-wave surfing as being solely about *life*. And I wanted to explore the possibilities to the fullest. Death, fear, courage, admiration, big figs and all the other publicity shit truly had nothing to do with the thing. It was a personal matter. If I could push myself to be the best that I could be – to live to the utmost extent through what I could do in the ocean – then I would have a good chance of becoming the best that there is.

BLOOD SPORT

All the existential reflection butted up hard against reality in the coming months. By the time the Pipeline Masters Invitational had rolled around, so had all of the travelling pros, along with the ASP circus. Not being an ASP full-timer as yet, it was no surprise that I wasn't invited. Nor was I competing in the World Cup at Sunset Beach. My 'job' in Hawaii was to simply surf as much as possible and to do my thing in front of Jack McCoy's lenses.

The '83 Pipe Masters was held during a very, very serious north-west swell. As is always the case during the best swells, there were long intervals between sets and the waves themselves were travelling at higher speed towards shore. They broke with such strength upon the reefs that percussive, pile-driver vibrations could be felt on the beach.

The peak day of this swell came to be known as 'Black Friday'. Chappy and I began the day watching the contest from the beach, as stoked as any of the thousands of other spectators.

A fine Floridian surfer, Steve 'Beaver' Massefeller, was driven into the reef head-first, fracturing his skull and putting him into a coma. He was barely clinging to life when he was dragged from the water. Onlookers and contestants alike were sickened as his ambulance sped away. It was obvious to everyone that he might not live.

After some considerable delay, it was decided the contest should proceed. Only minutes later, local surfer Chris Lundy surfaced after a violent wipeout, screaming in agony. Again, the lifeguards were called upon to save a life. Chris was carried ashore with his whole lower leg facing backwards. He was alive, but Pipe had ended his career. His ambulance chased Beaver's up the Kam Highway.

All and sundry were pretty fucking rattled by this shocking spectacle. There was palpable sympathy all over the North Shore for both guys. Especially for Beaver, since there was every chance that he wouldn't make it. As it turned out he did survive, but his pro career was also finished and he struggled with side effects from his brain injury for many years.

That afternoon, Sunset was in its glory. Fifteen feet and rising, but with offshore winds just a little stronger than ideal. As always, the line-up is a bit less crowded at this size than when it's a few feet smaller. Rabbit and Shaun Thomson were already stalking the west peak when Chappy and I paddled out.

It was a great session. I'd decided to catch one more and head home when massive lumps loomed out wide to the west. The other guys were way inside of my position. It was clear that we'd all have to paddle like men possessed to avoid having this monstrous set break right on top of us. It took me four or five deep strokes to get up the face. I free fell off its back and looked up from the trough at the sheer, blue bulk of the mountain that followed it.

I was the only one in position to ride it and the blokes inside were screaming like banshees. I was convinced that I'd make it as I threw my trusty Hot Stuff beneath my feet and felt the familiar weightlessness of a freefall drop. It was impossible to see through the spray blowing into my face from the wave in front.

My vision cleared just in time to see a guy abandoning his board about four feet below me. There was no avoiding a collision and the nose of his board speared into the outside of my left knee with a loud thud. For the briefest instant I thought I was okay because there was no pain. Then my leg collapsed uselessly beneath me like a numb, dead weight. I fell flat onto my back, headfirst, skimming across the floor of the tube. I focused on my beautiful Hot Stuff as it led me in being sucked up the spinning vortex. The long trip up to the full height of the barrel's roof seemed to take forever. After a brief suspension at the top, the journey to reef was all but instantaneous.

Once the rest of the set had rolled over me, I surfaced in a cloud of blood. I reached down to check my knee and was horrified to feel moving bones, meat and ropey ligaments. Big flaps of skin hung on either side of the wound. I looked around for help. Rabbit, who had seen what happened, was about fifty metres away and heading in my direction.

'Bugs! I'm fucked!' I screamed, disconcerted at the panic in my own voice. I felt the strange sensation of water pouring into my calf and gathering in my ankle.

'Can you get to the beach?' he yelled back

I answered that I could and he signalled that he would come and get me once we'd reached the sand. Another set was coming, so it was too late to do anything else. The effort to get back onto my board tore the skin further apart. I bounced to shore on the broken whitewater, battling the urge to scream as water rushed into my thigh and calf. My whole leg felt like it would burst like a balloon.

I rolled around in the shallows, desperately looking for Rabbit, Chappy or the lifeguards. My leg had a hole the size of dinner plate in it. I could see bones and flesh and quivering tendons. Not good. I became really dizzy.

It was a pity that Bugs didn't get to me first. The poor bastard was battling his own problems, having been washed away to the west in the current past Val's Reef. Two bearded guys looked down at me, commenting on my injury. Through blinding agony, I could tell they were stoned. Takes one to know one. I grasped the slippery flaps of skin with shaking hands and sat there trying to pull them together amongst the gore.

Unfortunately, a tripped-out hippy happened to be riding her horse along Sunset Beach at exactly the wrong time. She offered me transport to 'healing'. Convinced by her wisdom, the well-meaning stoners heaved my half-dead carcass up onto the arse of this fuckhead's trusty steed, despite my feeble insistence to wait for the lifeguards. Beyond belief, unless you're from modern Byron Bay or certain places in California. People wonder why I'm not too fond of hippies.

I was in a panic as the idiot's nag took off. I saw the lifeguards, sprinting from Sunset, screaming 'No!' from one direction, and Rabbit, sprinting from Val's, screaming 'No!' from the other.

Predictably, I went flying onto the sand at thirty kilometres an hour. Although now a matter of huge hilarity, it was this bizarre development that fucking near killed me just as much as the preceding shit fight in the water. Sand was now packed solidly into the hole and underneath my skin. You fucking beauty.

After shooing away my 'first-response' rescuers, the lifeguards applied a tourniquet while Rabbit and Chappy comforted me until an ambulance finally arrived. I was extremely lucky, as it was the last one available, such was the carnage of the day. Bleeding to death was a distinct possibility.

True to form, I quite enjoyed the morphine and groggily mused about how radical it was to be following Beaver and Steve to Kahuku Hospital, just outside of Honolulu. I tried to ask the paramedics whether Beaver was okay, but I couldn't get any words together.

Before I faded out, my last conscious thoughts were of Jeff Hakman. The year before, during my first-ever minutes in Hawaii, the great man pointed to a big building. 'I went there after I got impaled on the reef at Sunset. That's Kahuku. It's one place on this island you do *not* want to visit, okay, bro?'

PILLS AND
HÄAGEN-DAZS

Surgeons in Kahuku took hours to remove the sand and grit that was blasted into my leg and hip cavity so they could repair the wound. Surfboard glass and matting fibres were also forced further up into my body, thanks to falling from the horse. They needed to replace a lot of blood.

Infection was the biggest danger. Miraculously, the muscles, tendons, ligaments and major arteries were mostly undamaged. Sixty-eight stitches were required to close me up.

Once it became clear that I was going to pull through alright, hospital staff joined my friends in finding the unusual combination of a surfing/horse-riding accident very amusing.

I was laid up at Kahuku for a week of antibiotics and close monitoring before I could put any weight on my leg. As soon as I could hobble to take a piss, I announced to my carers that I was leaving. They objected, but I argued that I'd end up in their mental ward should I spend one more second in hospital.

After heated debate, I was finally released into the tender care of nurses Bartholomew and Jennings. They were under strict instructions to ensure that their patient remained completely immobile and that the utmost attention be given to sterility and cleanliness.

The surgeon skeptically handed me a pile of prescriptions for powerful pain relievers, anti-inflammatories and infection control. He wished me luck and forced me to promise that I'd return to him weekly for a few months. I pumped his hand with heartfelt thanks, knowing that I would be doing my level best to never see him (good bloke that he was) or the Kahuku Hospital (fine facility that it was) ever a-fucking-gain.

The boys dumped me in my bedroom and fussed around like a couple of old women. I thanked them but politely asked that they fuck off and go surfing. The last thing I wanted to do was to interfere with their enjoyment of an epic Hawaiian season. They complied reluctantly, leaving me with a pile of magazines, several tubs of my favourite Häagen-Dazs ice-cream and a TV. I could smell, hear and see the ocean through my open window and it drove me mad. So I shut the window, closed the drapes and settled into my miserable lot.

It took about two hours for me to look at the big plastic bag full of pharmaceuticals on my bedside table in a new light ...

The next three weeks dragged by in a slow-motion haze. Because I'd collected a few months' worth of prescriptions in one hit, I gobbled pills from their containers like Tic Tacs, without giving a shit about which bottle was which. There was no pain, that's for sure, so they were working pretty fucking well as far as I was concerned.

All the while, my door and window stayed shut. Many friends and wellwishers entered my putrid, fart-filled cell and were immediately commanded to fill even more prescriptions and bring back Häagen-Dazs while they were at it. I requested beer, but most people were too sensible and 'forgot' to pick it up for me.

I was smashed on drugs and eating litres of ice-cream a day. I actually forgot why I was confined. I started to enjoy myself, as American football, painkillers and Hokey Pokey became my whole life. It wasn't rehabilitating, it was *wallowing*. Nude the whole time save for a tangled mass of filthy bandages, angry boils erupted on my arse cheeks. At least they distracted me from the compulsion to itch and tear at my leg.

My nearest and dearest would hold their noses and enter the room, hopeful of getting some salad into me, or of cleaning my wound. If they didn't present with ice-cream or drugs, I'd throw empty Häagen-Dazs tubs at them and rant abuse.

So, I wasn't an ideal patient.

After three weeks, a collection of my friends, both Australian and Hawaiian, had a kind of United Nations meeting and concluded that an intervention was necessary. Rabbit and Chappy entered my room when I was sleeping and removed all the drugs. They even opened the window and removed the TV. I had no choice but to buck up.

Quasimodo was finished, Kong was back. It was tough getting off the painkillers, but it was honestly tougher weaning myself off the ice-cream. I was motivated by looking in the mirror for the first time since my accident. I was fucking fat. So bloated that I could barely squeeze into the clothes I hadn't worn for a month. Fortunately the crazy cocktail of medicines I'd been gulping down worked on my leg. Walking wasn't easy, but the swelling was down and the stitches had done their job.

I cleaned up and lumbered my blubber down to Backdoor one afternoon, just in time to see Jack film Richard Cram score one of the longest tube rides ever recorded for *The Performers*. That really got me going. There was no way I was returning to Australia yet. I was going to surf in Hawaii that season again if it killed me.

I visited good old 'Dr Dan', the North Shore's local GP who attended all the various little ailments suffered by surfers. I asked him to remove the stitches.

'No way, man,' he said. 'You are *not* surfing on that leg, Kong, period.'

There was no swaying him. He ordered me to get back to my surgeon for a check-up, warning me that although the wound had closed and that I appeared to be clear of infection, I had still suffered serious trauma. Like everyone, I loved Dr Dan and respectfully pretended to take his advice.

The next day, I bandaged a plastic bag around my stitches and strapped my knee up nice and tight. Before anyone had a chance to talk me out of it, I paddled out at Sunset and caught a few dozen ten footers. Bull was firmly in my mind. I'd never known him to take a day off work due to illness or injury, and he did much harder stuff than surfing.

Rabbit roused on me for being so stupid as to surf with sixty-eight stitches in my leg, but I was okay. The most pain I felt was the stinging of the giant bedsores on my arse. I surfed again the next day before returning to Dr Dan.

'I've already surfed, Doc. You may as well take the fuckers out. I'm alright.'

'You stupid, stubborn bastard!' said the medico, stating the obvious.

After a thorough examination of my leg, he laboured expertly for an hour to remove the stitches, one by one. There was a ridiculously gnarly scar and I'd battle with stiffness and nerve damage on and off for years, but it felt wonderful to symbolically put the long weeks of hell behind me. Mentally, I'd recovered. It was time to get back on the horse. Not fucking literally, of course.

It was late season, and many of the top visiting surfers had drifted back home or off to their pro commitments. Jack stayed behind with me to shoot sequences of me for *The Performers*. The waves were excellent, though the 'performer' was carrying a lot of extra ice-cream baggage hanging over his Quiksilver board shorts. The footage was great, maybe because I was surfing like a man who knew he'd dodged a bullet.

Beaver and Chris Lundy weren't so lucky.

AMATEUR AMATEURS

If I had a dollar for every time someone told me I was crazy for not going straight to the 1984 ASP World Tour after I returned from Hawaii ... well, I could have bought Al Green out of Quiksilver. I wanted to join the Tour, but not until September, when I planned to join the European leg of the 'big show', once I was freshly crowned as World Amateur Champion in California.

I needed to stay sharp competitively and I started by winning the Kirra Pro Am, followed by the last of my Queensland Open Titles. I'd now won five Queensland Junior and Open Titles in a four-year period.

I added the JJJ Pro Junior in Sydney to the winning list, but only after a hard-fought final against Ross Clarke-Jones. Like Chappy, Ross was very quickly to change from rival to best mate. What a great bloke is RCJ.

There I was behind the contest tent, intending to spend the half an hour before the big final psyching up and stretching my muscles. A throng of kids were asking for autographs and I had my head down signing t-shirts and event programs when a very large, hairy and ungrommet-like pair of feet entered my field of vision.

'Carn, mate – whaddya say to a quick choof?'

I looked up to see none other than my fellow finalist, sporting his trademark evil grin.

'Does the Pope shit in the woods?' I replied.

Ross didn't always drive a Porsche. In fact, we spent the vital half an hour before one the world's most important pro junior events lounging in the back of his ancient ex-mail-van, sucking mull from a blackened plastic bong.

To say we 'clicked' is a bit of an understatement. We were hysterical at all the things we had in common within minutes of lighting up. Apparently, the contest organisers made three unanswered requests for our presence over the PA system before some local grommets who knew where we were found the guts to knock on the van door.

We ran guffawing from the car park in a trailing cloud of smoke to collect boards and jerseys before making it into the line-up a full twenty minutes after the scheduled start. Our surfing didn't suffer. We traded waves furiously until the hooter sounded. I'd won, but only just. As we climbed the podium to front fans, sponsors and collected media, the irate contest director pulled us aside. 'Next time you two clowns pull a Cheech and fucking Chong act, I'll be giving these to third and fucking fourth!' he said, slapping the trophies into our chests.

In addition to sharing similar surfing styles and senses of humour, Ross and I were due to hit the pro Tour at around the same time. We decided that would be a good thing – 'good' having a pretty loose meaning at times in the years ahead!

The World Amateurs were a few months away in California. I'd have to make the Australian team beforehand, which wasn't to be taken for granted, despite my grand visions. The Australian Titles were being held not far from Chappy's place, on the NSW Tweed coast at Cabarita. My form held and I won the Australian Open Title, despite the stupidity of staying amongst Chap's local nocturnal haunts during the event.

I wonder if my old headmaster at Mooloolaba High School, Mr Law, was proud of me when I was named 1984 Sunshine Coast Sportsman of the Year? Although maybe he didn't recognise me on the front page of the newspapers – I *was* wearing a cream three-piece suit and beige shoes. Actually, I don't think even Bull knew who the fuck I was.

Australian Open Champion. California, here I come.

I wasn't a great chance to win the World Amateur Title in 1984. To be fair, I'm not sure the stitch-up was entirely personal. Star-studded teams and brilliant individuals from both Hawaii and Australia barely made the semis. A series of last-second changes to competition rules, coupled with judging that was – to put it diplomatically – *unkind* to Hawaiians and Australians, meant that the Team USA bus would had to have burst into a fireball on the way to the beach for them to be beaten.

Maybe I'd have been wise to keep the friendly banter about the big-wave credentials of my American NCAA contemporaries to myself. Wisdom isn't always my strong suit. In any case, Mike Parsons came out of the college program and he's done a pretty good job of shutting me up over the years!

Some Hawaiians took the farce pretty hard and responded by dumping a bucket of urine over the judges on the final day.

We Aussies were as outraged as everyone else, but managed to enjoy ourselves despite feeling like extras in the USA's victory parade. I developed a lasting affection for the town and the locals of Oceanside, California, thanks to being billeted at nearby Camp Pendleton. Ditto Californians and California in general.

I ended up placed fifth behind new World Amateur Champion Scott Farnsworth of the USA. Scott is a fine surfer. I should make it clear that I'm not aware of any competitive surfer who directs ill will towards their opponents if there's unhappiness with judging. It's just how it goes in a subjectively decided sport. Surfers don't set the rules, surfers don't give the scores – we just go out there and do our best. Nothing can be taken away from the victors. Kooks do not win World Titles.

Although I was bitterly disappointed not to achieve my goal of being World Amateur Champion, I was philosophical about the way things worked out. Delaying my pro career had given me two long seasons of priceless education in Hawaii and bought me time to feature in some successful movies.

The next afternoon I departed LA for France's Côte Basque, and the European leg of the ASP World Tour. The long wait was over.

OOH LA LA

Many aspects of my arrival in France to begin life on the pro Tour went exactly as I expected them to. After making my way to the iconic seaside resort town of Biarritz, I quickly settled into a customary couple of weeks of partying at the Quiksilver team's house at nearby La Barre. Rabbit was the unofficial team 'captain' and, as a veteran of many visits to the French Atlantic coast, it was a given that he'd show the new boys such as Gary Green (a radical surfer and drinking machine from Cronulla) and me the ropes.

The 'ropes' weren't too different to the ropes anywhere else.

'Here's where you find the best mull.'

'Here's where the best waves are.'

'Here's where the best bars are.'

'Here's where you find girls who you will have the best chance of having sex with.'

'This is how you order a sandwich in French.'

While the priorities were familiar, the outcomes of my introduction to all things French were a total revelation. Within a day, I had fallen completely in love with the place.

I was blown away by the ancient, living history that presented itself on every little street in every little village. Having grown up amidst ultimate natural majesty, I'd never considered that a man-made environment could be so overwhelmingly beautiful. Buildings, castles, boulevards, even simple things like old stone fences and footpaths captivated me.

It so happened that a thumping swell was smashing the Côte Basque from the deep waters of the Bay of Biscay, so all the local surf breaks were on fire. At home, I was used to pushing my way past Bull to jump off the trawler for a surf, not tiptoeing through an obstacle course of gorgeous naked women to the water's edge.

Nude people. Nude people everywhere.

Not disgusting nude people who should not be nude, like the nude sunbathers who scurry around seedy secluded coves in Australia or California, but glorious, glorious specimens. People who are nude not as a perverse, alternative lifestyle but because being nude on the beach is an everyday, normal part of life for the uncommonly beautiful people of southern France. Talk about an eye-opener. There's probably ugly people in the area, but I've yet to see them. Maybe there are ugly guys, but they're totally invisible amongst the supermodels sunning themselves all over the place in their birthday suits.

My motley crew of mates and I took two seconds to decide that board shorts were an unacceptable impost on genuine self-expression in the surf. Dumb move. Our arses were burnt to a crisp and we were extracting stubborn wax balls from our pubes for a week. Of course, Rabbit – the veteran – wore Speedos. Ridiculous, but wise, very wise.

In keeping with my highly addictive nature, I became instantly attached to 'real' coffee. I consumed syrupy espressos copiously in between surfs, along with lashings of the finest Moroccan hashish, which could be smoked publicly without anyone raising an eyebrow.

Après surf in the evenings, I'd actually 'dine', as opposed to shovelling down fish and chips or a meat pie. This wasn't a function of any pretence or wankery but simply because fast food did not exist. One eats 'well' in the Basque country or not at all. What a shock. What's more, I was introduced to red wine, something I had previously considered the exclusive domain of derelicts. Mind you, it took several years for me to understand local tradition and refrain from guzzling the sacred drop like a parched bag-lady at every opportunity.

What an unbelievable three weeks after my recent disappointments in the US! Overall, my first taste of life on Tour as a bone fide pro surfer couldn't possibly have been better.

It did get better, though. I thought that a taste of France had changed my life already. Ha! A couple of hours' drive north, Lacanau was about to make all that came before it an understatement.

I came a credible eighth at the unfortunately named Tutti-Frutti Pro. A satisfying result first-up, made even sweeter by defeating Rabbit along the way. I'd noticed a massive change in his behaviour during the week preceding the contest. He separated himself from our circle of immediate mates and was not to be seen mucking around in the usual manner. I was told he was training, which amused me greatly. I hung good-humoured shit on my old mate behind his back, alternately referring to him as either 'Rocky' or 'The Phantom'.

Come contest time, there was no advice or best wishes extended my way from the champ. He looked through me like I was made of glass before our heat. I was distracted by his attitude throughout the whole match-up. Victory came through the good graces of the ocean gods, who sent more waves my way than Rabbit's.

Though I was stoked to overcome my idol and mentor – especially with his weirdness and all – the tension I felt during our mini-battle stayed with me. Our friendship returned to normal after the contest, but something had shifted all the same. I resolved to get to the bottom of it when the time was right.

As I departed the Lacanau/Bordeuax area for the next Tour stop in Cornwall, England, Rabbit's mercurial antics were not at the forefront of my mind. Neither was winning the Foster's Surfmasters, or anything else I was employed to do. For the time being, I was trapped in a real-life, cheesy, romantic chick's movie. In addition to everything else that blew my mind in France, I just had to lock eyes with Pascale Roby, didn't I?

It was so close to not happening at all. I was walking past a café in Lacanau, speaking crap with Mark Occhilupo and enjoying my morning caffeine and hash buzz. She sat near the door talking with some guys, but looking straight at me. Like she was expecting to see me. She was a classically elegant, perfectly beautiful woman. I'd never seen such a spectacular girl. Not even in pictures, the movies or in my imagination. Dark hair, flawless olive skin. Knowing eyes that looked into me with a playful invite the second I saw her.

I *had* to stop and speak to her.

She began to smile as I veered away from Occy, leaving him obliviously bogging on to nobody. By the time I reached her side I was in love. Would you believe she held my hand like an old friend before I even ruined the word 'bonjour' with my Aussie twang?

There you have it. From useless debate with Mark Occhilupo about the shitfulness of the Cronulla Sharks Rugby League club, to in love with Miss Universe. Hang in there, Hugh Grant fans. This 'love at first sight' bollocks could happen to *you*.

SLOP

Pascale and I spent nearly every second together before I departed France. It was a love affair in the truest French tradition and we were enraptured with each other – mind, body and spirit. I loved her before I knew she was 'Miss Bordeaux' and a successful Parisian model. I know she loved me before she had any idea about my surfing credentials. But I couldn't have cared less about her modelling and she sure as hell couldn't have given a *merde* about surfing.

I got to know the guys Pascale was with on the first day I met her in Lacanau. Manu, Jean Michel Gue and Thierry Fernandez are still my dear mates to this day. These guys eased my shock when Pascale told me she had a boyfriend back in Bordeaux. They confirmed that the relationship was troubled and that the guy was *un idiot*. Although I'd never been one to deliberately 'cut a bloke's grass', I couldn't help but continue to love her.

Taking the plane to England was as wrenching an experience as I'd endured to that point in my life. There were no promises of faithfulness. Still, we promised our hearts to each other, come what may. I phoned her every day, no matter where I was in the world. And that was when you had to find a phone box! I sent her postcards and we exchanged letters every week.

Were it not for the cyclical, frenetic distractions of life on the Tour, I would have gone barking mad with my need for her. Without the endless lines of coke, without the bottomless jugs of beer, without the weekly challenges of surfing at my best, without slutting myself around like a moral-less ape, I could quite well have lost my mind. More than anything, without the good-natured camaraderie of other young blokes dealing with their own loneliness, separation and new-found celebrity on a rollercoaster ride around the globe, I would have lost the plot.

I don't mean this as an endorsement of bad conduct, but it worked for me at the time.

It was a sensational time to be a travelling pro surfer. The surfing part wasn't such great fun, but everything else was.

In the early eighties there were as many as twenty-eight events on the annual ASP World Tour. Therefore, it was virtually impossible for all the top surfers to get to all the top events. Usually, the best guys picked the events with the biggest prize money and the most amount of Tour points on offer. There were so many events that the 'season' was actually a full twelve months long. The ASP surfing schedule was weird, beginning the season in Japan during May and usually ending the year in Sydney during April.

Because I started late in the '84 season, I only contested eleven events. Even so, I was at a pro contest somewhere in the world at least a couple of times a month. Unlike these days, we were on the road constantly, only seeing home a precious few times a year.

The waves were a 'quantity over quality' proposition, that's for sure. Locations were selected based on which areas had closest access to the largest populations. This was great for the profile of the sport, which at the time stood alone as what we'd now call an extreme sport. It was common to have over 20,000 people attend every day of a contest and all events would receive extensive mainstream media coverage.

The fact that none of the world's excellent waves conveniently roll into the central shopping, tourist, media and business precincts of the world's most populated areas wasn't of pressing concern to surfing's governing body. The Association of Surfing Professionals needed as many events in as many major cities and tourist areas as it could possibly wring out of the sport.

In the days before social-media marketing, electronic publications and the commercialisation of the internet, the ASP World Tour was by far the best way to sell surfing products. After all, if what my rivals and I did on Tour was not selling t-shirts, board shorts, wetsuits or sunglasses, there would be no Tour.

So, pro Tour contests were usually held in appalling surf. Strange, but true. For every Hossegor, Bells Beach, Burleigh Heads, Pipeline and Sunset, there were five duds. The gruelling schedule meant that no waiting periods were possible. A couple of days surfing crap somewhere and then off to the next crap wave before you knew it.

The problems afflicting the sport didn't register in my mind. Mostly because I was either smashed on dope, booze and cocaine, or pining away for Pascale during that whole first year. Even had I thought about it, I wouldn't have had the slightest complaint that the ASP was deciding who its best surfers were by using some of the world's most fucked waves. I'd made some great mates and we were usually on the same flights and staying in the same hotels. A bunch of us hung together almost every day. And night. Tom Carroll, Martin Potter, Mark Occhilupo, Gary Green and Cheyne Horan. Ross Clarke-Jones had yet to join the circus full-time, but he and Chappy were often present, surfing through the trials.

Those were the days before the reality of AIDS had fully taken hold. Sex and drug binges were a part of my working week, and that was just on the aircraft. I once knocked the toilet door open with my backside while a young Texan lass and I were enjoying our youth high over the mountains of Central Asia. It was embarrassing, but we were past the point of no return, as it were. Later, a flight attendant castigated me, not for the bestial stage show, but for leaving a joint butt unflushed.

Gentler times … it makes you feel old when you can remember being allowed to smoke ciggies at the rear of an airplane.

A bunch of us all but demolished a heritage-listed landmark guesthouse in the historic village of Newquay in Cornwall, England. Antique furniture wound up in the fireplace. Rugs, vases, books, paintings and sculptures were smashed, torn and otherwise decimated. Some silly bastard got his head stuck in a jousting helmet.

That's what happens when you accommodate a few dozen immature numbskulls in a museum with a mountain of 'consumables' and an army of local female admirers. I'm regretful of wrecking things, but the episode is indicative of the times. Rock 'n' roll, man. Televisions in swimming pools. All that stuff.

No, the idiosyncrasies of the Tour weren't troubling me at all. I was getting paid to surf, travel and indulge in all manner of depravity, while ensuring that the 'market' knew what clothes, sunglasses and wetsuits I was wearing while I was doing it. I'd never had a higher profile, which meant that I had a very happy set of sponsors.

The only interruption to the fun was that I couldn't rid Pascale from my thoughts, no matter what I was doing. Even when I was surfing in a final or sleeping with other girls, I could never go a minute without thinking about her. Whenever I was alone, with only my thoughts for company, I would miss her to a point of physical nausea. I guess this partially explains why I spent so much of 1984 and 1985 as a social animal, nearly twenty-four hours a day.

THE NEXT LEVEL

By the Hawaiian winter of '84, I'd fallen into the habit of measuring the passage of time by my annual visits to the North Shore of Oahu. Touching down in Honolulu had already begun to feel like a homecoming.

And 1984 also marked the first year that I had meticulously envisaged what I intended to accomplish in Hawaii. I'd spent a week in October at Hot Stuff's factory in Currumbin, working with Al Byrne on my first serious quiver of serious surfboards. They were specifically tuned to individual waves and conditions.

I'd made a conscious decision to dedicate more time to Pipeline, Waimea and Haleiwa that year. The Pipe Masters and the Sunkist World Cup were still specialty events in 1984, 'invitationals' to which I was not invited.

Quiksilver had booked out an entire resort of bungalows at Ke Iki to accommodate its local and international team of sponsored surfers for the duration of the season. It was the first time a big surf company had done this, so our compound created a fair bit of interest. The arrangement gave Jack

McCoy the ability to coordinate filming of *The Performers II* with some degree of efficiency. Even so, getting blokes to be present in the right places at the right times was still akin to herding cats for the poor bastard. Rabbit, Chappy and I took up residence under the same roof yet again.

Sunset lifeguard Darrick Doerner continued mentoring me in '84 and played a decisive role in my future. Derrick didn't just surf with me. He paddled me around to every inch of the Sunset line-up and pointed out dozens of land-based navigation points up on Comsat Hill, behind the beach. These indicated to within feet where I was in the water.

I already had what I thought was an extensive knowledge of the character, colour, shape and nuances of the currents and reef system. The addition of these exact physical coordinates, far away on shore, gave me inside knowledge at Sunset that would've taken years to accumulate. There are at least thirty different 'dead reckoning' reference points on land which form a sort of treasure map of the world's most inscrutably shifting surf break: 'If a set approaches from x direction, at x size, on an x tide, when the wind is blowing from x direction, paddle to the spot where x rooftop lines up precisely behind x tree.' That kind of thing. It reminded me of how Bull used to navigate our trawler through the reef up and down the Queensland coast. I took to my lessons with huge enthusiasm. Familiarity and comfort evolved to the same levels I felt at Alexandra Headland, as improbable as that seems, since Alex Headland is hardly likely to pound anyone to a bloody pulp. I became respectfully confident that I would only ever be punished at Sunset due to arrogance or error, not due to a lack of understanding.

I dedicated many days to Pipeline in 1984. Although I'd surfed it extensively in the past, my preoccupation with Sunset had sucked up most of my curiosity. The drive to educate myself at Pipe wasn't what it should have been. It was tough to force myself to ignore Sunset when it was good, but putting in the effort to master Pipeline's subtle but deadly nuances paid off in a big way.

I stalked local big-wave legend Marvin Foster around the line-up like a suckerfish, watching his every move: the timing of his reactions to an incoming set, where he paddled to, when he delayed bottom turns, when he raced the section. I badgered Rabbit and Tom Carroll for their thoughts on positioning and decision-making.

Riding Pipe adequately is not particularly difficult for a surfer of excellent quality. The all-time Pipe Master, Gerry Lopez, famously described it as a 'cakewalk, if you know how'. But riding Pipe excellently – being a stand-out – is an extremely taxing, dangerous and precise art form. They're completely different characters, but Pipe has its own malicious ways of slapping down complacency, just like its cousin Sunset Beach.

The extreme shallowness at Pipeline makes appointments with the reef inevitable. It's ironic that the fiercest bashing I received that year happened after I hammed up a casual upright stance in a six-foot tube, while an army of photographers gawked at me from point-blank range. The lip clipped my head. I hit the reef at least three times and was jammed into the jagged lava bed until I saw stars. Note to self: don't be a wanker at Pipeline. A day spent threading fifteen-foot giants on Pipe's famed second reef (the outside lava platform that breaks only during the biggest swells) capped off my Pipeline experience that year. I was officially in love.

Paddling into maximum-size Waimea Bay is as much an exercise in luck as it is in skill or knowledge, even for its best and most experienced riders. The Bay is a place that can wipe you from existence like a bug if you allow excitement to overpower sense. I enjoyed a few classic Waimea sessions when it claimed its traditional role as the only rideable break during wild swells that close out the rest of the island. A surfer's progress at Waimea Bay is measured in years, not in waves or sessions. I was happy to put more time, more incremental successes and more punishment into my Waimea kitbag during 1984.

BIG CHARACTERS

The Ke Iki Resort was gated on three sides and fronted by a rocky, lava reef beach, just around the headland from Waimea Bay. It was a standing joke that the fences were to keep the 'inmates' separated from the public, because the goings-on were usually more like an asylum than a resort. Surfing to a standstill every day, boozing and drugging every night – everything about the usual cycle was always more intense in Hawaii.

We had a huge party for Christmas that year at Ke Iki; Mum, Bull and my siblings even came over to spend the festive week with us. Christmas Day nearly killed Rabbit. The inmates of Ke Iki had devised a truly ridiculous game of the kind that's common amongst buzzed-out stoners and drunks the world over.

The shore break out the front was very similar to Waimea Bay's. In other words, it was a hellish, grotesque triple-up, which sledge-hammered onto Ke Iki's jagged, exposed lava reef. At night, under the dodgy lights of the resort, we'd wait for a set to finish then race after the receding water down the sharply sloping sand and out onto the reef. The object was to be the deepest person to touch the fully receded water line, then race madly back across the reef and up onto the sand to avoid being atomised by the next set. Of course, contestants were disqualified for spilling their beers or getting their joints wet.

The booby prize of being sucked around the headland into Waimea's pitch-black line-up with only a can of Primo for flotation tended to focus participants on the task at hand. Ke Iki Matador: definitely *not* a game the whole family can play. In fact, not a game *anyone* should play.

Rabbit – being the most competitive person I've ever known – announced drunkenly on Christmas Day 1984 that he would take Ke Iki Matador one step further by surfing a gruesome, square left that peeled into the shore break. It would have been unusually cruel to throw a barracuda into the water that day. It was eighteen feet if it was a foot, but he couldn't be talked out of it.

Only someone with world-champion credentials could have made it out the back, drunk or not. The wave Rabbit got was the gnarliest shore dump I've ever seen. To the horror of those on the beach, he somehow made it off the bottom and raised his arms in victory before the twisted, quadruple-ledged beast broke an inch behind him. He was shot through air and onto dry sand like one of those cannon jockeys at an old-time circus – too bad there was no net. Classic.

Merry Christmas!

Madonna and I hung out during that Hawaiian winter.

Madonna.

She was on Oahu shooting a video and needed some surfers as extras, so her production people made contact with Quiksilver. The shoot was happening around the west side and, since Chappy and I were acceptable foreigners around there, we got the gig.

There was a small army of technicians, assistants, dancers and musicians on site. Friendly and down to earth, Madonna was especially curious about surfing and welcomed us with warm, easy conversation. Her project lasted for weeks, and even after we'd finished our minor segment she personally invited us to private parties in Honolulu nightclubs.

There were often top bands playing when the pro Tour was in town. I'd developed friendships with quite a few rock musicians, such as Michael Hutchence and Ronnie Wood – it's curious how many entertainers love surfing. Peter Garrett of Midnight Oil became a good mate. But with due respect to the big fella, he ain't quite as sexy as the 'Material Girl'.

Madonna and I talked for hours one night in Honolulu about stuff that had nothing to do with either music or surfing. I'll admit to being one of millions of guys to fall more than a little bit in love with her. It was great to get to know Madonna for a few weeks and it was nice to know a mega-celebrity who was also a lovely, fun person who took a genuine interest in other people.

Incidentally, I don't think the music video she was filming ever saw the light of day!

Ray Street is an enigmatic guy few surfers have ever heard of. There should be a photo of Ray in the dictionary under 'hard core'. The North Shore has more genuine one-of-a-kind individualists per square metre than any other surfing location in the world and Ray Street is perhaps the most interesting of them all.

A highly decorated 'Black Ops' US Special Forces veteran of the Vietnam War, Ray retired from the military to a gentle life of surfing, shaping and glassing boards on Oahu. Very occasionally he'd speak of the horrors he'd experienced in war, after which you'd realise where his self-reliant demeanour and the quiet though gung-ho attitude came from. No wonder he lived as though each day was a miraculous bonus to him.

Chappy had picked up some boards from him the year before. The two had become friendly, which was uncommon for Ray, who was a noted loner. Chappy told us about this interesting bloke who was an unintentional inspiration. So we were very excited when – on a rare flat day of surf – Ray invited Chappy to 'bring a couple of buddies' on a hike. We were going up into the jungle of Kaena Point, the high isthmus which separates the North Shore of Oahu from its West Shore. It would be great fun to go for little day hike up to the top of the mountains and look down at our favourite waves. Really, it didn't *look* like it would be a particularly taxing thing to do. Mont, our old mate from Mt Woodgee, came along for the jaunt.

Ray greeted us at the base of the Kaena Point Sanctuary and Nature Reserve early in the morning. He explained that he often spent weeks at a time 'living rough' up in the Kaena wilderness. Experiencing the jungle and the sights would give us a better understanding of the energy of the island.

'This will help your surfing,' he said seriously.

A huge bag of magic mushrooms was produced and shared around.

Within half an hour, it was abundantly clear that this was no pleasure trip. The terrain was pathless, steep to the point of 'climbing' rather than 'walking' and very densely vegetated. Our jovial good humour evaporated as the job of keeping up with Ray turned into a Delta Force entrance exam – a hallucinogenic, psychedelic battle for survival. The jokey banter between Chappy, Mont and me gave way to grunting, sweating and a rising panic that we would become separated from Ray then lost in a claustrophobic green maze. The field of visibility was about three metres in any direction.

I was appalled when Mont wheezed that it was just after 2 pm. We were tripping and we were thirsty. Ray was always moving invisibly above us, only audible when he whistled softly to give us a direction to follow. The relief was incredible when the ground finally levelled out and we saw Ray crouching in a small clearing ahead. We collapsed beside him on the wonderfully level ground, happy to look up at blue sky after hours of being blanketed by the jungle.

'Okay, not far to go now, you pussies,' he whispered.

The whispering was really unsettling. Why whisper?

With that, Ray got up and walked in a dead-straight line across an open space and into the next line of thick ferns and vines. He waved us towards him from his position, which was maybe ten metres away.

'Walk where I did. Don't look down.'

Our guide had just strolled across a natural rock bridge straight out of an Indiana Jones movie, thirty centimetres wide with a sheer drop each side into the canopy of the jungle *a hundred metres* below.

'Fuck off, Ray,' I hissed back in a weird 'shout' whisper. Why the fuck I was whispering I'll never know.

'This is the secret. It's the only way to the top, Kong. *Do it*, man!'

We Aussies looked at each other forlornly. A happy, cruisey day had turned into a warped fucking nightmare of Stephen King-like proportions. What a fucking ridiculous, useless way to die. I knew we'd never get down from here without Ray, but the idea of walking across a slippery sliver of rock with certain death on each side and a gutful of magic mushrooms on board paralysed me. They would never even find our corpses if we slipped.

I went over on hands and knees, shaking like a leaf and looking into Ray's insane eyes, hoping that they'd act like a magnet. I made it. Mont did the same, big droplets of sweat rolling off his forehead and disappearing down the chasm. He'd aged visibly.

Chappy looked down halfway across and froze. He collapsed to his belly and gripped the edges with his fingernails and toenails like claws. It wasn't funny. I felt sick for him. I felt sick for us. Mont and I looked at Ray hoping that he may lighten things up, but his face was locked in a deathly skull's head grimace.

'*Do it*, Chappy. Get it *done*. Get the fuck up and *get it fucking done*, man!'

The little guy looked us in the eye, got himself onto all fours and scurried over into our arms. We all hugged each other for a long minute in total silence. Then we laughed. We laughed like never before. The compulsion to whisper left us and our cackling echoed deafeningly around the ravines.

There was another half an hour of upward travel together, all the while Ray telling us that this was the only path to the top and we'd be rewarded for the effort. The clearing we finally broke into was a heavenly intersection. The North Shore's famous line-ups spilled away far below to our right and the sun had begun to descend behind the West Coast far below to our left. The surf was flat inshore yet colossal swells, kilometres long, were bypassing the island way out to sea. The curve of the earth was visible horizon to horizon. It felt as though we were standing atop a *living thing*.

The energy was religious. We were moved beyond words. A lifetime moment was shared between us. Handfuls of mushrooms were passed around and we ate them in absent-minded, awed silence.

Then the cosmic sense of peace degenerated into chaos. Ray wigged out into a full-blown combat flashback. 'They're coming! They're *fucking coming*!'

The urgent whispering returned as he dive-rolled into the nearby underbrush. Chappy, Mont and I experienced a sort of flashback of our own. It wordlessly dawned on us that we'd just eaten another handful of brain-bending fungi, *while we were watching the sun begin to set.*

We had to get off this mountain! Fuck!

We ran to Ray and attempted to short-circuit the trip he was taking. No good. Panic sets in as quickly as love under the influence of mushrooms and unfortunately we were all loved out.

Decisions needed to be made. Mont thought it best to convince Ray that it wasn't 1972. Chappy and I thought it best to get the fuck out of there while there was still some daylight. The three of us agreed in no uncertain terms that getting back over the rock bridge was not going to be much fun. Ray warned us that 'they' would pick us off, one by one, if we separated. The haze had set in.

Chappy and I broke the impasse by bolting back down from the summit. A night spent re-enacting the final scenes of *Apocalypse Now* on the roof of Oahu didn't hold much appeal. As much as the ascent was a gruelling, inch-by-inch test of willpower, the descent was a mad dash of tumbling, sliding and surrender to fate. In our altered mental state, getting to the bottom before dark became a race against the grave. The mortifying rock bridge was crossed upright, at virtually a full sprint. We took turns testing our memories to pick the same paths down as we'd taken up. Thankfully we didn't fuck it up, and we made it back to sea level as darkness fell, rattled to our bones but in one piece.

Mont and Ray were only five minutes behind us. Chappy and I followed Mont's white t-shirt down through the final few hundred metres, yelling encouragement and good-natured abuse. The tension of the intense hallucination at the summit turned into intensely joyful tripping at the bottom. We embraced each other in a four-man circle, yelling and laughing into the night like primal mad men.

Our adventure created a close bond between the four of us. Sure, we can look back and laugh at the tale, but there's more to it than that. Ray was right. It helped my surfing. It helped my life.

I'd seen Hawaii for the tiny dot of beautiful reefs and greenery it was, unprotected by a continental shelf and perched helplessly in the vast, pitiless North Pacific Ocean. It was proof that planetary power can never be physically dominated. Surfing itself seemed frivolous, let alone contests and accolades and sponsors and money.

It evoked the feelings I had when our trawler dropped behind the horizon after I'd taken the little boat to surf open ocean reefs. I was a microscopic spec on a gigantic blue orb. It's no bad thing to remember how small you are in the ocean, even when you make a living out of pretending you're big.

The year 1985 stretched out ahead as Chappy and I departed our trashed bungalow at Ke Iki and nursed our trashed old Pinto up the Kam Highway to the airport for the journey home from Hawaii.

As was our habit, I drove and Chap rolled the joints. Throughout the long winter in Oahu, he persisted with an awful tradition of placing every dirty used butt into the Pinto's glove compartment. By late January, there were hundreds in there. On our final drive out of the North Shore, he pulled apart all these rancid roaches and rolled one last trombone from the contents. We smoked this disgusting ten-inch joint all the way to the 'No Parking' section adjacent to the Qantas counter. The Pinto was abandoned where it stopped and we dragged ourselves to the departure gate.

It had been a truly great Hawaiian season, filled with new experiences, as always. And fun – lots and lots of fun. So much so that the hard-earned reputation of 'Kong', the 24-hour drinking and drugging dynamo, had captured the imagination

of the surfing world every bit as much as
reputation of 'Gary', the rising pro surfer. May

Surfers everywhere loved buying into tall ta
about the 'rage all night/surf all day' hard charge
movies, ads and magazine articles, but a little hard to   ..tain
in real life. 'Kong' and 'Gary' were officially at odds, and
Kong's priorities were getting too much attention. It was as
easy to see as it was to ignore.

CLEARING THE AIR

There were a couple of treasured weeks at home for the first time in half a year before the commencement of the Australian late summer events. I got to hang at Mooloolaba with my mates, putting on kegs of beer and getting wasted on whatever came my way for days at a time. Mum spoiled me with comfort food and I was stoked to kick back in the garage at home, talking trawling with Bull and David. I raved about Pascale like a love-struck loon to my family. Mum and Bern were fascinated; Bull and Dave made a passable job of pretending to be.

Falling into my old bed with my heroes looking down at me from the walls nearly made me cry. The famous photo of Mark Richards top-turning at Haleiwa on his classic red and yellow Lightning Bolt really set me off. I'm not completely sure why.

A cyclone swell struck Queensland during this sabbatical, so I fired up the Sigma (my celebrity and new contracts had yet to result in an upgraded car) and sped down to Kirra. I stayed with Rabbit.

One night after an evening of barbecuing up at Nick's place on Mt Woodgee, we were relaxing with a joint and talking our usual shit about tubes made and wipeouts survived. I broke a moment's silence by raising the subject I'd been bristling to bring up for months.

'Listen mate, what's going on with you?'

'What do you mean what's going on, you tool?' Rabbit chortled jokingly.

'You know what I mean, come on. Stuff's been weird between us since France.'

'You *really* want to talk about that, mate?' he asked, turning serious.

'Yeah, I really fucken do.'

'Okay, mate, o-fucken-kay,' he threw his joint onto the grass, 'but you need to *want* to listen to this shit.'

'Whatever … yeah … I told you I do.'

Rabbit took a deep breath and stared off into space for a long beat before looking me straight in the eye. I recall every word that was spoken during the following twenty minutes.

'You're wasting yourself. You're one of the best fucking surfers I've ever seen, but you've got no fucking respect for your own talent. You're a dickhead.'

All of a sudden, I was totally sober.

'Well … you're not a dickhead, but you act like one. Do you know what most people would give to have your natural ability, mate?'

Before I could answer, he continued. And continued.

'Ninety-nine per cent of surfers will never have what you've got. But it's the other one per cent who'll send you back to the trawler if you don't get smarter very fucking quickly.'

He had my complete attention now.

'You think that Curren, TC [Tom Carroll], Pottz and Occy don't have your talent?'

I was dumbstruck.

'Well do ya? I'll tell you mate, they fucking do. They've got it in fucking spades and if you're satisfied with going around and around the world like a rock star, those boys will *take your life away*. And if not them, it will be someone else.

'Why did I ignore you in France? I'll tell you fucking why. Because you may be my mate, but you're good enough to *take my life away*. I've got nothing but winning as a surfer. You know I came from nothing. Fucking *nothing*, man. You've got trawling as a backup. That's great, but is that what you want to do? Is it?'

Rabbit had begun to shout, although there was no anger at all. I answered his question weakly. 'No.'

He caught himself and returned to normal volume. 'Look, Kong, you'd best start getting fair dinkum about the things you need to do to win. You've got the whole Hawaii thing wired, which is great. But that won't keep you off the trawler. Neither will being any company's number-one party animal and publicity slut. Beating blokes is what counts, just like in the old club days. It's *all* that counts. Otherwise you're going to end up another burnt-out next big fucking thing.

'Every bastard will tell you what a sensational surfer you are, because it's the truth. But you'll always be a sensational surfer whether you're the World Champ or whether you're working prawns. I'd be the exact same surfer as I am right now whether I was working fixing dings or whether I was World Champion. But I'd sure as shit have a different fucking life. For fuck's sake mate, think about your life, not just about your surfing. Do whatever it takes to make the most of what you've got.'

'I fucking *am* making the most of myself, mate!' In my typical way, I had begun to feel lectured, which always rankled me. I was getting flashbacks of Bull's frequent outbursts as the nets were being raised.

'*Are* you?'

'I'm fit, you know, Bugs. No-one out-paddles me. You don't earn a black belt in Zen Do Kai if you're not bloody fit,' I said finally. I rarely reference the martial arts influence of Paul Pascoe upon me, but it seemed appropriate at the time.

'I know you're fit. But are you as fit as TC? That mongrel looks like a fucking condom full of marbles.'

We had a good laugh at that. Everyone loved Tommy Carroll, the muscular little bloke from Newport who was about to win his second World Title. Everyone also knew he was the strongest, fittest man on the Tour.

'Seriously, Kong, Tommy works out so hardcore because it gives him something special upstairs,' Bugs said, tapping the side of his head with his fingers. 'It's his edge. Blokes know that he never stops thinking about winning, not just when he's in the water. He's doing things differently. Preparing, planning, scheming to stop blokes like us taking *his* life away.'

'Yeah, you're right.'

'Fuck oath I am. Do you think Cheyne [Horan] is riding those crazy boards and living in a fucking tree house because he's relying on his radical natural talent? Edge, mate … edge. Every fucker who thinks Cheyne's a mental case is missing the point. He's smart, they're dumb. He's doing things his own way … making his opponents wonder about what he's doing and why. And what they're *not* doing. Edge.

'Every time you let your competitors see inside of you, you're giving away another small part of any edge you have. You can't help but let every bastard on earth see everything about yourself, Kong. Every night of the week. Well, that's great for making friends. But most of the friends you're making need to beat you in the water to stop themselves from fixing dings or laying bricks. *Or catching prawns.* The partying is fucking great. You need to do it. We all need to do it, but never forget that it's an illusion, man. The fame and the celebrity and all that stuff. Totally temporary. You can party at home. You'll be a legend at home from now on, no matter what you do. But you can't win a fucking World Title sitting in the pub at Mooloolaba.'

That really cut through. I got what Rabbit was saying, but I couldn't apply the logic to how I could possibly change myself. 'What … are you saying I can't fucking hang with my mates on Tour?'

'Of course not! I'm just saying that you need to start understanding what's really going on. We're all only ever a few last-place finishes from being out on our arse. You're not gonna make a living by being Mr Fucking Sunset, and I'm not gonna make a living forever by being the '78 World Fucking Champ.'

We had a laugh at that, which broke the tension.

'If you think the business heads are gonna keep laying money on you for being everyone's favourite coke head, you're fucking dreaming. They love you partying it up now, but it won't keep selling t-shirts for them if the winning stops, trust me.

'I know how worked up you get about Sunset. You need to get focused on every contest like you get focused before a surf at Sunset. What is it that you have to do to find that focus, that intensity? *What do you have to do?* Know what I mean?'

'Yeah,' I lied. I thought I knew what Rabbit meant, but every subsequent year that I spent on the Tour put more meaning into what he was talking about.

'There's a fucking universe of money about to roll onto the blokes who own those stickers on our boards, mate. Greasy, Al Green, Claw and Singo. They're the next Adidas and Nike and Puma. Just you wait. You need to be at the top of this little anthill we're sitting on when the coin starts rattling. I'm too old now, but you'd better be perched up on top of the other ants soon mate, mark my words. There's blokes out there hell-bent on stopping you.

'*What do you have to do, Kong? What do you have to fucking do?*'

Tom Carroll was '84/'85 World Champion, untouchably so, and setting the pace for all to follow. I'd finished twenty-sixth in my rookie year, after only eleven events. A good result, though hardly reflective of the potential I'd arrived on the Tour with. Still, my sponsors were stoked with my profile and my results. My stature and notoriety were way beyond my ranking after half a year.

Twenty-sixth? I was a happy man but the figure gnawed at me all the same. There may have been twenty-eight contests in a year, but there were still eleven I could have won. There was a difference between being happy and being satisfied. Were there really twenty-four blokes between my ability and TC's?

Tour life ground on, contest to contest. It dawned on me, as it does eventually to all pro surfers, that each contest represented the biggest annual celebration of surfing in each town we visited. The biggest party of the year, every week. New hotels, new waves, new brands of beer, new friends. The constants were my travelling comrades, ironically joined together as rivals and friends. And the mull and cocaine. Constant companions.

My surfing continued to improve and my sponsors remained delighted and supportive of me, in the water and out. I was climbing the rankings and getting plenty of global exposure.

All good. Though a faint, creeping sense of doubt had begun to dilute my usual optimism. I was getting exhausted. Tiredness and repetitiveness were registering. I never considered that over-indulgence in drugs was eating away at me mentally and physically.

In rare moments when I wasn't occupied competing, rushing around or partying, I thought about the success of my peers. The fitness of Tommy Carroll. The mysterious, solo preparations of Tom Curren. The lateral thinking and individualism of Cheyne Horan. The idea that I might need to change some things surfaced, though I dismissed it. Why fix what isn't broken? During those rare moments, Rabbit's echo usually had the last say.

What do you have to fucking do?

CLASH OF THE CULTURES

I was less nerve-wracked by surfing the Côte Basque for ASP Tour points than I was by seeing Pascale for the first time in nearly a year. The anticipation was killing me. Our phone calls and letters developed an urgent tone as the Californian leg of the year concluded. Only days to go!

Little did I know that Pascale was dreading my arrival. Minor detail: she'd never dumped her boyfriend. As a matter of fact, she'd become engaged to him. Apparently, things just sort of 'drifted beyond control' with the guy. As I was obsessing over her from one side of the world to the other, she was being tortured by her involvement with two blokes.

She broke the news after we'd made love on the night I arrived in Lacanau. I felt like she was gouging my guts out with an old soup spoon. It wasn't the sexual jealousy; I was the last one who could feel aggrieved by that. It wasn't even the deceit, which didn't actually occur to me in the moment. It was the love. Surely she couldn't love this joker like she loved me? Surely this magic we shared wasn't a lie?

The solution came easily to me. So easily that it had come out of my mouth before it had finished organising itself in my brain.

'Right. That's it. We're getting married,' I announced. It wasn't a question.

We spoke for hours about our obligations to star-crossed destiny and the poetic urgency to spend eternity with each other. She felt crushed by guilt and the terrible task of breaking the news to her French fiancé. I, too, struggled for one agonising second over the ethical implications of dropping in on *le bâtard*. By dawn, Pascale Roby was engaged to two guys. One of them was about to get his heart broken, the other was about to start living with quite an important split-second decision. The drama! Vive la France!

I did okay in the Lacanau Pro, getting edged out by Curren in the quarters. But France was all about our engagement and the explanations and celebrations. Just about all of my friends and family thought I was joking when I told them the good news. Literally – most people laughed at me. After the look on my face told them I wasn't joking, the look on *their* faces told me that they thought it was a bad idea. I don't suppose you could blame them. We didn't know each other well. She was sophisticated, while I was a prawn trawlerman. We were too young. I'd never tone down my partying ways. She didn't care for surfing. I couldn't speak French.

However, our engagement had a great effect on my surfing. Maybe it had nothing to do with Pascale at all, but regardless of the causes, I went on a tear of good form in the following months. I made the quarters in England, Wollongong and at my favourite US haunt in Oceanside. Tom Curren stopped me in two of them. He, South African super-talent Martin 'Pottz' Potter, Occy and I had begun a cycle of rivalry in the late rounds of contests.

Between England and California, I won my first ever ASP Tour event at Wrightsville Beach, North Carolina. It was a relief to stand at the top of the podium knowing that I had beaten a mix of my heroes and 'younger crew' rivals. When your goal is to win every heat you enter, relief is the first emotion that sweeps through you once there's no-one left to beat. The fun happens later. The Record Bar Pro may not have been blessed with great waves, but the celebrations were first class. My friends and rivals seemed almost as happy as I was.

In the short Tour break before the next Hawaiian season, I arranged for Pascale to visit Mooloolaba to meet my nearest and dearest. She would get a great taste of Aussie life and I had high hopes that all would go swimmingly. Such high hopes that we agreed she would arrive in Australia a week before me while I finished some competition obligations.

High and very foolish hopes.

Poor Pascale was dropped onto another planet from the time Mum and Dad picked her up from the airport. Likewise, my folks had taken an alien under their wing. Aside from struggling to comprehend our Queensland nasal drawl, the complete absence of European decorum spun her out. It was difficult for her to converse and to comprehend the up-front way Aussies interact.

The proximity of the bush to our home in Tombarra Street terrified her. We take spiders, snakes, giant mosquitoes and all manner of bugs and grubs for granted. Cockroaches the size of mini-skateboards are a fact of life, while Pascale was a girl who screamed blue murder at a mere glimpse of the tiny, benign insects which occasionally show themselves in France. Naturally, her fears were dismissed in good nature by Joan and Bull.

'You'll be right, darlin', we won't let the snakes eat ya!'

This is the dry, humorous way of Aussies. My fiancée interpreted it as callousness. She hardly slept a wink the whole week and was frightened to go outdoors. Oh boy.

From Mum's perspective, I'd found myself one hell of a stuck-up, pompous little princess. Pascale was welcomed with open arms and with all the warmth the household could muster, but she was sulky and unhappy. And all dressed up from morning to night like she was in Paris, not the Sunshine Coast.

What an idiot I was to send her home without me. I could understand that she was well out of her comfort zone in unfamiliar – even intimidating – circumstances. It was stupid of me to assume that she would adapt to travel and such a radically different environment as readily as me and my mates did on the Tour.

I could also understand that my family and friends might be horrified to discover that I had fallen for such a seemingly spoilt, rude girl, who so obviously didn't value the effort everyone was going to. They saw our relationship as being a monumental mismatch.

Most blokes get over these thoughts pretty quickly. Bull, Dave and my mates embraced the time-honoured male maxim of 'if you're happy, I'm happy'. Nice and simple. Besides, Pascale was so incredibly good-looking that all else was forgiven!

Like any mum, anywhere in the world, Joan was a completely different kettle of fish. Her lad was making a big mistake and she was not inclined to sit back and let him do it. I arrived home to a disaster.

I spent the first days de-bugging my bedroom to surgical standards and sealing off every microscopic crack to the outdoors so that Pascale could sleep. She was tired and cranky. When I wasn't soothing her I was trying to convince Mum that the ungrateful prima donna I'd chosen to marry was not the person she appeared to be. How relaxing. I wound up spending as much time as possible away from the debacle with my head buried in a bong or in a beer, which made me even less popular with both women.

One thing was for certain: Mum and Pascale disliked each other. The abstract thoughts I'd been having about making changes in my life were beginning to take on some clarity. For starters, it was impossible to marry Pascale *and* make our home in Australia. They were mutually exclusive concepts.

It was a relief to get on a plane and get back to the chaos of the Tour. The familiar, comfortable, *bad* chaos.

PAST THE LIMIT

I let myself down badly in Hawaii in 1985. Basically, I descended into full-on cocaine addiction within weeks of arriving.

I felt all of the usual excitement and anticipation for the waves. My preparation was good, my form was good and my boards were great. However, I was still studiously ignoring my biggest shortcoming. 'Kong', the superhuman party animal and indestructible surfer was actually a stupid outfit worn by Gary Elkerton, the totally human kid with a terribly addictive personality. I was like a guy living sealed inside one of those hilarious football mascots. I'd been doing it for so long and with such success that the big foam gorilla suit and I had become one. I was about to get a rude shock.

Cocaine was especially plentiful in Hawaii that year. I joked that I had to walk a kilometre to buy food but only 250 metres to top up on 'blow'. That amounted to a lot of short walks because I did a lot of topping up. Any embryonic intentions I'd formed about making changes to my routines and about the settled years ahead with Pascale evaporated the second I arrived in Ke Iki. Rabbit's wise words – having just started to take root – were ripped up and flung into the shit can. I was an arrogant, foolish young man with talent, celebrity and opportunity but without a shred of respect for my blessings.

The problem, of course, is that cocaine is the perfect enabler for just this kind of dickheadedness. I'm given to binging on alcohol and cannabis. Coke made it possible for me to consume five times more booze and mull. It fooled me into thinking that minor details like food and sleep were unnecessary.

I spent more time in Honolulu hanging with new people who loved to tell me how fucking good I was as much as I loved hearing it. There were no pre-dawn missions at Sunset or Waimea. I woke midmorning every day, needing a 'bump' up my nose to get me into the ocean.

Surfing-wise, it would have taken someone who knew me very well to notice a difference. But there *was* a difference. I was weak from poor eating and sleeping. Partying sessions started at 2 pm rather than 9 pm. While the cameras still clicked and the backslapping kept coming, I was privately losing my confidence at surf breaks in which you cannot hesitate. Positioning suffered when my usual paddling strength failed me. Even so, there was no thought that I should cut down on the drugs and booze. Just a disgusting, shameful desire to get my surfing 'out of the way' so that I could return to my lines of cocaine, my beers and my weed.

In previous years, I'd enjoy a terrific wave at Pipe or Sunset then I'd paddle back out as hard as I could, hurrying to get as many rides as possible until total darkness. In 1985, I'd catch a couple of great waves that I knew were photographed or filmed then go ashore and reward myself by getting shitfaced. Talk about fucked-up priorities.

The event I'd been amping on all year, the Billabong Pro, was blessed with epic surf at Waimea Bay in the heats. I couldn't have asked for a better opportunity to capitalise on my preference for larger waves in the most high-profile and important contest of the year. Tom Curren, Ken Bradshaw and Joey Buran kicked my pathetic arse into last place in heat two. I was deservedly consigned to the sidelines, as the immortal Mark Richards secured the first of his legendary consecutive victories in the event.

Everyone on Tour is a fantastic surfer. Everyone at that Billabong Pro was a fantastic surfer. I'd have needed to be at my absolute best to beat Tom, Ken or Joey in that heat. But I'd lost weight, lost focus and lost respect for my rivals and myself.

And I had utterly lost my way.

My stay in Hawaii came to an early and inevitable conclusion in the first week of January. My frailty had begun to manifest itself in my gaunt, strung-out appearance. My behaviour became erratic, even by my rather high (or low) standards. I was breaking into random, red-faced sweats. I told those around me that I was fine, though they could see me reacting with ill-disguised panic to frequent episodes of a racing heart rate, inability to breathe, spontaneous vomiting and even fainting.

Eventually, several of my mates stepped in. I love these guys for many reasons, but their care for me in '85 saved my career, if not my life.

By the time Pottz and Tommy Carroll insisted that I pack up my shit so they could drive me to the airport, I couldn't help but agree that I was a mess who needed to get off the island and out of the whole circus. Before they arrived to pick me up, I sucked up as much of my stash as I could ingest, like the junkie I was.

I barely made it to the departure gate, but this time it wasn't as a stoned, trumped-up and triumphant hard charger. It was as a sad, clapped-out imbecile who had forgotten what he had in life and who he was as a person.

My years of excess had been very public. The damage to my health was hidden by success, approval and bravado, until a tragic outcome was all but inevitable. I was alive, though darkly embarrassed to be so. I was lonely and distressed as the plane took off. A few valiums begged from a nearby passenger allowed me a troubled sleep most of the way back to Brisbane.

DIGNITY

I woke up an hour or so before the plane touched down in Brisbane feeling lower than a brown snake's knob. I was so ashamed of myself that I couldn't even face Pascale. We agreed that I'd go to her in France for a few weeks after Hawaii, but my breakdown and early departure had changed the plan. She was unaware of recent events, because my phone calls to her from Oahu were the upbeat smokescreens typical of a druggie in deep denial.

Was *this* the life I had in mind when I dreamt of getting off the trawler?

I fought back tears as I collected my bags and found my way onto a bus to the Sunshine Coast. No-one was expecting me and I had no idea how I would explain my unexpected arrival home.

Mum and Bull were happy to see me of course, but they were surprised by my haggard appearance and my subdued demeanour. They were most worried by my reluctance to get out and party with my old mates. I just wanted to stay at home, watch cricket on the TV and eat Mum's cooking.

They accepted my explanation of 'burnout'. So did Pascale, begrudgingly, when I told her I needed to be around family for a while.

Bull cottoned on to to my real problem, although he perceived it through his own experience. 'You've been getting on the piss too much, hey, son? Living the high life, hey?'

'Yeah, something like that, Dad.'

'There's more important things in life than the grog. You have a good day on the boat. You have a good day in the surf. The pay-off is looking back at the work it took to get you there. What the good day means for you. Food on the table. Knowing you do your job well. Doing things right. That's the pay-off, mate. Not swimming to the bottom of a fucken bottle. I know, I've been there. You know ... you know I have.'

'Yeah, Dad.'

'You'll be right, son,' he said, rubbing my head just like in the old days.

My old man doesn't talk too much, but that short conversation helped me a lot. He's a man of private addictions and selfish passions like me, I guess. But he's lived a really honest, really admirable life all the same.

Bull could easily have said that I'd be welcome back on the boat anytime. He probably thought it. Had he said it, I may very bloody well have given into my feelings of weakness and considered the offer.

'Get your act together, Gary. Win that fucking World Title, okay mate?'

He couldn't have said a better thing at a better time. Have I mentioned how much I love the crusty old bastard?

The first person I reached out to after my immediate family was Paul Pascoe. It felt comforting to ride a bicycle to the surfboard factory. I shared the full truth of my last few months with Paul and he listened to my self-inflicted troubles in silence, staring at me with scarcely a blink.

'You've lost your respect. You've lost your *dignity*,' the last word was emphasised with a sharp finger jab to my sternum.

'Training tomorrow morning at six.'

The next eight weeks were a rebirth. I humbled myself at the Zen Do Kai dojo before my *sensei* and he pushed me harder than I'd ever been pushed in my life. Whole days were spent revisiting every nuance of every *kata* until I collapsed exhausted. Night-time sessions were contact sparring bouts during which I was kicked, punched, thrown and locked in submission holds again and again. And I remembered how much confidence and enjoyment I got from doing punishing, painful training.

Addictive personalities can work for you as well as against you. This is one thing that Paul drilled into me during the first months of 1986. Best to be addicted to the things that help you achieve your goals rather than the things that work against you.

'You'll fall off the wagon a lot, Gary. Forgive yourself. Just make sure you never lose your dignity again. Kong's a nickname mate, it's not some way you have to fucking live.'

It was the first time that I'd consciously considered that 'Kong' may be a bit of a problem for me.

'You're a fighter, mate. Don't let people divert you or stop you. Especially yourself! You want to be the World Champion? Well, everything that stands in your way should be treated like an opponent standing opposite you on the mat. Respect it. Fear it. Fight it. *Put it down before it puts you down!'*

Incredible that Paul had offered me guidance so similar to Rabbit's precisely twelve months before. Different in delivery, but uncannily alike in context. I decided – albeit belatedly – to start acting on good advice from good people.

THE NEW KONG

Quite a few of the guys phoned me while I was recuperating, which was really nice of them and very much appreciated. Generally, I laughed off their concerns and promised them they'd better 'fucking watch out next contest', or some such smart-arse comment, just to reassure them that I was my old self again.

But I wasn't my old self at all. I was physically stronger and fitter than I'd ever been, after two months of training three times a day, a good diet (for the first time ever) and nothing nastier than sharing a bottle of XXXX with Bull once a week. The biggest change was in my attitude. Having been thoroughly shaken up after Hawaii, I'd figured out the answer to Rabbit's nagging question. I now knew *what I had to fucking do*.

First, I recognised that I'm hopelessly incapable of denying my raging appetite for grog and drugs when temptation is so often presented. Maybe I could let myself off the chain on occasion to enjoy a private beer or puff on a joint. But all-night raging every night of the week had to go. Which meant that hanging with my touring comrades all year had to go too. Most of these guys knew when to stop and when to avoid the throngs of hangers-on. I didn't. My major problem was a childish aversion to missing out on a good time. I hated listening to radical stories of fun nights or hilarious misadventures when I wasn't in the thick of it.

In any case, the very same guys who I so loved to be with were also the people who were doing their best to piss me back off to the prawns once the starting siren sounded. There was no getting around it. They were all great blokes but they were also incredible surfers. If I allowed my respect for them as surfers to be blurred by my compulsion to socialise, I'd suffer.

These guys were professionals who could balance their lifestyles. Clearly, I couldn't balance mine. 'Spring break' cannot, by definition, go for three hundred and sixty-five days per year.

Secondly, I promised myself to fear being ashamed again. I visualised facing my surfing opponents at the karate dojo. I should fear them like I'd fear physical punishment on the mat. This translates to positive aggression. I had to recognise them as respected opponents who were out to damage me. I resolved to prevent them from doing so.

Scraping the bottom of the barrel in Hawaii was the making of me. I'd come within a whisker of being 'that big guy from the Sunny Coast who was on those couple of Jack McCoy films'. There were many people who supported me in a way that lots of surfers over the years haven't been, people who pulled me up on my dangerous excesses. People who cared enough and were mature enough to worry about me as the person underneath the façade of the surfer. Underneath 'Kong'. I was utterly determined to pay them back.

For some of them, it meant they had a reinvigorated, sometimes aloof 'new' rival.

The final events of the '85/'86 World Tour were in Australia. My nemesis in many a contest that season went on to win the World Title in emphatic style. Tom Curren is a surfing genius.

He is one of many blokes from the era who would stamp his personal style on surfing forever. He had a unique brand of 'smooth'. I had wanted to beat his perfect flow with raw gouging so bad ever since our amateur days. I'd had my mini-victories over him, but he held sway over me that season like he did over everyone. I was burning for a chance to meet the champ from Santa Barbara in a big final. That was going to take a while if the bastard kept wiping me in the semis!

Throughout the final Aussie leg of '85/'86, mates and competitors stirred me up about my change in demeanour. I didn't carouse around the VIP area before heats. I wasn't to be seen at the usual mid-contest piss-ups and parties. It was the start of a process I'd finetune around the world in the upcoming year.

I finished eleventh in the world at the conclusion of my first full season. It was a result I was happy with, since my goal was to make the top fifteen. But I wasn't completely satisfied, thanks to thoughts of what 'might have been' had I woken up to myself earlier.

I was frothing for the commencement of the '86/'87 Tour and training my guts out.

THE BUBBLE

My results at the start of 1986 were uneven, but my fitness, focus and general surfing were really good. Pascale accompanied me to the first two events, which were in Japan and at Sandy Beach on Oahu's South Shore. It was during this period that we made some big decisions as a couple.

We locked in our plan to marry at Waimea Bay in January of '87 and we decided that we would set up home in France afterwards. The decision to move to France was an easy one. Not only did I adore my fiancée, but I was totally enthralled by her home region in France. Also, Lacanau presented as a fresh start for me as I fought hard against my ingrained bad habits. We were excited about setting down our roots as a couple.

I passed on the South African leg of the Tour while we spent some time together in France throughout July. The time wasn't wasted. We rented an apartment overlooking what was to be the contest site in Lacanau. I trained ferociously and surfed the stretch of beach several times a day, acclimatising to every shift of tide and wind.

When the ASP circus arrived in August, I met up with my mates and thoroughly enjoyed catching up on Tour gossip over a few drinks. But not too many. The Lacanau Pro of '86 commenced without the traditional partying presence of 'Kong'.

I spent the time before my early heats pacing the floor of the apartment, looking out at the contest bank and listening to AC/DC on my headphones. I built myself up into a frenzy, focusing on nothing but the destruction of my opponent. The excellent surfer who would send me back to prawn trawling. Who would ruin my life with Pascale. This was hard fucking core. It was a fight for life.

I would not give them the opportunity to even look at me before a heat. I'd arrive at the beach just in time to pick up my contest jersey and paddle out.

No-one was getting anything from me. This was a one-on-one combat sport where the winner takes all, not a gentlemanly game of croquet. Handshakes and camaraderie were for later. Until then, all bets were off. Fuck you for trying to hurt me!

Curren beat me resoundingly in the semis and went on to thrash his compatriot Mike Parsons in the final. While I seethed at being booted out by my personal Mr Fucking Kryptonite, I was pleased that my new mindset sat so comfortably. It felt right and, above all, it worked.

My working concept of one-on-one competition became that of a boxer. Competition surfing, like competition boxing, is not throwing lovely combinations at a punching bag. You beat your man. You beat him to a pulp before he does the same to you. And you sure as shit don't stay in the same hotel rooms and live cheek to cheek with him. Ali and Frasier weren't roommates.

I retain the same rituals during competition to this day. I picture myself in a bubble, totally self-sustained and separated from anything that diverts me from dealing with the threat of my would-be attacker.

In the water, some guys smile at you. I look through them. Others want a chat. I ignore them. When they want to get all aggro I'll go out of my way to paddle right over the top of them, hoping they'll start a fight that I'll finish. Verbal battles get me really pumped up.

Some of the guys were a bit put out by it. They thought I was trying to intimidate or bully them. But those who knew me well understood that my coldness and aggression were not about them, they were about me. It wasn't unsporting or disrespectful. It was what I *had* to do to remain competitive, to stay on the Tour and to keep my life. Those who didn't understand could go get fucked. I had enough mates.

The next event was the Foster's Surfmasters in England, where I beat Occy in the quarters before *again* being eliminated by Tom Curren in the semifinal. There's no dishonour in losing to Curren, but the scoring was very poorly adjudicated.

A quarterfinal finish in the mid-season OP Pro at Huntington Beach kept me in the title race. Occy won the thing in front of a gigantic crowd on the last day.

The 1986 Marui Pro at Hebara Beach in Chiba, Japan holds a special place in my memory, and not just because I won the contest in small surf so unsuited to my style and physique. I treasure the memory because I prevailed over one of my most sentimental childhood heroes and over two of my most respected friends and contemporaries on the way to victory: Shaun Tomson, Occy and then Martin Potter in the final.

I went close to finishing last, not first. On my arrival in Tokyo I was held in customs for thirty hours thanks to my visa expiring. Luckily, the local Quiksilver boss was best mate of the Japanese prime minister's son. Strings were pulled. I waxed my board on the way from the airport, jumped from the limo, pushed through the huge crowd and paddled straight into my round-two heat with Matt Kechele.

I relaxed my spartan touring routine after the win, much to the amusement and good-natured ribbing of my Tour mates as we attacked downtown Tokyo. The prize money was paid to Pottz and me in a pile of US dollars. There wasn't much left of it twenty-four hours later. Pottz and I bought a street florist's entire stock and distributed bouquets to horrified downtown motorists. Later, at a nightclub of dubious repute, a stage show of exotic beauties showing off their wondrous buttocks in skimpy g-strings was infiltrated by Queenscliff's Rob Bain. His god-awful underpants pulled tight up his hairy arse crack did nothing for the sensuality of the performance, but it amused the large audience no end! The celebratory night in Tokyo proved that I could enjoy myself without necessarily giving in to a perpetual state of unjustified celebration. This was as personally important as the contest victory itself.

I made the quarters on the Gold Coast and at Wollongong, where I was shaded *again* by Curren. I'd be lying if I said I wasn't just a little sick of the guy.

Despite the reigning World Champion's mid-season ratings lead, I was looming as a chance for the Title when December – and the Hawaiian Tour events – cycled around.

OL' YELLOW

Pascale and I rented a modest Hawaiian bungalow at the quiet end of Sunset Beach, a few streets back from Darrick Doerner's lifeguard tower. It was a little love shack that Pascale added some personal touches to, most unlike the grottoes of filth and debauchery I'd inhabited (or, rather, created) in previous seasons.

I made sure to pay respects to my Hawaiian friends, such as Mickey, Eddie, Marvin and David, but heavy socialising was replaced by the continuation of my training and preparation routines.

I surfed religiously at first light, then divided each day between eating, sleeping, two more surfs, a run, some karate training and a midday chat with Darrick below his tower. I got to know every little chip of paint on that tower as it became my major hangout during any downtime I had. Darrick and I became even closer.

I was happy to connect with my old Grajagan buddy Mike Miller soon after we settled in. Although Mike lived at Sunset Beach, he was a true-blue authority on Waimea. I was grateful to have him paddle me around the 'line of sight' reckoning points at The Bay. If anything, these secrets were even more exacting than Sunset's, literally down to centimetres. I filled a notebook with the information and studied it, as I had with Darrick's and Jeff's tutorials at Sunset.

One afternoon, Mike showed me an old, bright-yellow 10' 6" Dick Brewer gun he had stored in his shed. He treasured it because of its radical 'banana' rocker and the strange story behind its creation. Apparently, back in '73 or '74, enigmatic surfer/shaper Owl Chapman had half-shaped the blank before wigging out on an acid trip. Master craftsman Dick Brewer completed shaping the board months later, before it was finally glassed. How many Dick Brewer/Owl Chapman combination hand-shaped guns are there? No wonder Mike loved the thing.

Mind you, he swore that it had too much rocker for Waimea. I begged him for a surf on it and he was nice enough to allow me a session in some solid twenty footers. It felt fantastic and I raved about its magic. I hassled him to allow me to buy it or at least borrow it for the season, but he just laughed and locked 'ol' yeller' back up in his shed.

The following morning, Mike set sail on his catamaran for Niihau, Hawaii's 'Forbidden Isle'. Presciently, he spoke of a 'major swell event', and charted a course for the remote waves of the little island's leeward shore. Mike's Waimea lessons and the old yellow Brewer were to play a major part in the week ahead.

The waves that season had already been as consistently big as I'd ever seen when the beginnings of an epochal swell feathered into the North Shore for the first days of the Billabong Pro. The trials and early heats were held at Sunset, building from twelve feet, to fifteen feet, to eighteen feet throughout the second afternoon. Just as Mike Miller had foretold.

By the time failing light halted proceedings in heat seven of round one of the main contest, Sunset was maxing out furiously, though perfectly, at twenty feet. Most people – even the veterans – agreed that they'd rarely seen it break with such pristine symmetry at such a size. My current high ranking meant that I was seeded directly into round two, so it was disappointing to miss out on my favourite wave at its best.

But there was no talk of Sunset.

Technical experts from the US Navy and other government departments predicted that the swell height may well double in size before it peaked the next day. Locals peered knowingly out to sea and thought that the eggheads were – for once – correct. There was consensus. The waves were going to get much bigger the next day. The Bay was *on*.

There were some very tense, nervous and subdued people around Oahu's North Shore that night.

The meal Pascale and I shared was interrupted by the vibrating of our plates and cups on the table as each new set broke on the outer reefs. The valleys and hillsides of the North Shore echoed with a constant loud roar, not like the usual distant rumble but like a jet taking off. No-one in the whole area could've been unaware that something very special was happening in this most special of surfing communities.

After dinner, I left Pascale to her romance novel and walked down to the lifeguard tower. The pylon I leant on twisted against my back rhythmically, like you'd expect in high wind.

But there wasn't a breath of air moving. I surveyed the ocean at Sunset, attempting to pick up some kind of pattern, but there was no line-up to observe. Just glowing white mountains of foam as far as could be seen. I closed my eyes and soaked up the raging noise, the vibrations through my feet and the contortions of the pylon.

After a long while, I returned to bed and thoughts of being below deck, riding out storms with the Bull.

I woke from a dreamless sleep at 3 am and was energised by a harebrained plan: I needed Mike's old Brewer. I must have it. If he were home, he would surely allow me to use it for this monumental day? Long before sun-up I stole into Mike's backyard like a common thief and used a broken old hacksaw blade to cut open the padlock on his shed.

I drove to Waimea in darkness, waxed the Brewer, attached a couple of two-metre leashes and waited for first light. It was a good thing that I couldn't clearly see the outside line-up as I sprinted through the twelve-foot shore break on a wing and a prayer. Because by the time I'd reached the take-off area, I saw that these were by far – *by far and away* – the biggest waves I'd ever been amongst.

My plan was to be the first out into the line-up. The idea was to tune up ahead of my heat and get my positioning straightened out. I also wanted to send a message to my fellow competitors that I was keen on the challenge. But all that tactical bullshit was forgotten as I became distracted from my flippant plans by a serious personal battle to survive.

What was I thinking? It was too dark to pick up my line-up references, but it was way too late to paddle back in. The height of the waves was immense, but it was their *mass* that worried me. I'd never seen this shit before. These fuckers were like fast-moving office blocks. Okay ... I'd get one then go back to the beach and reassess.

I caught the biggest wave I'd ever caught – which was the smallest wave of the set – and started to drive into the vast face. I then realised why Bay veterans don't use leashes when it's 'big'. The bastards felt like parachutes behind me. I was pitched in the lip, having achieved no downward momentum against the galactic forces of upward drawing water and the terminal drag of two thick ropes of polyurethane. The leashes snapped like dental floss anyway, as I was driven so deep that my ears popped. At Waimea you kind of wish for the familiarity of a reef upon which to be minced.

When I finally surfaced, my thoughts turned to an unpleasant body surf through the shore break to safety. Then they turned to Mike's unique board.

Unfortunately, the Brewer was not washed up on the beach. In fact, it was hundreds of metres away, disappearing out to sea in the violent current at the far end of Waimea Bay. There was no avoiding the mortifying task of retrieving ol' yellow, so I resigned myself to death as a preferable alternative to fronting Mike Miller with the news that I'd first stolen, then abandoned his favourite keepsake. And 'death' is not an exaggeration.

The Bay had started to close out.

CONTEST OF CONTESTS

Darrick Doerner's advice to stuff a small swim fin down the back of my board shorts seemed like a pretty overdramatic tribute to North Shore folklore when he first suggested it. But in those days before jetski support and guardian angels in helicopters, the little flipper proved to be a godsend.

I recovered the yellow Brewer and went on to ride three of the greatest waves of my life to date – each one bigger than the last – before returning to shore for breakfast at about 7 am. I was exultant and relieved at the same time. Most likely I would never surf waves like these again, because I just couldn't imagine that it would be possible to run the contest that day. The swell was building by the minute. It was already closing out just about everywhere on the whole island.

Normally, contest sites are buzzing with excited conversation, while organisers, officials and surfers rush around this way and that. The scene at Waimea that morning was more like a funeral. Everyone stood on the grass or in the car park, gawking in awe at the ocean. The Bay was bigger than it was during my early morning session. It was also *better*. The lightest offshore breeze cleaned it up and the swell direction had altered ever so slightly, so that each set peeled perfectly. Imagine your favourite local wave on its best, most glassy three-foot day. Then turn yourself into GI Joe or Barbie's boyfriend, Ken, for correct scale.

No-one was surfing. The beach itself was viciously awash. There was even a sense that onlookers weren't totally safe up on the grass. Many of us contestants stood on low concrete benches in front of the car park. There wasn't a lot of conversation on the perch I shared with Gary Green and Bryce Ellis; they were as white as ghosts. I probably was too. Rob Bain, who was due out in the first heat, paced up and down, chain-smoking.

Strangely, there was no debate about the size of the waves. It was at least thirty feet on the Hawaiian scale, which was all anyone needed to know. That's sixty feet wave faces, or about double the height of a ten metre diving platform. Late, great Waimea Bay expert Mark Foo had coined a phrase, 'The Unridden Realm', which was his description of waves that were physically impossible to paddle into. There was a general feeling that this was what we were looking at.

As each set continued to build bigger than the one before, comforting whispers spread amongst the surfers that a postponement of the contest was inevitable. Girlfriends and wives were freaking out en masse. Everyone was shitting themselves. That's a fact.

Which is why the entire scene was electrified when contest director Randy Rarick announced that the contest was on. Fuck, boys. Here we fucking go! The biggest day of competition surf in the history of the ASP World Tour was underway.

Mum would be stoked to know that I said my first and only prayer of thanks to St Brendan. Had this day occurred a year earlier when I was a drug-soaked wreck, I'd have died for sure out there. No joke.

It was eerie to watch my friends Rob Bain and Ross Clarke-Jones walk down to the water's edge with living legend Mark Richards and Brazilian triallist Alex Salazar for that heat. The swell was still building. It had to be well over thirty feet – *Hawaiian* – but nobody bothered to even mention the size any more, let alone put a measure on it.

Competition stops and human nature starts when you know that one of these blokes could easily die in the next half an hour. No jetskis. It was agreed that board caddies shouldn't be endangered in conditions like this. Lifeguards were on hand, but there was no way that they – or anyone – could help a distressed contestant. The boys were on their own.

Everything turned to shit within a few short minutes. MR had miraculously paddled through a gap in the current and was a hundred metres further out from the other guys when spectators on the cliff tops began pointing to the horizon. Their shrieking and yelling horrified those of us below. Fuck knows what it did to the four surfers in the water.

From ground level, it was difficult to see over the seething white water in the foreground. The microscopic figure of MR could be seen in the distance taking a dozen desperate strokes up the vertical face of the first wave. The rest of the set was visible *behind* it. Think about that for a minute.

This set wasn't peeling – it was closing out the North Shore of the island of Oahu. In that moment, Randy Rarick must have believed that he'd just sent four young men to their deaths.

MR made it over them all, each wave threatening to pitch the four-times World Champion backwards into oblivion. The other guys were annihilated.

The same waves thundered through the foreshore, washed over the grassy bank and into the car park. The crowd bolted in a panic for higher ground. Surfers and fans sprinted to save their cars as water powered over the bitumen. It was mayhem.

Alex was pulled from the shore break. Fortunately, he was smashed towards land. He appeared lifeless as rescuers worked to resuscitate him. The lifeguards eventually revived him heroically. Rob and Ross were rumbled by the entire set, wearing its whole force in a succession of two-wave hold-downs. Both guys have told me many times that they thought they'd definitely drown and were preparing to die as the waves bore down on them. It's a tribute to both men that they eventually caught a wave to safety.

While he ran out of oxygen, listening to gigantic boulders on the ocean floor crash together like marbles, Rob formed the opinion that he ought to quit smoking. I've never seen him with a ciggie since.

Meanwhile, Mark Richards ripped. He ripped the biggest heat of the biggest day ever on the ASP World Tour. Enough said.

That famous set proved to be the peak of the swell.

I was amping to slay the dragon. The contest had become about guys who *wanted* these waves and guys who were *coping* with these waves. During the thirty minutes of my win in round two, every second played out in the kind of sharpened awareness that only exists on the border between life and death. The 'fear of feeling fear' beforehand was the worst. Worrying about my friends and waiting to paddle out was more stressful than being in the water.

When the time came, it was actually a relief to start the process of staying alive. The mass of the waves bore no resemblance to anything I'd experienced before, including the beasts I'd ridden before breakfast that morning. Without any adequate reference point in my memory, being so physically *minimised* in this titanic environment was literally surreal, as though I was a prop on a Hollywood special effects set. Rather than fear, I felt an odd kind of *wonder*.

The spell was broken by the first wave I caught. I willed myself to go for it, though conscious thought screamed in favour of self-preservation. I freefell the first twenty feet before connecting about halfway down. Some more big S-turns got me to the bottom, where a grim race against four storeys of deadly foam saw me through to the safety of deep water. A skier, centimetres ahead of an avalanche. Once that was out of the way, I was mentally focused on winning the heat and the contest – I was just too busy to be scared. I left *that* to the crowds onshore and TV viewers.

My study of Waimea's line-up markers worked. Inch-perfect positioning amongst the terrifying craziness proved decisive. Just knowing where I had to be and when helped give me something to concentrate on other than the mortal danger at hand. Pottz helped too.

There was aggro developing between Pottz and me, since we were so close on the ratings. We had an almighty paddling dual while thirty-foot bombs landed all around us. I paddled him a little deep on one wave and he was pitched in the lip. He lived, so no harm done.

I won my quarterfinal, which included Curren, pretty easily. I'll concede this seems like an arrogant statement, but it's honestly how I felt. I was tuned in and firing on all cylinders, absorbing every second of the experience, because I knew deep down that a big final in these conditions would never happen again. I couldn't very well bitch about contests being held in one-foot slop then not make the most of this, could I? My long, dramatic day ended on a huge high, both as a surfer and a competitor.

There's a special camaraderie between the guys who competed that day. The heat sheet is a who's who of the last great era of paddle-in big-wave surfers. This was pure surfing competition. Just surfers with their boards, experience and skill up against each other and against the full fury of 'survival mode' Waimea Bay.

I feel sorry for the guys who chose not to contest their heats. Despite the fact that *everyone* was considering whether they should paddle out after witnessing what happened to Alex, many people still questioned the courage of those who forfeited. I'd like to dump these armchair experts into the line-up at thirty-foot Waimea Bay with no boats, jetskis or chopper backup. Such idiots deserve a punch in the head, but they'd be better served by 'walking the talk' – paddling in – at The Bay.

The semis and final of the Billabong Pro concluded the next day at Sunset, which was as big and as flawless as it can be.

I came a close second to Mark Richards in the semi and was also pitted against the great man in a nail-biting final. I relaxed and enjoyed each second of the decider. Ronnie Burns and Glen Winton tactically opted for smaller boards and the inside bowl. Mark and I chose longer equipment and the outside peak.

The waves at Sunset were right up my alley and I felt in top form, especially after the previous day. Of course, perfect, maximum Sunset Beach west peak is also right up MR's alley and his form is permanently switched to the 'on' position! I have to say that I loved watching MR during our final. He inspired me to position myself deeper and deeper, since I would have to ride some unlikely tubes to beat the master.

It was fun. MR did his thing and I did my thing. After the final siren went, we paddled to each other and embraced warmly, reflecting on what an unbelievable couple of days we'd been through together.

Mark Richards won, enhancing his already peerless reputation by coming out of retirement and surfing through the trials to victory at the Billabong Pro for a second straight year. I was stoked for him, I was stoked to be a part of it, but that final was still very bloody close all the same. I thought I might have won it and MR might have quietly worried that I did too, but I've never been so happy to come second. After all, MR was still stuck to my bedroom wall at Tombarra Street!

Pascale and I celebrated the long emotional and physical distance I'd covered between the shame of Ke Iki in '85 and the pride of the Billabong Pro in '86. But it was the last time I was ever over the moon about being the 'first loser'.

WEDDED BLISS

It's sounds ridiculous to describe a contest at Banzai Pipeline as an anticlimax. But any contest that followed the '86 Billabong Pro would have been a slight let-down. Even so, the Pipeline Masters went off in excellent waves and carried its customary aura, characterised by First Reef powering away just metres in front of a beach full of cheering crowds.

Derek Ho won the contest, while Tommy Carroll and Brian McNulty were the other stand-outs. My run finished in the semis with a fifth placing overall in my first Pipe Masters.

We had a wonderful Christmas Day as guests of Randy Rarick, along with Mark Richards, Shaun Tomson and their wives. You could imagine how I felt in that company. Eddie Rothman's New Year's Eve barbecue was terrific, as usual. Other than that, we were fairly quiet and 'loved up', as they say.

I was in serious trouble with Mike Miller though. He didn't take kindly to the theft of his surfboard, though I returned it undamaged. Mike gave me a fearsome verbal battering and banned me from visiting him again. I was terribly sorry and suitably put down by the episode. I really looked up to Mike, but you don't respect an elder by doing childish shit like that. He forgave me a couple of weeks later at the urging of Jack McCoy. In fact, a few years ago Mike actually gave me the board! These days it's stored in Hawaii under the awesome protection of Ray Street. Can't have any prick stealing it now, can I?

Pascale and I kept the details of our wedding close to our chests, since we were trying to avoid the negativity of Mum's objections.

I needed my birth certificate in order to be legally married in the state of Hawaii. Mum wouldn't send it to me even though I told her I needed it to organise a visa. I think she smelled a rat about our wedding, especially since David was on his way over to visit us. We argued mightily on the phone, but she eventually relented, just in time.

The day of our wedding did justice to the depth of our feelings. Pascale and I had a few close friends present. I would have liked to have had some Tour friends and best mates, such as Rabbit and Chappy attend, but the ASP had moved on. We wanted to keep the ceremony quiet and out of the spotlight, and I was stoked to have David stand beside me throughout.

Waimea Falls Park was a picture-perfect romantic paradise, set just behind the majesty of Waimea Bay. Eddie Rothman sourced wedding rings for us and I was touched that he and a few of my other Hawaiian mates worked to make the day such a special one.

Wedded bliss had begun.

HOME EN FRANCE

My second in the Billabong Pro and my fifth at Pipeline kept me squarely in the race for the World Title. Pascale and I returned home in early February. Home ... to France.

We lived in an apartment right on the beach at Lacanau, which is a completely different village in the middle of winter to the raging summertime resort I'd known during the surf contests. We were two of just 450 residents. It was gorgeous, rustic and colder than anywhere else I'd been to. Winter swells in France are much stronger than they are in summer and crowds are non-existent.

My first surf as a Lacanau 'local' was hilarious. I hurried into the water, excited by the powerful, empty perfection. 'Life's getting better all the time,' I thought, until my cranium was crushed by the icy water. After two duck dives I was forced to retreat in agony. My 3/2 millimetre wetsuit wasn't going to cut it! Pascale laughed her head off as I sat beside the fireplace thawing out. There'd be some adjusting to do, but I was falling more in love with my wife and our new home by the second.

I couldn't have been in a better environment to continue my training and my new-found commitment to the things that mattered. I surfed and exercised hard every day. I explored the food, fine wine and culture of the region, while I worked diligently, but hopelessly, at my French. It was liberating to be separated from temptations that I couldn't resist, particularly at that time of year down in Australia.

My daily fifteen-kilometre run took me through a misty section of the local forest. Snow was frequent and I made quite a sight in my two sweaters, beanie, scarf and long johns, stylishly packed beneath a bulging tracksuit. Icicles formed around my mouth and nose. I revelled in my new surrounds because they focused me so clearly on the changes I'd made and why I'd made them. Rabbit's mantra played in a loop over and over, in time with the beat of my strides.

What have you gotta do? What have you gotta do?

Tom Carroll forcing himself through a million chin-ups. Cheyne twisting his frame with yoga. Curren doing whatever the fuck he did to be the enigmatic freak he was. Occy, Pottz, Gerlach. All of them.

What have you gotta do? What have you gotta do?

I knew I'd turned a major corner when I didn't cast a single thought to the wild goings-on at Torquay's world-famous pub when we went down to Bells Beach. I'm pretty sure that I didn't pass a word to any of my mates until after the consistent American Dave Parmenter dusted me in the quarterfinal.

Nicky Wood won the event, however all of the other frontrunners fell before I did, meaning that I was still a mathematical chance to win the World Title when the season concluded at the next Tour stop – Manly in Sydney. But for that to be a reality a lot of guys had to bomb out and I would have to go all the way to the final.

It wasn't to be. Nicky Wood eliminated me in round one in crap waves on a tight split decision. No point blaming the judging though, because other results blocked any long shot that I had anyway.

Tom Curren secured his second World Title in row. He was definitely the best surfer of the year. Actually, Tom could easily be the best surfer of any year. It's a good thing for the rest of us that his competitive fires weren't always on full burn.

I finished fourth in the World. Considering that the World Champ seemed to be on a personal mission to beat me by narrow margins in quarters and semis during the whole year, I couldn't be too hard on myself. Ratings aside, my objective was to reclaim respect and dignity, which I did.

From twenty-sixth to eleventh to fourth in two and half years on Tour. The next step in the sequence was up to me.

ALL OR NOTHING

Mum didn't take the news of my marriage and permanent move to France very well. I didn't help matters by avoiding the uncomfortable phone conversation until after the Coke Classic at Manly. Pascale made me face the music before we flew out from Sydney.

'Hi, Mum. Listen, you've probably heard that Pascale and I eloped. Well, you see, I won't be coming home this time around. I'm going to go to France between Tour stops from now on, okay?'

I was too gutless to say, 'I've moved to France.'

Mum was a loving, caring, beautiful person, but she disliked Pascale. Yes, Pascale had behaved poorly on her first visit. And yes, Pascale was usurping Mum's traditional role of chief supporter, minder, moral guardian, manager and travel agent. But I was madly in love with Pascale and I was completely taken with my new home in France.

Not to mention the crucial advantages that a new life away from my addictions and weaknesses held. How could I tell Mum about the complexities of my drug problems? About the vital role that my new relationship and my new home played in the protection of my health, let alone the wellbeing of my career? I didn't have the maturity to articulate these awful revelations without breaking Mum's heart. How could I tell her that the son she was so proud of was actually a fucked-up coke head with no self-control?

So, I broke her heart anyway by saying that my gravitation to France was 'just the way it was'. She thought that I was throwing away my family and that I'd been led by the notoriously unreliable judgment of my penis into a life of 'glamour' in France. Nothing could've been further from the truth, but in the absence of complete honesty from me, I can't blame Mum for thinking so.

My Mum and I were extremely close. We suffered an estrangement over the following year that hurt us both, but which – happily – didn't diminish our love for one another. Bull was caught in the crossfire, as were Bern and Dave, I suppose. The 'bubble' I created for myself had probably gone too far. But there was no turning back.

I was professionally committed to winning the World Title in 1987. Carrying through my training from the year before, and with my contest preparation routines wired, all the supporting elements were in place.

At last I was an adult, with an adult's responsibilities. I had my own home and a wife. I had to make my own way, keep a roof over our heads and pay all the normal household bills, which meant that I had to succeed at my profession. And 'success' – to me – meant that I had to be the best.

Surfing is a low-paid job unless you're at the very top. Accolades, magazine articles, movies and occasional victories don't mean much if you can't support a family. Riding waves is lightweight compared to what my father and grandfathers did to make something of themselves. I was determined to avoid the life of a failed pro surfer, trading on a couple of Tour wins and consigned to repping board shorts for a crust. I had to win an ASP World Title. All or nothing.

The year started in my happy hunting ground of Japan, at the Mauri Pro on Niijima Island. I had a lot of pent-up energy to release in this contest, so much so that it's fair to say I was the dominant surfer of the event for all but the last thirty seconds. Who else but Tom Curren needed the wave of the contest to pass me as the head judge was reaching for the siren? Second place was still in line with the plan I'd set. If I could place no lower than ninth in every contest outside of Hawaii, I'd have my best chance to establish a lead at Sunset, Waimea or Pipe.

A ninth at gentle Sandy Beach held the plan together.

During an early gap in the tour schedule, the famous Quiksilver film *Mad Wax* was shot. What a hoot. TC, Bryce Ellis, Ross Clarke-Jones, (the late, great) Mark Sainsbury and I had a blast hamming up the storyline and ripping some great waves all over the place. Pascale was none too happy about my character (the bad guy, of course) having a sexy female cohort close by in every scene. I still enjoy watching *Mad Wax* occasionally. Good times.

Every surfer had to drop his two worst results from each season's total points tally. Often, guys opted to skip two contests and use the break to prepare, recover from injury or simply to avoid going somewhere they didn't like. The two last place finishes don't count anyway. In '87 I again chose to bypass the two South African contests. My reasons were varied. I believed that passing on the South African leg gave me a rare chance to be at home with Pascale for at least four straight weeks. Since she now travelled with me, it also gave her an extended time to be with family and friends.

It wasn't a holiday for me. The brief respite from travel and contests allowed me to intensify preparations before the American contests.

Volunteering to come last in two events – which therefore automatically became my 'throwaway' events – was a calculated risk. I weighed the benefits against the chance of injury or form loss later in the season.

My results in the USA were pleasing, considering the poor waves. As usual, I enjoyed being at Oceanside for the Stubbies USA Pro, where Shaun Tomson gave me a wave selection lesson in round three for a ninth placing.

Huntington Beach was a mass of fans for the OP Pro. It was like a Superbowl! I was aggrieved to lose by 0.7 of a point to Barton Lynch in the quarters for fifth place.

I pinned a lot of expectation on my performances in the three French events. I already considered it my home and the local press was full of stories about their 'adopted' pro surfer. The heartfelt support I received was out of this world, full-on European soccer-style fanaticism.

Because there's never been an ASP Pro Tour event on the Sunshine Coast, I never got to feel the way the Sydney boys do when they get cheered on in Sydney, or the Hawaiians in Hawaii, or the Californians in California. It was so uplifting to be embraced as a local, but I couldn't quite repay the outpouring of goodwill. Ninth placings in Lacanau and Hossegor were an overall 'pass' mark, but I set out to win every heat. To win every contest. Ninths did nothing but keep me within reach.

The contest in Cornwall, England, separated the Hossegor and Biarritz events in '87. Coming third in the UK Surfmasters made me feel a lot better. Losing to Curren in the semi didn't.

The Biarritz Anglet Offshore Surfmasters was my last chance to win on 'home turf' for the year. On the final day, the enveloping cliff tops, boulevards, resorts, cafés and bars at Biarritz's Grande Plage were packed to capacity. Most competitors agreed that this was as close to surfing in a stadium as we could get. The atmosphere in the water was supercharged. There were tens and tens of thousands – who knew how many – in the crowd.

In solid ten-foot surf, I was helped by wild support to a comfortable victory over Tommy Carroll in the semi and a hard-won shootout with Damien 'Dooma' Hardman in the final. The crowd went friggin' beserk. It was a happy day to be a winning 'Australo-Frenchman'! The trophy was a huge lump of solid brass which I struggled to lift. I was so exhausted that I bloody near dropped it into the crowd, which definitely would have splattered one of my new *bons amis*.

There was no time to celebrate because the Hang Loose Pro in Brazil was due to start three days later and we had to leave for Florianopolis almost immediately. My left ankle was throbbing uncomfortably when I went to bed. I remembered twisting it slightly doing a close-out floater on the last wave of the final, but that was last I thought of it. I was so tired that I didn't ice it and thought I'd 'sleep it off'. No big deal.

It was a big deal when I woke with extensive bruising and swelling. The diagnosis was a medium-grade ligament strain. Nothing snapped or broken, but it would need some rest and treatment. The Hang Loose Pro was out of the question – which was *not* in the plan.

The ankle was fine for the Tour's return to Japan three weeks later. Dooma 'returned serve' from France by downing me at Chiba in our second close final in three events. I was stoked to have maintained peak form despite the injury setback.

After locking in a pair of ninths at the springtime Aussie events at Margaret River and Newcastle I had achieved nothing less than a ninth in every event I'd competed in during the season, plus a win and some seconds and thirds.

There were about four of us vying for top spot before Hawaii. For the first time in my career, most pundits were expecting me to excel in Hawaii and hit the home stretch to the World Title with the wind in my sails. The expectations sat comfortably, because they were the same expectations I had of myself.

PAY-OFF

There were three North Shore contests scheduled in four weeks, which was an unprecedented opportunity for me to cash in on my love for Hawaii and the personal devotion I'd given to my development in her waves. The pay-off was profound.

The Hard Rock Café World Cup at Sunset picked up the start of a series of beautiful north-west swells which lasted nearly all of December. I arrived at the beach before each heat as ready to win as I've ever been. The specialist small-wave gymnastic rippers had had their run for the year. My turn now.

There was a strong sense of destiny attached to my charge through the Hard Rock to victory.

Every element felt so dialled in that I was able to both enjoy surfing fifteen-foot Sunset *and* focus on defeating my opponents. It's not always easy to combine the two, but 'enjoyment' was the major lesson I had taken from watching MR at such close quarters the year before. I was also using boards which were slightly larger than anyone else's. By the semi and the final I was establishing a position outside of my rivals that went unchallenged, allowing me two 'tube sections' per wave and considerable speed advantages for big moves in the steepest sections.

Occasionally a surfer will enjoy such a rich feeling of confidence that he doesn't want a contest to end. The Hard Rock was such a contest for me. I was stoked that I only had to wait a few days before the Billabong Pro commenced at Sunset Beach. I stayed in contest mode during the brief break, even to the point of hiding my Hard Rock trophy. I promised myself I would enjoy my long-awaited first Hawaiian win at my favourite wave, but not before the Billabong Pro and the Pipe Masters were over. There was work to do.

Conditions at Sunset remained in my favour and I was humbled to win the Billabong Pro in fantastic waves from Glen Winton, Martin Potter and the evergreen Shaun Tomson. If anything, I was more tuned in, more fluid with my re-entries and more precise with my fades and bottom turns that I was in the Hard Rock.

Two ASP Tour victories in a row – two victories in a row at pumping Sunset Beach. From the day I first opened a *Tracks* magazine I had dreamt of winning a pro event at Sunset. Two consecutive first places was beyond the dream. If I was still a kid, I'd have *me* on my wall, for sure. A pretty silly thought to have while lifting my second trophy in two weeks.

I was only half-joking when I lamented that the Pipeline Masters couldn't be staged at Sunset.

I came within a whisker of making all three finals in Hawaii but settled on a fifth placing at Pipeline, well beaten by locals Derek Ho and Ronnie Burns in the semi. In any case, nothing could've stopped Tommy Carroll from winning his first

Masters. His shredding was superhuman. It was tremendously sad to hear that Tommy's sister had been killed in a car accident just days before the event, which says so much about the character of the bloke. A champion in every sense of the word.

I finished first, first and fifth in the three Hawaiian contests, which secured my first Hawaiian Triple Crown title, second only to the ASP World Championship in prestige. I was the first non-Hawaiian to achieve the honour.

We kicked back at the Hilton and allowed ourselves the luxury of a party. Plenty of friends and wellwishers dropped by with congratulations. The guys who knew where I'd come from in '85 were especially great. By the time Pascale and I were alone, I was bit choked up.

My love of the ocean had led me to so many places and driven me through so many phases. Now I was the reigning Hawaiian Triple Crown Champion, leading the ASP Tour rankings and racing down to the wire for the World Title in the months ahead. My name and Sunset Beach would be linked in history, which pleased me as much as anything. Like Lance Armstrong and the Tour de France. Bjorn Borg and Wimbledon. Tom Brady and the Super Bowl. The honour couldn't be taken away.

We had another month in Hawaii before the O'Neill Coldwater Classic in California. It was not to be a completely relaxing time.

Al Byrne and Paul Hallas had parted company at Hot Stuff. Al had formed his own company, Byrning Spears, just before

I organised my Hawaii quiver for '87. It was a tricky situation because my business arrangements for free boards were with Hot Stuff, but the sensational craft I so relied upon were crafted by Al. In the end I sidestepped the conflict by paying for my quiver from Al. When I received them, his new board logo was positioned in the nose area of the board where I was obliged to place Quiksilver's brand mark. I had little choice but to cover a large part of the Byrning Spears logo with Quiksilver's.

Al was furious and harsh words were exchanged between old friends.

We both had an understandable position. These things happen in the industry, though at the time neither of us were overly philosophical. We parted company on sour terms. There wouldn't be another sleek Al Byrne shape beneath my feet for many years. I'm very happy to say Al and I resolved our problems in time and we're good mates once again. I was gutted by our misunderstanding, not just because of my respect for Al as a supreme craftsman and surfer, but because I truly value our friendship.

A happy ending, but as 1988 was welcomed in at Eddie Rothman's annual barbecue, I had a serious situation on my hands. I needed good boards, fast. A call to Nick at Mt Woodgee eased my mind. I'd already ridden his boards and loved them. We'd surfed together a lot too. He started on an awesome new twenty-board quiver of Mt Woodgees then and there. What a relief. The last thing I needed was to worry about my boards during my surge for the World Title.

I thought ahead to future Hawaiian seasons by introducing myself to local master shaper Pat Rawson. Mark Richards –

a superb shaper in his own right – had been recommending Pat to me since our Billabong Pro showdown in '86. Tommy Carroll also raved about his quiver of guns. I started working with Pat before I departed Oahu in January.

Over two decades later, I'm still riding Mt Woodgees and Pat Rawsons.

BUSINESS IS BUSINESS

Results in Santa Cruz didn't alter the standings, so the Australian leg – Bells Beach, Wollongong and Manly – would decide the Title. It looked a dramatic set-up and so it proved to be – and then some.

We arrived in Australia with a few weeks to spare before Bells. I took the opportunity to head up to Mooloolaba in the hope of discussing things with Mum and collecting a few personal effects from home, like old trophies and so on.

Once again, I didn't think things through. Just lobbing up without a conciliatory letter or phone call was insensitive. I copped an earful from Mum, my aunty, and even Bern as I attempted to remove a few boxes from the garage. Pascale didn't help by yelling French insults from the car. Jerry Springer would have been stoked.

Dooma eased ahead of me in the rankings by winning the Bells Easter Classic. I couldn't even apply any pressure thanks to one solitary wave sensationally underscored in round two, which was the end of my contest. That upset was utterly dwarfed by other bizarre developments during the contest.

Massive ructions were at play behind the scenes in the surf business. Quiksilver had changed enormously since I had first been invited to join the promotional team as 'number two' behind Rabbit. The company had relocated its headquarters to California, and American licensee Bob McKnight was now CEO of a fully corporatised, global business.

McKnight and Al Green visited Pascale and me in our Jan Juc rental home just after I was eliminated. My contract had expired and a new one was due. I was still on $15,000 per year, plus airfares and accommodation. This was the same arrangement that I'd started my pro career with. I needed other sponsors and prize money to make ends meet, let alone have any security or comfort.

I certainly wasn't complaining, but given the exposure I'd achieved for the company and especially because of the continual improvement of my Tour results, I was expecting a friendly, congratulatory meeting. After all, I *was* leading the Tour heading into the Aussie leg and I *had* just won the Hawaiian Triple Crown in commanding fashion. Within a month, I could well be World Champion. I was front-page news for months on end, right across the surfing world. I'd cleaned up my act and I was surely Quiksilver's number-one promotional tool, particularly in light of Rabbit's imminent retirement.

I was very much looking forward to continuing my loyalty to Quik and to securing my financial future with the company. Al looked pale and sheepish when Bob proudly announced that I deserved an upgraded contract: $20,000 a year for three years. A $5,000 per annum pay rise. Sixty thousand dollars in total over the *whole* duration of the contract. First and final offer, no negotiation. I was dumbfounded. And I was cut very deeply.

Two-time World Champ Tommy Carroll was newly back on board as Quik's nominal 'competition figurehead' and a substantial budget had been allocated to him as the launch vehicle for their new range of wetsuits. Bob disregarded the changes I'd made since '85 and explained that I was still 'very important' as good old crazy Kong, the promo party animal. The 'great' new contract reflected my value to the business.

It was quite clear that they were simply not going to spend big money on both Tommy and me. One of us had to go.

Of course, I had no choice but to reject the offer, which was the obvious intent of the company. This was considered a resignation, Quiksilver would therefore not have unceremoniously dumped a loyal and successful servant. Officially I had 'quit for more money'.

It didn't hurt me to ask Bob to leave my house, but it bloody near killed me to ask Al Green to depart. I thought we'd be celebrating a new deal with a quiet beer, not going through this terrible trauma. I sat there in shock for half an hour, staring into space. After all of the effort I'd put in – let alone my recent contest achievements – the cold brutality directed my way was unbelievable. Literally, I could not believe it.

Now I can look back on the affair as a positive. It obviously worked for Quiksilver – you only have to look at the incredible success the company enjoyed post 1988 to know that Bob McKnight is a shrewd guy. I still strongly believe that I was wronged, notwithstanding that so much budget was deservedly heading in Tom Carroll's direction. But I accept that a CEO who was instrumental in building a multinational giant out of t-shirts must make more wise calls than dumb ones. I was livid with Bob for some time, though I came to respect the fact that a guy in his position can't avoid upsetting people. I also came to respect him for being man enough to front me in person.

I've never been dirty at Al. He was part of a big machine by that stage. It took a lot of guts to accompany Bob McKnight that day and it was a task that would have made him as sick as it made me.

From my perspective, I'd just graduated with honours from the University of Surfing Business after a ten-minute crash course. McKnight did me a big favour. Once you realise that you're a 'unit of income' you will never be hurt again by the surf industry.

It's a harsh business, premised on the sale of two dollars' worth of cotton for seventy dollars. The idea is to convince non-surfers that they will magically become part of the physical activity of wave riding should they buy a t-shirt with a special logo printed on it. This marketing ingenuity helped support me for many years, so please don't think I'm criticising.

Pro surfers hold a volatile role in the brand-building exercise. If smart businessmen don't think you can help them create and maintain perceived value in a ridiculously expensive t-shirt, you'll be out on your arse in a heartbeat. The side issue of surfing doesn't always figure in the process. Your job is to surf your best. Theirs is to sell t-shirts. Sometimes the two jobs don't sit neatly together. Business is business.

I was forced out of Quik because they calculated that paying both me and Tommy Carroll what we were worth wouldn't sell 'double' the product. Fair enough.

I picked up the phone and was promptly invited to join California's Ocean Pacific on $80,000 per year plus all expenses and super-generous incentives. Just like that. OP were a gigantic company at the time and my teammates included Todd Holland, Lisa Andersen, a grommet called Slater, and none other than Tom Curren.

The next day, OP stickers were on my boards and every thread of Quiksilver apparel I had on hand was distributed around the local grommets or tossed in the bin. Business might have been business, but I didn't have to enjoy being treated like a kook.

Quiksilver and 'Kong' were tied together in the public's mind, so I'd change my name to Johnny B. Dogshit before I'd give those guys a ride on 'Kong' moving forward. Anyway, I was sick of the public connection between the Kong persona and my old partying ways. The gorilla received a very public execution. OP were getting Gary Elkerton, professional surfer. No hairy alter egos.

Within a week, my solicitor had informed the ASP, the surfing press and the mainstream media that I was no longer to be referred to as 'Kong'. A drastic step, though one that reflected the strength of my feelings.

The World Title was well and truly enough to set a fire under me ahead of the next contest in Wollongong. I was pumped by the immediate opportunity to repay Ocean Pacific's belief in me. Did I also want to stick it up Quiksilver? My fucking oath I did!

Dumping me with two events remaining to decide a World Title. Unbelievable. I counted the seconds until the first siren blew in Wollongong.

SHOWDOWN

I paced around on the balcony at our rented Wollongong apartment, working myself into a rage before each heat. It didn't take much effort.

I beat Sunny Garcia, new team mate Tom Curren and Glen Winton on my way through the finals to victory. On the last wave of the final, I fell just short of perfect scores with a huge close-out floater in the shore break. Hundreds of photos of the OP decals on the nose of my board went around the world. I was in such an aggressive mental state, I wished I could've surfed against everyone on the Tour that afternoon, but I'd have to wait a week.

Dooma Hardman made the quarters in Wollongong, which set up a perfect showdown for the Coke Classic at Manly Beach. Whichever of us went deepest into the contest – the highest placed – would be World Champion. Dooma won Bells. I won Wollongong. Manly, in Sydney, was 'high noon' and the media frothed over our clash of styles. The nimble, lighting-fast vertical specialist verses the power surfer.

I suffered from severe nerves throughout the whole contest, a new and unenjoyable experience. I felt nauseous the whole time I wasn't in the water. The crowds at Manly were huge and every single one of them were barracking for local lad Damien Hardman. Especially the Narrabeen boys, who were predictably rowdy. I blocked it the best I could and prepared as usual in our suite at the Manly Pacific Hotel.

The waves in the event were bad, but my form held and so did Dooma's. Our paths met in the semifinal. Winner take all.

Sloppy right-handers dribbled into North Steyne Beach on a weak south swell. My nerves vanished and I felt focused and energetic from the start. Dooma and I traded waves, punching and counter-punching until the heat clock ticked into the final minute. I only required a low-scoring ride to overtake him and win. A couple of little turns and I was World Champion. I was paddling back out and Dooma was outside of the break when the most important little wave of our lives wobbled into the contest area.

It broke well in front of Damien and closed out across the sandbank he was counting on. There was no way he could ride the wave to score any points. He was left fifty metres from any workable face. The ocean gods smiled on me as the tiny wave stood up and presented me with enough blue water to score the points I needed. I reeled off three or four carves down the line and soaked up the roar of the crowd. I'd done it. I'd won.

The crowd wasn't cheering me. They were cheering Dooma.

He'd swung around and got to his feet in the folded-over, foamy slop, a hundred miles from me and where the face was breaking. Dooma trapped me in a technical violation of the interference rule. As the rule stood, I was deemed to have dropped in – to have stolen his wave. It took a few seconds for me to understand what was happening. My score did not count. Damien Hardman was World Champion.

I don't blame Dooma one bit for using the rules to his full advantage. Good on him – he was one ruthless, clever competitor. I wouldn't even have *thought* to use the interference rule like that, let alone actually *done* it. It was exactly analogous to a 'mankad' run-out in cricket – deeply cynical, but within the letter of the law. More fool me.

I stormed off the beach as quickly as I could before someone said something or did something that caused me to start throwing punches. Being around people chanting Dooma's name wasn't a good idea. I attended the podium presentations (Damien went on to win the event) and I managed to front the ASP Ball a few nights later, when the new World Champion was officially crowned. We left for France the following morning.

They say circumstances like this are 'character building'. It's standard for professional sportsmen to spout feel-good bullshit about how dealing with injustices like this makes you a better person. Let me tell you something: *winning the 1987 World Title, as I deserved to, would've made me a better person.*

I'm not buying into platitudes or weak-as-piss pop philosophy. All the farcical interference situation did was to leave me feeling justifiably robbed. But lessons were learnt. Foremost of them was that the ASP didn't waste any time in changing the interference rule. If you weren't practically blocking someone's wave or physically preventing them from surfing naturally, you weren't interfering. Too late for me. So glad I could help though.

It was also the last time that the ASP World Title race would finish in shit waves. All future seasons would conclude in Hawaii, the birthplace and spiritual home of the sport. Cold comfort for me. Would I have lost a World Title showdown against Damien Hardman in large Hawaiian surf?

I would've won the World Title had I advanced from even one heat in South Africa, or had I not been injured for Brazil. Moral of the story? No more skipped contests, because you can't dismiss the possibility of injury. Regardless of events at Manly, I can only blame myself for this misjudgment.

Grief and anger ate at me so hard that I barely uttered a word for days. Coherent thought wouldn't form through the searing frustration, so I couldn't even express myself. I was gripped by a desperation to escape. A few weeks spent on the grog, mull and coke would fix me. I seriously considered leaving Pascale at home for a while and going to some non-surfing place like London or New York where I could anonymously medicate away the pain.

Life since my big triumphs in Hawaii had been radically hectic. Fights with family, upheavals with boards, shafted by Quiksilver, welcomed by Ocean Pacific, a win at Wollongong and the debacle at Manly. No wonder I needed an escape.

My old mate Chappy had gradually drifted away from the Tour and life as a pro. Likewise, Rabbit had cut back his commitments and was retiring. I'd deliberately distanced myself from my other close Tour friends. My time-honoured cure-all of throwing myself into socialising wasn't the option it once was.

Home at Lacanau was all the medicine I needed. The serenity of our village separated me from the 'world' of surfing. The steadiness of Pascale's love and the familiarity of home ratcheted down the drama, which was exactly what I needed.

It was glassy and six feet for my first surf at home. There was nobody on the beach or in the water and the simple joy of riding waves bubbled back to the surface. Life wasn't so bad after all. Great wife, great home, great job. I wasn't going back to the trawler any time soon.

I may not have been World Champion but I now knew that I could be and should be. I didn't need drugs, I just needed my surfing. And another opportunity at the Title.

For the time being.

REGROUP

I reconciled with my family by phone before the '88 season commenced, although the antipathy between Pascale and Mum never abated. Mum reached out to me after the disaster at Manly. It was a load off my mind to be able to regroup for the new season without worrying about how I would clumsily attempt to repair our relationship. It was so comforting to know that I had Mum and Bull firmly in my corner, no matter what.

There was a lot of regrouping required, not just by me but by everyone on the Tour. In order to realign the contest schedule with a calendar year finale in Hawaii, twenty-four events were squeezed into seven very short months.

I augmented my karate, weights and forest running with hill climbing and soft-sand sprint work. Pascale's brother, Stefan, also changed my life by introducing me to snowboarding. You could see the snow-capped Pyrenees from most of the local surf breaks, so it made sense to use them for cross training. I wasn't much good to start with, but the exercise was great and I became a massive fan of the sport from my first downhill slide.

During this cold winter of preparations, I also developed a very unlikely friendship. Tom Curren had also relocated to France. Like me, he also happened to be married to a beautiful local girl, Marie. Pascale and Marie naturally gravitated to each other as the Tour wound its way around the world. Although Tom and I carefully avoided each other during competition, we were regularly the only two surfers sharing Hossegor's seriously sized winter swells in the break between ASP seasons. Remarkable that so often the only two 'recreational' surfers on a quiet French beach were foreigners who were deadly rivals for the world professional title. Throw in the fact that we were OP's leading team members and it was impossible for us to ignore that we had a *lot* in common.

It was wonderful to share waves with Tom and to chat away easily (in English, I might add), just like two normal surfers enjoying some good-natured camaraderie. And with our wives, the four of us shared many a pleasant dinner together over the years, though never during the months away on Tour. The deep respect I always had for Tom grew to genuine fondness for his company. We never became close friends and we always kept a sharp edge to our competitiveness, but I found it hard not to like the laid-back champion from California. Unless the freakish arsehole was wearing a contest jersey, of course.

I was gratified to discover that he worried about coming up against me as much as I did him, though we agreed that we both loved the challenge. We'd shadowed each other for so many years. In the past I'd often wished that Tom had grown up in Detroit rather than in Santa Barbara! They say you're 'defined' by your rivals at the top of professional sport. I'm extremely fortunate to have been defined by all of mine, none more so than Tom Curren. The bastard.

Every drop of sweat shed during training was needed to power through the breakneck pace of the 1988 Tour. Half a dozen of us battled it out before Barton Lynch claimed the World Title in a thrilling finish in Hawaii. I was out of contention by the last event, the Billabong Pro, despite coming second to Tommy Carroll in the final of the Hard Rock World Cup at Sunset.

I made a concerted effort to put Manly in '87 behind me. My objective was to make the semis in every contest and then drive off that for victory when the opportunities presented. In hindsight, I should have allowed anger from the year before to take more of a hold, because my fifth place finish for the year precisely reflected my 'measured' plan; I finished with a lot of fifths and sevenths. The process was valuable nonetheless as 1988 was my most consistent year – contest by contest – to date.

My 'pre-season' training in '89 was interrupted – or perhaps augmented – by a chance introduction. Steve Bell was an expatriate Victorian from Torquay who lived in France and ran a successful surfboard company called Euroglass. I often bumped into him and fellow expat Victorian Maurice Cole when I was down in Hossegor. Steve was mates with a bloke called Xavier Audouard, who was a motocross entrepreneur. Xavier was based in Biarritz and owned Pro Circuit Racing, a company that customised professional motocross bikes.

I was still a huge motocross nut, so Xavier secured himself a big fan in Lacanau's only pro surfer. Xavier in turn introduced me to Australian motocross legend Jeff Leisk, who was also based in the Biarritz area and competing in the Motocross GP series in Europe. Now these were my kind of new mates! Jeff was nice enough to drive me to Xavier's private sand track and allow me to cut loose on a borrowed bike.

Within days I'd bought myself a nice easy Honda XR600 four-stroke to reacquaint myself with riding. Days after that it was joined in the garage by two spanking new, beastly Hondas, a CR250 and a CR500, both expertly tricked up to racing spec by Xavier's Pro Circuit workshop. I discovered that the old axiom 'you never forget how to ride a bike' is completely true. My childhood passion, so long pushed into the background by surfing, was revived under the supreme tutelage of Jeff and Xavier. I was like a pig in shit.

My home in France had turned into the ultimate theme park for an adrenalin junkie: pumping waves, world-class snowboarding and thousands of acres of dirt-bike forest trails, all within minutes of home. Talk about cross training. And I was stoked to have a new circle of mates to relax with, both in the snow and on the bikes, who were outside the complexities that came with my surfing friendships. I was also stoked to discover that my close mate since childhood and the Mooloolaba grommet days Reid Pinder was moving to the area as a bigwig for Billabong. His presence was always a real comfort to me.

I maintained a 'bubble' of competitive focus on my surfing career, but I'd also found some excitement and release away from my profession that didn't involve sucking powder up my nose or smoke into my lungs. 'Kong' still craved these pleasures, but 'Gary' kept himself so busy that the ape was subdued. The '89 ASP season was dominated by a man who'd kept himself equally in check.

'Best-of-the-best' super world champs like Kelly, Andy Irons, MR and Curren might've had more dominant seasons on the scorecards, but Martin Potter's blitz in '89 sticks out in my mind for the high-risk, balls-out, *radical* surfing he executed during contests. Pottz built a bridge between traditional big-turning power and the emerging predisposition to reward acrobatics and stunts. It was a landmark year of transition and Martin wrote his name on it by smoking everyone at everything. Maybe only Nat Young's effort in 1966 to build a bridge between elegance and power was of similar importance. And all this from a guy with impeccable credentials as a charger at Waimea, Pipeline and Sunset Beach. Martin's was as magnificent and as landmark a performance over twelve months as I've seen, and I believe it is too often forgotten as one of the greatest World Titles ever won.

Okay ... enough about Pottz!

I was actually happy with how I performed in '89. I placed highly throughout the season and positioned myself nicely coming into Hawaii, as was my usual plan. Though it was mathematically impossible for me, or anyone, to catch Pottz for the World Title, I focused on the three contests of the Hawaiian Triple Crown.

I nearly drowned during the semifinal of the Hard Rock Café World Cup at Sunset in the first leg of the Triple Crown. Though it was 'only' twelve feet, the extreme west swell created a treacherous outgoing current that surged up the face of every wave. And although the waves weren't as high as they can get, they were uncommonly powerful thanks to an extra-long, eighteen-second swell interval.

I didn't know that I was already safely through to the final when I got to my feet on a jacking wave, just as the siren sounded. I was launched in the lip, outward and upward before belly-flopping on impact. I skipped for three massive bounces without being able to penetrate the water. It was an awful feeling, as contests and careers were forgotten. All I wanted to do was to pierce the surface and escape the terrible pounding. I didn't have a scintilla of oxygen left in my lungs when my wish came true.

Suddenly I was driven into the reef, with less air in me than a popped balloon. I blacked out briefly. The board caddies and lifeguards frantically searched for me in the impact zone while I rolled ashore on the beach, coughing blood. The emergency settled down and I'd just gotten off an oxygen mask when the final – which I'd just qualified for – began.

I was pretty fucked up mentally, but I rallied late to come a close second behind Hans Hedemann, who scored an excellent win. Normally I'd have been dirty on myself for wasting a chance to raise another trophy at my favourite wave, but I was honestly just relieved to be on the podium. I was lucky that my favourite wave didn't drown me.

I was tremendously encouraged by the wild conditions that prevailed for the start of the Pipeline Masters. It was extremely difficult to overcome the 'Pipe specialist' goofy-footers when the waves were perfect. Guys like Derek Ho, Ronnie Burns and Tommy Carroll were nearly untouchable on big, smooth tunnels.

But for this contest the reef had a little too much sand on it and the giant swell was being generated by a low-pressure system that was just a little too close to land. Swell intervals were not ideal at just ten to twelve seconds. Some waves broke on the second reef, some on the first.

Pipe was an inconsistent, choppy, uninviting and deadly mongrel, spewing awesome, unreadable power onto its lava reefs at maximum size under crosswinds and grey skies, nothing like the textbook blue-green funnelling perfection that had made it a household name. Had the contest not been necessary, nobody would be bothering, as there was no enjoyment factor. It would simply not have been worth the risk.

The early rounds were a lottery of luck and guts. Early on the morning of the final day, a large crowd – including participating pros – watched the empty, dead low-tide line-up from the beach. It was spectacular, but nothing that anyone was too keen on experimenting with. Pipeline frequently killed people on perfect days, let alone in this crazy shit.

I'd decided to stamp a psychological edge on proceedings by paddling out. While I was waxing my board, the beach suddenly began to buzz. Tom Curren had beaten me to the punch by opting on a lone 'warm-up' surf of his own. I thought I had the edge on him with this kind of thing – calculated psyching in chaotic surf. My respect for Tom went up one more notch. I went out anyway and we managed a knowing bleak laugh at each other as we dodged death and made a few drops. Common sense eventually overrode competitive instinct and we both made our way back to shore and waited for the tide to fill in.

The last rounds began as the incoming tide created a surfable situation. It was classic 'Pipeline theatre'. I beat Tom Carroll, Liam McNamara and Sunny Garcia on my way to the final against Vetea 'Poto' David, Cheyne Horan and Ronnie Burns. It was gigantic, it was scary and all the finalists chucked themselves over some truly ridiculous lumpy ledges. There was a macabre Colosseum type of dynamic between the finalists and the crowd. I was happy to come through unscathed. I was happier to be the Pipeline Masters Champion at the end of the day.

The swell dropped for the Billabong Pro, which played out at Sunset the following week. It was smallish and very shifty during the quarterfinals and I was outpositioned and outsurfed by Sunset local Mike Latronic.

Fifth place, combined with my previous second and first, secured my second Hawaiian Triple Crown. A season of close eliminations in the finals had ended on a massively satisfying high. My final ranking of sixth was a letdown of sorts, but I was still confident that I had a World Title in me, if I could catch some better luck in the semis during 1990.

'YOU'RE OUT, FUCKER'

Tom Curren launched a comeback to the full-time Tour in 1990 after spending the previous eighteen months or so competing sporadically and pursuing other interests. We took up combat right where we'd left off in thumping waves at Steamer Lane in Santa Cruz, California, the year's first event.

The script was obeyed, fair and square. Curren first, Elkerton second.

Fair and square went out the fucking window at Burleigh Heads in the second event. The high drama continued and we met again in the final in spitting low-tide barrels. I got out to a lead inside the last five minutes and held priority when the decisive set wheeled around the headland and into the cove.

I was outside of Tom and in dominant position when he threw a tactical 'Hail Mary' and blocked my line by paddling directly in front of me. It was a classic 'snake' move, executed aggressively and contrary to etiquette in free surfs. Definitely illegal in competition.

The wily bugger was taking a long shot that I'd back off, but he must have known deep down that was never going to happen. I had nothing to lose. If I paddled over the top of his back and into the wave, I ride down the point and win. If I didn't get over the top of him, we collide, he gets called for interference and I win anyway. So I gritted my teeth and paddled as hard as I could straight up his backside.

We went over the falls together in a tangle of limbs, boards and leashes. Recovering our boards wordlessly, Tom gave me a little grin as if to concede defeat.

The interference call went against me. Curren first, Elkerton second.

Judging was starting to depress me. I'd been putting tight split calls behind me for a couple of years, but true resentment for the faceless men in the tower now took hold. *These* blokes were taking my life away. Unlike my rivals in the water, there was little I could do about them except try as hard as I could to focus on the 'controllables'. Still, I wasn't mentally right for the remainder of the first Aussie leg.

My mojo was back in Durban where I placed third. The mid-season run through Europe, the US, Japan, Brazil and springtime Australia went in similar fashion. Lots of thirds and fifths – narrow-margin losses in the semis and quarters. The Seland Pro in Spain typified my year: a loss in the final to Sunny Garcia by 0.3, though that was a veritable thrashing compared to some of my results. The pattern had become a talking point around the traps: I either won heats by huge margins or lost by a hair's breadth.

I resigned myself to the necessity of establishing big, obvious leads early in every heat because, whether it was me or whether it was the judges, the results were plain: I hadn't won a nailbiter for years.

I was perched comfortably in second place, so it was down to Curren and me for the World Title. He'd have to underperform and I'd have to excel in Hawaii for the positions to be reversed at season's end.

Tom bombed out in round one of the Hard Rock at Haleiwa, so I had my chance to pounce. Haleiwa turned on fantastic competition conditions and the standard of surfing was excellent. I was tuned in and amped to reel in Curren. Although Derek Ho and Barton Lynch beat me into third place in the final, I'd managed to chop off a big chunk of Tom's lead. A similar result at Pipe would set up a showdown for the World Title in the last event at Sunset Beach. Momentum had turned my way at last.

Both mainstream and specialty media had done their calculations and built up incredible anticipation ahead of the Pipeline Masters. The traditional rivals were going head-to-head for the World Title in the last two events, at the two most famous waves in the world.

The tale could hardly have been better constructed in fiction. The returning former World Champion trying to hold on after an amazing year of winning through from the trials, unseeded in every contest. The 'master' of power surfing roaring at the champ's back, determined to claim an overdue World Title on his favourite stage. And that's how it went in the first two days. Just like a novel.

Pipe was a lovely, sunny six to eight feet. Curren couldn't fight his way out of the trials. I had a clear run. A fairytale climax beckoned. I only had to make the quarterfinals for Tom and me to head to a surf-off at Sunset. But the end of the 1990 season wasn't orchestrated by a romance novelist.

I hadn't counted on the importance of the Hawaiian Triple Crown to Derek Ho. Having won the Hard Rock, Derek was leading Barton and me in the race for the Crown. In those days, all three contests were top-rated ASP Tour events. It was a genuine 'title within a title'.

In 1990, I was still the only non-Hawaiian winner. Naturally enough, Hawaiian competition surfers weren't thrilled with the idea of me leaving Oahu with a third Crown, especially since local lad Derek was out in front. Fair enough too.

Tragically for me, this welcome and healthy competitive spirit was taken a step too far by Derek's older brother, Michael Ho, in our round two clash at Pipe. Early in the heat he grabbed my leash as I paddled into a solid wave. I was flung into the reef and received a cut to my elbow which later required twenty-seven stitches. Despite the laceration, with a few minutes remaining I only needed a three-point ride to progress through to the quarterfinals and an appointment with Curren the following week.

I had positioning priority over Jeff Booth and I was completely comfortable that an adequate set would arrive in time for me to do the few turns required of me. A nice inside wave duly stood up and I took off.

Michael Ho was paddling out. I was mortified to see him swing around on the shoulder and drop in, heading right on this left-breaking wave. I was astonished as he ran into me with a shove.

'You're out, *fucker!*' he said, as I was rolled away into the foam and a zero score. Mike not only blocked my wave in contravention to rules and etiquette, but he finished the job by physically tackling me. He was called on a deliberate interference.

Many people on the beach were almost as distressed as I was, though I couldn't talk to the dozens of them who commiserated with me. I was so distraught that my knees wobbled and I was supported in a kind of mass 'group hug', as friends, rivals and fans rallied around in a state of disbelief.

Eventually, Pascale pushed her way through, tears streaming down her face. We were shepherded into a car, me still bleeding, wet and unchanged from the heat. Back at the Turtle Bay Hilton I shut the drapes and turned on the TV, trying desperately not to think about anything at all. A doctor came and attended to my elbow. The phone rang continually but I barely heard it. Out of nowhere convulsive sobs burst out of me. I cried myself to sleep in Pascale's arms. Some tough guy.

My heart was broken. I felt like flying home straight away, but pride drove me to collect myself and compete at Sunset Beach with some dignity. I was in a bit of daze though I forced myself to embrace the contest for the pleasure of surfing. But there was no ignoring how deflated and dispirited I was. I finished seventh in the contest. Curren – on a carefree victory lap – finished ninth.

All I wanted was a fair chance at the World Title. Michael's infamous decision paid off: Derek Ho went on to the quarters of Pipe and the semis at Sunset, which secured him the Hawaiian Triple Crown. I would gladly have forfeited against Derek in the quarters or semis at Pipe if that's how much it meant to the Ho brothers. I didn't have to be taken out of contention for the World Title by a foul like that.

Friends like Eddie, Mickey, Marvin, Darrick and Mike Miller sympathised with me and reassured me the malice didn't extend all the way through the local Hawaiian community. I questioned myself all the same. Did I *deserve* that treatment? Had I disrespected my Hawaiian Tour rivals? I didn't think so, but *something* must have driven Michael's actions.

The answer was many years in coming and it was quite obvious when I thought about it, free from anger. Brotherly love. The incident was less about me being a haole who had the nerve to claim expertise in Oahu's surf and more to do with Mike Ho looking out for his brother. No culture wars. No complex vendetta. Just as simple as blood being thicker than water.

I've made my peace with Mike and Derek. These days they count amongst my very closest friends in surfing and they're the first guys I visit when I get to Hawaii. Strangely enough, the shared experience of the controversy may have brought us together – though it didn't happen for several years.

The events of 1987 and 1990 have been terribly difficult to live with at times. My friendship with the Ho brothers in our 'post-Tour' lives has played an important role in helping me maintain perspective. They are both great blokes. I'll never get another crack at the 1990 World Title, but life goes on, like it or not.

Tom Curren was World Champion again. I was second – controversially – again. As in 1987, spiteful, torturous questions kept nagging away at me. What if even some of my semifinal losses by less than a point had been wins by less than a point instead? How would the year have panned out had Curren been called for his interference on me at Burleigh?

Would Curren and I have finished in the positions we did at Sunset if the real pressure had been on? Could I have won Pipe? What if Mike Ho had been out the back, not paddling past, when my winning wave came through?

The questions of 1990 melted into the questions of 1987. They barked at me without pause, long after we returned home. I lost my appetite and I was too anxious to sleep properly. I felt exhausted, even though I spent the first few weeks back in Lacanau in bed. I'm now told I was most likely suffering some sort of mild state of shock.

When Pascale wasn't at home, I took to smoking hash again to empty my mind and give me some respite from the anguish. Before long, I was rested enough to resume surfing, training, snowboarding and bike riding. Season 1991 was about to start and I couldn't very well avoid it.

Anyway, getting back on Tour beat the shit out of being alone with my disappointment.

ONE LAST SHOT

My ASP efforts in '91 and '92 were almost carbon copies of each other; both years were cursed by fairly crappy surf, which seemed to stalk us from one side of the world to the other.

My early performances in 1991 were listless. It was a real struggle to maintain my routines and discipline. I did so begrudgingly and I also battled a new-found fatalism, which both annoyed and drained me. 'What's the point of all this hard work, all the denial of my urge to party, when everything I fucking do is in the hands of the kooks with the score sheets? Besides, if I allow myself to believe in a World Title, I'll only be gutted by fate again. I'm not *meant* to win.'

I didn't really believe that fate was against me, but the thoughts persisted. It was a challenge to psyche myself into staying positive. I made the judges' jobs easy up until mid-season by surfing poorly. I didn't even make a quarterfinal until France. The World Title was effectively out of my grasp by this point. I decided that if I was to salvage anything from the year then I would treat France as my last stand – the 'Hawaii' of '91.

I trained maniacally and isolated myself from absolutely everyone for weeks before the Quiksilver Lacanau Pro. In my mind, I turned winning Quiksilver's contest at my French hometown into a blood feud. Damien Hardman was adjudged to have beaten me by 0.4 in a final that I know I controlled from siren to siren.

The next week, Tom Carroll and I *tied* the final at nearby Hossegor. He won by 0.5 on a countback, meaning his average wave score was marginally higher. This double kick in the guts took the wind out of my sails.

Seventh, ninth and ninth was the best I could do in Hawaii and I finished eleventh for the year. Damien Hardman won his second World Title.

I started '92 knowing that there was only Pipeline to look forward to at the end. Thanks to changes to contest licensing, scheduling and marketing arrangements, Sunset Beach (or anywhere else aside from Pipe on Oahu) was finished as a top-rated contest for maximum Tour points. The younger crew had begun to ride strange super-rocker boards by this stage. Scoring criteria had started its permanent shift from rewarding traditional power to what were previously called 'tricks' – aerials and tail slides.

I got a bunch of fifths, a few thirds and a couple of second placings, to finish sixth for the year. Boy genius Kelly Slater charged through the year to win his first World Title in spectacular style. He actually redefined the scoring system single-handedly, as judges began using his unique manoeuvring as the new ASP benchmark. For some of us, aping Kelly was just not possible. I could no more surf like him than he could surf like me.

The promotional influence of this one-man headline matched his prodigious talent. We met in the final at Hossegor that year. To my knowledge, the conduct of this final has never been reported.

Hossegor was messy and surging at eight foot plus with severe cross-currents. As a local, I knew that it would take several minutes to paddle through the chaos and a few more to make good position before the heat started. Fifteen minutes before the scheduled start, I began paddling out to the contest area. Strong effort was required to maintain position against the rip, but I had made it to the best spot right on time for the siren to sound.

The clock ticked past siren time, but there was no siren. Kelly had not shown up. I paddled my guts out for a further fifteen minutes before he arrived. Then I paddled my guts out for seven minutes *more* while he made it out the back with me. *Then* they blew the siren to commence the final.

The entire event was put on hold and the rulebook flushed down the shithouse for one competitor. Heats start when they're scheduled to start. If you're not there, too fucking bad. I should have had an unassailable lead built up by the time Slater got into position. Instead I'd been paddling flat out for nearly forty minutes before officials were satisfied that Kelly was nice and ready.

I stayed competitive, but it goes without saying that he had more in the tank at the end of the final. It was a fucking outrage and I wasn't the only person having my say in the 'frankest' possible terms afterwards.

A revolution was at hand and I didn't need to be Einstein to figure out that I was probably going to be 'revolutionised' clean out of the fucking picture! I'd become more outspoken in my criticism of judging, swearing and venting to the media, the ASP and the judges themselves about obvious inconsistencies and perceived bias, which was a stupidly self-defeating way of perpetuating my dissatisfaction.

At twenty-nine, I was caught between the generations. I began my career when the 'Bustin' Down the Door' generation of legends – Rabbit, Shaun, MR – were finishing theirs. My surfing philosophy was premised on 'moving water' – doing the biggest, heaviest, sharpest full-rail turns in the steepest parts of the wave. In the mid-eighties, when blokes like Cheyne, Pottz, Occy and me mucked around by breaking out our fins, or popping airs like we did on skateboards, we were told that we'd be scored *down* for losing control of our lines. True story. There was no more Sunset Beach or Waimea Bay to count on at year's end, just the one Hawaiian contest at Pipe.

Unseeded surfers battling through the trials were also a thing of the past. A two-tiered system meant that lower-ranked surfers who used to have to survive up to four rounds of trials before earning a place in a main event were now automatically seeded into the top flight via a secondary tour.

Times were changing, but could I change with them? Did I even *want* to? For many reasons, I knew deep down that 1993 would probably be my One Last Shot.

I prepared accordingly. The first thing I did was to put aside all the introspection and get back to focusing on my opponents. The close defeats and especially the two second placings for the World Title had turned my attention inward too much.

I convinced myself that I had one year left to be World Champion – no point leaving any bullets in the chamber. It was time to let out every bit of built-up aggro. I didn't care about going back to the prawns any more. These pricks were taking away my World Title. I'd fucking earnt it and I was coming after it one last almighty fucking time.

I had a new major sponsor for '93, French company Oxbow. Sadly, Ocean Pacific – despite its size – had without warning descended into financial difficulties in '92, so much so that its team couldn't be paid. OP's big names were juicy pickings for its competitors.

Oxbow was a great fit for me. Its owner, Fabrice Valeri, was a great guy from up my way in Bordeaux. Many of the Oxbow-sponsored snowboarders and motocross pros that I knew spoke very highly of Fabrice and his company. Nat Young, Laird Hamilton and my Tour mate Robbie Page (a Wollongong lad now resident in France) were on the surf team. It was refreshing to have a dynamic and enthusiastic new sponsor for my big 'push'.

As fate would have it, Derek Ho and I battled it out all year. Had I not been in the eye of the storm, I would've found the '93 Title race as gripping as did the rest of the sporting world. For the third time in my career, my chance at the Title came down to the bitter end.

I jumped the Hawaiian at the start of the year with third at Bells and a very emotional, emphatic victory at the Gunston 500 in Durban. I was an angry, pumped-up machine in South Africa, ghosting in and out of the contest site, growling and snarling like a cornered wolf. It was no act. Anger worked for me. I was in career-best form in mid-season.

I was murdered by the judges in an absurd loss to Kaipo Jaquias in my hometown of Lacanau: my rich vein of form was halted in the quarters by 0.01 of a point. One one-hundredth of a fucking point. Fifth place, when I've never been more confident of winning a contest. I decided to vent my rage on my opponents instead of stewing on it.

Alas, the next one I faced was Curren in *his* hometown of Hossegor. He got me by 0.6 in round three, leaving me in seventeenth place for the event. Derek, meantime, had also placed fifth and seventeenth in the French contests. I had 630 points over him and led the tour at the halfway point.

I maintained form and consistency, but Derek picked up his in the second half of the season. I had a run of fifth, ninth and fifth. His was third, fifth and third. Still, I led him by 180 points heading into the second-last contest in Brazil.

In Rio, Derek bombed out in round one, which meant thirty-third place and minimum Tour points. I had my chance to wrap up my World Title right there. A win for me in Brazil would put the title out of Derek's reach. If I finished anywhere from the quarters up, he'd still need a minor miracle at Pipe to reel me in.

Someone called Jojo Olivenca created history, of sorts, beating me by 0.07 of a point in round three. Perhaps there was an element of local bias, which tends to happen everywhere. Perhaps it suited the powers that be to have themselves a showdown for the World Title at Pipeline. Perhaps it was simple incompetence. Whatever it was, *I won that heat.* Everyone who watched it knew it. Apart from the guys with clipboards.

Whatever. For the first time, I had a World Tour ratings lead heading into the last contest at Pipe. Derek Ho was a

Pipeline local. Past Pipeline Master or not, he had the wood on me at his home break.

There was a lot more than the usual tension and atmosphere on the beach at Pipe. Every Hawaiian was on tenterhooks, hoping and praying that their man would become the home of surfing's first professional World Champion. Regardless of my self-imposed isolation since killing off 'Kong', there was a huge amount of sentimental support for me too. A massive crush of fans, fifteen or twenty deep, shouted encouragement as security cleared a path for me to the water's edge. I was even feeling a lot of love from the Americans in the crowd. They thought it was high time I got my just rewards. I did too. I was as calm and centred as I've ever been when the contest got underway. Pipe was an excellent eight feet.

Derek had his fingers crossed that I would bomb out early. I had my fingers *and* toes crossed that he'd exit straight away and gift me the Title. But neither wish was ever bound to be granted. We met in the semifinal – it was a surf-off for the title of ASP World Champion.

I led the Tour ratings by 440 points. I had to miss the final and Derek had to make the final for him to beat me. All I had to do was to get through to the final. Even if Derek won the contest, he couldn't overtake me if I came first or second in this semi. The four-man semi had three former Pipeline Masters. There were two Aussies, Tom Carroll and me, and two Hawaiians, Derek and Pipe specialist Larry Rios. The tension on the beach was palpable, though I still felt at ease. Worked up, but not debilitated by nerves at all. I told myself to relax and enjoy the process. 'You can do this. Don't just go for second … *win!*'

Tommy started proceedings by shredding his first wave to the massive roar of the crowd. I can't remember what he scored but it was really high. All I saw from behind were massive explosions of foam as he smashed a couple of huge snaps down the line. He'd established a big lead and stamped himself on the semi right from the get-go.

What happened next is one of the gutsiest, most selfless expressions of friendship I've heard of, let alone experienced. Tom paddled past me and said, 'Right … leave these blokes to me, mate.'

Larry obviously had the job to tactically hassle me out of waves. Tom took it upon himself to both block Larry's efforts and to move Derek out of position. They couldn't ignore him, since he'd established a lead. It was classic two-a-side club surfing, just like Tommy and I had grown up with as grommets.

I want to make this known for posterity: Tom Carroll could quite well have won his fourth Pipeline Masters later that day. Instead, he did everything in his power to help me win a World Title. I still get goosebumps thinking about what that level of mateship means.

It was a battle royale, with the local boys starving me out of the best waves for most of the heat. The window was still open to me in the last two minutes. I didn't need much to overtake Larry into second place and the World Title. But I did need a wave.

The semi was becalmed as the seconds ticked by. And by. My heart sank as I looked at my watch's countdown timer sweep into the last thirty seconds.

No waves were coming. It was all over. The whole thing. Over.

It was all fucking *over.*

Tom had sacrificed himself into fourth place for me. He paddled over with a few seconds remaining, looking crestfallen.

'Oh … mate,' was all he needed to say, before he hugged me. It was good to have him there as the final siren unleashed the thunder of thousands of Hawaiians going crazy with joy.

Derek went on to win the contest and the World Title on a famous day for Hawaiian surfing. Deep down, I was actually happy for him and for the locals in general. He won courageously and fairly, a wholly deserving World Champion. One of us had to come second.

And that one of us couldn't bear 'second' any more.

There was only so much I could take. I watched the victory ceremony with appropriate decorum and respect, but I was raw and hollowed out inside.

The competitive fire that had burned uninterrupted within me since age fourteen went out.

POPPING THE BUBBLE

I blocked out my third second placing altogether. I blocked out the first two as well. I *had* to, in order to stay sane. I was so psychologically shattered by the ordeal that I packed up the pain into an airtight mental container and shoved it into the farthest corner of my mind. Stuck right in beside the few things I'd learnt at school.

I got so fucking sick of people telling me I deserved a World Title that I developed an acute sense of when the subject was about to come up in conversation. I always cut off discussion with a laugh and something like, 'Yeah, well, shit happens,' or some such deep analysis. That always stopped people asking me how I felt.

I hated that question. Actually, I was *frightened* by that question. Self-preservation prevented me from asking it of myself. What was I supposed to say?

'Well, let's see. I *feel* like screaming until I pass out. I *feel* like tearing the flesh off my face in frustration. I *feel* like killing my-fucking-self. That's how I *feel* about losses by 0.01 of a point and about bullshit interference calls and about deliberate drop-ins and about dumb-arse decisions to skip events. I *feel* like sticking my face into a bowl of cocaine until I suffocate. How's that, fuckhead? Is that a good enough answer for you? Could have. Should have. Fucking *didn't. Shut the fuck up.'*

A jovial 'shit happens' worked a lot better.

Whenever the three second places leaked into my thoughts I hammered them back into quarantine by reminding myself of the quality of my rivals. Kooks do not win World Titles.

But sometimes champions don't either.

It was this tiny, tiny morsel of self-belief that kept me competing on the ASP pro Tour.

On the surface, I deluded myself that I could still achieve the ultimate prize. I willed the fire to return. I willed myself to believe that my Tour opponents still obstructed me from what was rightfully mine. However, there aren't enough fluffy self-help books on earth to reignite what was extinguished in me. More importantly, it was impossible to change my physical fundamentals.

I'm a heavy-set man, lucky enough to be custom-made for 'heavy' surfing. My style is all about blowing a wave to bits, aiming turns into the lip which carve out as much water as possible using as much rail as possible, while continuing to maintain stored power and speed. That physical predisposition lends itself to large, powerful waves, though I'd worked bloody hard over the years to translate my technique successfully into weaker, smaller surf.

By 1994, the physical advantages that helped propel me to the top of the surfing world were working against me. In Olympic parlance, I was a like shot-putter suddenly recruited into the figure-skating team. A silverback gorilla taking mighty air swings at a screeching pack of taunting, nimble gibbons.

In preparing for the '94 ASP World Tour, I spent hundreds of hours executing aerial moves and slides. Anyone who has surfed for a living as long I have can do this stuff easily enough. The question was whether I could do so instinctively under competitive pressure and whether I could do so *better* than my young opponents. Or, I should I say, *opponent*. The answer to the question was a resounding 'no'. I'd seen quite enough of Kelly Slater to know that ponderously reinventing myself was mission impossible.

A changing of the guard had occurred from Rabbit, MR and Shaun Tomson to Tommy Carroll, Tom Curren, Mark Occhilupo, Martin Potter and me – abridged by the remarkable career of the Cheyne Horan. Now the relentless march of time had wrenched the baton from us and given it to Kelly. A new generation embodied in one surfer.

Long may it be that the sport of surfing morphs with each passing generation. It's always been a 'youth movement', after all. Otherwise, we'd *all* be opting out by riding longboards.

I decided to stick with my strengths and hope that each ASP Tour event threw up waves which suited me. I may have been a dinosaur, but there still wasn't anybody who could outpower me. Fuck the grommets!

So I deluded myself, draped myself in the lie of 'shit happens' and pushed on. I was a professional surfer, therefore I kept surfing.

* * *

The ASP competition seasons '94 through '96 flew by. I guess that's because I wanted them to. I finished nineteenth, twenty-fourth and thirty-sixth respectively on my way out the trapdoor. Generally I finished up the leader board in challenging waves, but the new benchmark criteria in smaller waves left me behind, bit by bit. Slater defined surfing and there were few opportunities for me to rewrite his destiny, even had I been able to. He won all the World Titles in my last years on Tour with ease.

Hawaii wasn't the advantage it used to be for me because Pipeline was the only relevant Hawaiian contest. And perfect Pipe was perfect for the perfect surfer. There wasn't the inscrutable doom of Sunset Beach or Waimea Bay to give an 'old boy' a chance to rattle the new champ's cage.

Burying the hurt probably wasn't a healthy way to deal with my career issues, but it did allow me to broaden my interests. I'd spent every season since '85 trying to shut myself off to anything that could've derailed my World Title chances. Once the train was off the tracks anyway, what harm could it do to loosen up a little? I'd been holding my 'bubble' shut with a death grip for eight years. I was tired.

I started taking a snort of coke here and there behind Pascale's back, especially when I was up in the mountains. I also packed a nice supply of hash to smoke every time I went into the forest with my bike. Before too long, I began to look forward to coke and mull and hash again. Which meant I was looking forward to being away from my darling Pascale. Even in small doses, drugs always manage to skew your priorities.

Snowboarding became something that I got pretty good

at very quickly. It was hard not to, considering that most of my boarding mates were top pros and some of France's best mountains were only a short drive away. Likewise my beloved motocross. There were no dark feelings to confront when I was dealing with vertical powder runs in the Alps or flying off motocross jumps.

Oxbow were fantastic. They encouraged both my hobbies and were always looking to use me cross-promotionally. I entered – and succeeded in – many of the first crossover boarding events. These were snowboarding and surfing contests – in the mountains one day, then at the beach the next. I loved them.

I emerged from my bubble on Tour too. I'd denied myself a *lot* of partying over the previous eight years. Pascale wasn't travelling with me as much, so I used our separations to get up to some old tricks.

Though I maintained discipline during contests, I just couldn't keep manufacturing aggression against my old mates who'd been on the merry-go-round with me for ten years. The new kids got both barrels but not my fellow veterans.

I drossed on about still having a Title in me, though the reality was that I'd stopped enjoying surfing shit waves. The company of long-time fellow travellers was the appeal. The lads were happily calling me Kong without so much as a raised eyebrow from me.

There were no orgies or foolhardy overdoses. The closest I got to genuine trouble was when Robbie Page saved me from surrendering my heart (and other organs) to a robust beauty in Papeete who had calf muscles which wouldn't have looked out of place in Samoa's awesome Test rugby front row. An Adam's apple the size of a baseball and a healthy chin stubble escaped my scrambled attention but were detected by Pagey just in time. Warning: Teahupoo isn't the only danger to worry about in Tahiti.

WAR ON WATER

In 1995, Pascale and I moved from one idyllic French location to another when we shifted from sleepy Lacanau down to Seignosse, near Hossegor.

The promotional stature of 'Gary Elkerton' was still very high in the sport, so my contract with Oxbow was lucrative and the dear old sponsor who'd stuck with me through thick and thin – Oakley – continued to value me, as did newer backers such as Gorilla Grip. Along with the contest prize money accumulated throughout my career, we were in good shape financially. We kept the beachfront apartment we'd bought in Lacanau and purchased a beautiful big house in Seignosse, replete with nice cars, bikes and jetskis in the garage.

It was obvious that I wasn't going to win the World Title. Actually, it was obvious in '95 that *nobody* was going to win the World Title in the foreseeable future other than Kelly, let alone a 32-year-old stowaway from the age of power surfing. Even so, the young 'King' and I still had a few of the heaviest man-on-man confrontations imaginable in a non-contact sport.

Make no mistake, Mr Robert Kelly Slater has not become the living god he is by being a lovely chap who takes losing with a laconic shrug of his shoulders. Along with Rabbit, Martin Potter and Brad Gerlach, Kelly is as combative a contest animal as I've encountered. The stand-out contest enjoyment I derived from my final two years was my heats against Kelly.

The ASP scheduled Tour stops at Grajagan, sponsored by Quiksilver, in my final two years. They were a great credit to the company. The surf was insane and it was a buzz to link up with Al Green during these amazing contests. I'd never lost my affection for him, Jeff Hakman and Harry Hodge, so I was delighted that these visionary events were so successful for them.

There were also contests at the intimidating long left-hand reef break of Saint-Leu on Réunion Island, held either the week before, or the week after Grajagan. Between the two mighty left-handers, a worthy backdrop was created for Kelly and me to conclude our hostilities in the water.

Now, professional surfing is a sport in which the use of psychological verbal abuse by competitors against each other (what Aussies call 'sledging') happens routinely. Would you believe some brutes have even said rather distracting things to me about Joan Elkerton? Shocking. Profane salutations of the sort that would embarrass a merchant seaman were exchanged between Kelly and me throughout our round-four heat at Grajagan in '95. I'd rate the swearing joust as a dead heat, but Kelly took the surfing points. It felt great to get some genuine anger back and I hoped for a return bout in good waves at the next contest at Réunion. The draw and the ocean cooperated and we came together in round four again.

Réunion Island was an Oxbow event in '95. Robbie Page (who had borrowed a board and ripped through the concurrent longboard event) noticed that I was low on energy as I waited for my date with Slater. Truth be told, I'd been thinking about his interminable winning streak against me.

'Mate, lift your fucking head. It's eight feet. No one – not even Lord Slater – can blast the back out of those things on their backhand like you can,' growled Robbie. 'Get yourself going, for fuck's sake. He might be screwing with everyone else's head, but surely not *yours*? These are *your* conditions! Take the bastard to school!'

With that, Pagey announced that he would be caddying for me and we concocted a plan to get the champ thinking about me and my tactics – straight from the Michael Peterson/ Rabbit Bartholomew textbook. A textbook that was having new chapters added by Kelly himself.

With forty-five minutes remaining before the heat, we quietly walked well out of sight of the contest area and began the painstaking process of tiptoeing our way over the urchin-encrusted reef, hundreds of metres behind the take-off spot. The swell was big enough for us to be unnoticed out to sea.

Slater paddled out in the usual fashion and was visibly confused by my apparent absence. He was looking inshore, wondering where the fuck I was, when I stealthily stroked into position behind him.

'G'day, arsehole. Looking for someone?'

For the briefest moment, he couldn't disguise a look of shock. It took him a few seconds to respond in kind, but I knew I had him. I never relinquished priority and I did – indeed – blow the back out of every wave while Pagey screamed encouragement from the channel like a demented boxing corner.

An easy win over Kelly Slater happens with slightly less frequency than the appearance of Halley's Comet. Pagey and I were suitably jubilant as we picked a path back over the spiky reef. Kelly made his way over to us and I extended my hand.

Rather than offering his hand, he instead offered me some frank and open advice about a range of personal issues. Decorum prevents me repeating it. Let's just say that Kelly raised a surprising number of diverse topics in a very short time: body fat ratios, personality disorders, the definition of good character, aged care and the extinction of the dinosaurs – all covered within a minute.

Of course, I blew up and aimed a punch at him. Fortunately for all concerned, balancing on the reef was difficult and Robbie chucked himself on top of me while Kelly made comically ginger haste away over the urchin beds. I shouted that I would knock his block off, but later I had to laugh at the bizarre turn of events. Man, that kid was competitive. And aggressive. And *smart*. He wasn't going to leave me dwelling on my win. He was going to leave me wasting my time dwelling on something else.

It was '96 in Grajagan before we were matched up in decent surf again, this time in the semifinals. The waves were out of this world. Kelly was frothing like a man possessed as we sat out the back waiting for the starting siren. He was looking straight at me, punching himself *hard* in the face. Whether he was trying to psyche himself up or trying to psyche me out, I'll never know. I only recently found out that Kelly's daughter was born that very morning, all the way back in the US. Maybe that's what accounted for the unsettling spectacle. Whatever the reasons, it was bloody radical.

'Keep it up, cunt, you're saving me the job,' I offered helpfully.

'Bring it the fuck on, man!' he said between masochistic uppercuts.

It was a great battle, waged on Grajagan's perfect battlefield. With ninety seconds to go, Kelly needed a nine to take the lead. Ever the consummate professional, he used priority expertly to take the last wave of a set. He ripped the absolute shit out of it and I could hear the response on the beach, even from hundreds of metres away. Slater pulls nine-pointers out of his supernatural butthole at will, so I accepted that my goose was probably cooked.

I then experienced a couple of 'firsts' in my career. With seconds to go, a G-land Special gifted itself to me out of the blue, totally out of sync with how the sets had been working in the heat to date. That was 'first' number one. I'd never enjoyed Curren's or Slater's psychic abilities to command waves to me in the past.

I bottom-turned very late and pulled into a stand-up backside tube that overtook me immediately. I stood there weaving big turns in the barrel. There was enough time to anticipate the fantastic feeling of being spat out of the tube mouth, which had bent away out of sight, despite my speed. It was like I was entombed in a massive emerald. I'm told that my bright contest jersey could be seen from the beach, flashing behind the curtain, but that it disappeared from view, seemingly consumed by the foam and impossibly deep. I was given up as gone by spectators and judges alike.

Sure enough, I was catapulted from the cavern with centimetres to spare before the wave closed out violently. Incredible that scarcely a drop of water had touched me on my journey across the entire reef. I hooted like a maniac. One of the best tube rides I'd ever enjoyed had occurred in a major contest during my last year on Tour.

Kelly got his nine-pointer. 'First' number two for me transpired when I was scored perfect tens. In all my years on Tour, even during my most dominant periods, I'd *never* been rewarded with a perfect score. It was nice to give the judges no room to move on style or on any other subjective measurement. If you ride a tube at heaving Grajagan from take-off to the end of the wave, it's a ten. I lost the final to Shane Beschen's terrific repertoire, but I was touched by how stoked everyone was for me. Almost everyone that is.

Kelly was nowhere to be seen after the semi.

I shared a bottle of red with Al Green at the conclusion of Quiksilver's marquee contest. Perhaps it was a little ironic, given I'd blocked their figurehead hours before, though it felt totally natural to kick back with an old mate under the circumstances. I was telling Al how disappointed I was in Kelly for not approaching me to acknowledge our epic semi. I didn't expect him to fawn all over me, but I thought that he might at least have offered some kind of personal indication that he respected a memorable heat, professional to professional. Actually, I might have been drunk enough to suggest half-jokingly that the 'grommet' was due a good clip around his revered earhole. Al and I had no sooner stopped chuckling about the headlines that would generate when Kelly appeared at the door of the cabin.

'Hey ... sit down, mate, we were just talking about you,' we said together, or words to that effect.

'No thanks, man,' responded the champ self-consciously. 'I just wanted to say, you know, congratulations and stuff. I really enjoyed today. Awesome heat, man.'

We shook on it and shared a brief uncomfortable hug. Then we stood back and looked dumbly at each other for a few seconds before laughing together at an unspoken joke that neither of us could define. I hoped that he might stay for a drink or two, but he left as quickly as he'd arrived.

After Kelly walked back into the night, I reflected on how hard it must be for a 24-year-old guy to carry this crazy, chaotic sport on his back. When I was his age I struggled under the weight of half the expectation, half the talent and a fraction of his mainstream global celebrity. He was handling himself beautifully, all things considered. Maybe a prickly bastard like me rattled his unflappable demeanour occasionally, but he generally carried himself flawlessly.

This guy was dealing with a life that almost nobody could comprehend. I could comprehend it and I didn't envy him. It wasn't just a sport he was carrying – that was a veneer. He was carrying a multinational textile industry. And it seemed to sit on him as lightly as the two-buck t-shirts he was turning to gold.

He wasn't just a young man with riches of talent, a warrior's will to win, and innate competitive intelligence. There was precedent in our sport for that. In my own way, I was part of that precedence. Kelly was already 'something else' in 1996. He had the calmness of character and the diamond-hard mental toughness to thrive on the messianic role he'd been drafted into by the corporate surfing community. His qualities as a human being, underneath those of the surfing phenomenon, are why I respect him so much. And the rabid mongrel pit-bull that barks beneath the silky smooth greyhound appeals to me too!

Al and I toasted the fact that Kelly showed his class after that final day of the '96 Grajagan Quiksilver Pro. We also agreed that he could very bloody well keep winning for as long as he was motivated to do so.

WOULD YOU CARE FOR ABUSE WITH YOUR CHICKEN?

Pascale and I had a new home and a comfortable life together. It was time for us to move on and start planning a new stage. I announced my retirement from the full-time ASP World Tour halfway through the '96 season.

The '96 Pipe Masters would be my last contest. I was completely dry-eyed about it. My pain was still locked up tight and it was being guarded faithfully by an ever-increasing use of my favourite drugs when Pascale wasn't looking.

I held a genuine expectation that I could go out with a bang by winning at Pipe. If it was big and gnarly, then I feared no-one on Tour at the place save for locals Derek Ho and Sunny Garcia, who would be their usual, formidable selves. To this day, I'll back myself against almost anyone paddling into severe waves. I knuckled down and prepared thoroughly, the fantasy of a Mark Richards-like exit from centre stage fixed in my head.

Banzai Pipeline was all of three feet.

My last heat as a full-time competitor on the ASP World Tour was against none other than Kaipo Jaquias, the surfer who eliminated me during my Title run in '93 by 0.01 of a point in Lacanau. In a fast-diminishing swell, Kaipo pumped me conclusively by a much more satisfying 4.85.

What was mentally and spiritually finished at the same contest in '93 was now physically and officially finished in '96. Mine was a long, enjoyable goodbye, but a 'goodbye' it was. There'd be no Currenesque comebacks from me. I was done.

The ASP annual awards banquet was held a few nights later in Honolulu. A gala event, attended by all the top pros, many past champions, industry luminaries, media pundits, business leaders and various blowhards and hangers-on. The World Champion is officially presented with his trophy and notable retirees are duly recognised.

It was the perfect occasion for me to exit my career as a venerated pioneer of the promotional corporate era, with the remarkable unofficial moniker of 'Best Surfer Never to Have Been World Champion'. I could depart the ASP Tour with dignity as a senior statesman.

The idea of confronting this inevitable discourse on stage with the master of ceremonies in front of a packed house caused me to consume two bottles of very good Shiraz within minutes of arriving. My *feelings* would have to be addressed in any valedictory speech. There was no getting around it. Feelings were not good. *Feelings were not fucking good at all.*

Newcastle's Simon Law and California's Jeff Booth were the other Tour veterans retiring with me. They were outstanding surfers with proven, noble records in life-threatening surf. I felt honoured to share the stage with them.

Alas, the main course was served as the 'retirees' segment of the evening's program commenced. Assembled guests were swapping their chicken for the beef and carrying on loud conversations as the formalities of farewelling Simon, Jeff and me were attempted. The MC pushed on with his preamble manfully while the throng carried on drinking and dining like he didn't exist.

We three retirees stood there onstage like spare pricks at a wedding. It was poor organisation. People were hungry, and our part of the ceremony shouldn't have coincided with the arrival of dinner.

It was the newer crew who most got under my skin. Tables containing older people were at least turning their faces to the stage; the kids weren't bothering. Not to mention the large number of young surf-industry types who were ignoring us. They may as well have been at the pub.

I squinted at them through the spotlight and imagined myself sitting there in front of the guys who were once stuck to the wall of my caravan bunk. I may have been an irreverent prick as a new pro, but I definitely wouldn't have laughed and talked while there was a ceremony taking place to honour them. Simon, Jeff and I deserved just a little respect, I thought.

Now, a sober man may have allowed this trivial slight to pass and been big enough to forgive the insult due to the general drunkenness of the gathering. But I wasn't sober and I had no forgiveness to offer. I looked at Simon and Jeff shifting their feet in embarrassment. I looked at one young pro surfer

(I won't name him) at a front table who had turned away from the stage in conversation. And I snapped.

I shouldered my way to the microphone and let loose.

'Oi! Howsabout you pack of fucking cunts showing a bit of fucking respect? Ya could at least shut up and stop feeding ya fucking faces for five seconds to listen to what's goin' on up here, couldn't ya?'

Simon and Jeff manhandled me away from the mic, while I used the foulest possible language to berate everybody for their shocking lack of manners. Tommy Carroll, Pottz and others calmed me down offstage. We vets all had a good laugh, though my outburst was no laughing matter. I made a total cock of myself, which I can live with. But I probably ruined Simon and Jeff's experience while I was at it. For that I'm eternally sorry.

At least I wasn't asked about my feelings. Maybe that's what was really behind my rant. A serenely happy man doesn't seriously want to rampage through the crowd at an otherwise happy function, knocking people out as they chew their Chicken Kiev.

Sure, there was a little provocation; however, responding to bad behaviour with bad behaviour is a no-win situation. I left the ASP World Tour with a bang after all. Winning a second Pipeline Masters would have been a slightly better way of doing so, but nothing about my pro career ever indicated that a heartwarming conclusion was likely.

QUIK STEP

Fabrice Valeri had sold the bulk of his interest in Oxbow to a large fashion umbrella corporation. I was stoked for him, though I was worried about the direction of the company in the context of my future, post-Tour. There was some soul-searching to be done about where my career was headed.

The relative comfort of full-time tow-surfing had yet to become a practical career choice. I could go on the Longboard Tour for Oxbow, but the very idea sent me to sleep. And there weren't enough surf/snow events for me to build a future around.

I was still keen on surfing and providing promotional value for sponsors, in a similar way that many of my recently retired contemporaries were. It was Pascale who envisioned the solution.

'Quiksilver never fired you, *cherie*. You resigned, remember? You still love Al and Jeff and Harry, *non*? Europe Headquarters is right next door. What harm could a visit do?'

I spoke to Harry, who immediately pictured a role for me in promotional work across Europe, as Quik rolled out their extensive retail network of themed stores from Russia to the

UK. There'd be coaching, promotional trips and selected contest wildcards. Harry was enthusiastic, though there was strong resistance from the top at global headquarters in California.

It was Al Green who stepped in to make the decisive call, since he'd always felt poorly about my first departure from the company. I'm told that he insisted that I be brought back to the fold, even if he had to pay me out of his own pocket. Al may have been a quiet type, but he still had a lot of weight to throw around when he was appropriately fired up to do so.

I was back with Quiksilver in '97. My new role was great, but I needed to adjust to having bosses, scheduled hours, set tasks and measurable responsibilities. Not that it was a chore, by any means! However, at age thirty-three, I'd lobbed into a completely novel environment in which my time was not always my own and in which most decisions about what I did with that time weren't either. Ha! Welcome to what they call 'life', sunshine!

The first few years in the job were educational and invigorating. I worked with Sydneysider Rob Rowland-Smith, the 'Sandhill Warrior'. Rob is one of the best physical trainers and conditioning coaches in the world. Quiksilver was innovative and wise to have retained his expertise.

Tommy Carroll and I teamed up with Rob to train Quik's European and Australian teams physically, mentally and tactically at regular training camps all over the world. I thoroughly enjoyed the interaction between the coaches, and the new-found challenges of being both friend and mentor to aspiring champions such as Miky Picon, Jeremy Flores, Danny Wills, Mick Campbell and the irrepressible Matt Hoy.

The flip side to the training, heat simulation and classroom work with the team was the promotional appearances and 'schmoozing' work associated with Quik's rapidly growing Euro empire. The expectation to be the life of the party, in keeping with my reputation, was fine by me. But it sure did clash with my role as the flinty coach demanding 100 per cent physical dedication from my charges at training camp. I was a bit like a beast with two heads. Once every so often I'd forget which head had to be screwed on in which situation.

Tommy and I sometimes enjoyed a little extracurricular night life on training camps once we were sure that our 'kids' were all tucked up in bed. I should add that these clandestine forays would often coincide with the presence of one Mr Ross Clarke-Jones in the vicinity. There was a certain schoolboyish thrill to ghosting off for a bit of fun when we were supposed to be in lockdown. And, like naughty schoolboys, a 'ringleader' and an 'innocently led lad' are always typecast when the inevitable bust happens. No prizes for guessing who was who on that score in Quik's eyes!

The job was hectic, but rewarding. Things at home, though, were not quite so rosy. Pascale and I had ever so gradually grown apart. The depth of love was still there, but the feeling of togetherness drifted as the nineties drew to a close. I've come to understand that there's no neat explanation for how great marriages sometimes become not so great. The simplistic answers so favoured by junk magazines rarely apply in real life. They certainly didn't apply to us.

It was as though our relationship was defined by the 'us verses the world' bubble we created for ourselves during the peak of my competitive career. Perhaps the 'Kong' that Pascale first met appealed to her as someone who needed saving. Perhaps the Pascale I first met entranced me as the saviour I needed. We were perfectly matched when we shared a passionate mission together. But once the 'war' was over, the dynamics between us changed.

I was neither the out-of-control animal nor the single-minded World Champion in waiting any more. Maybe she didn't quite know what to do with the man in between the two extremes. She wasn't the passionate, protective muse any more. Maybe I didn't quite know what to do with the challenges of normal domesticity. There were no raging fights. Love remained. But communication waned in imperceptible units, week by week.

We'll probably never know what impact our inability to have children together had on us. A rare genetic mismatch made conceiving both difficult and prohibitively dangerous. Maybe we didn't acknowledge this to each other enough.

In the years '97 to '99, the frequent promotional partying and travelling that was my job spec with Quik wasn't helpful to the growing estrangement inside our marriage. Sexual temptation was everywhere, though I restrained my compulsions to stray. I don't give myself any credit for knocking back string-less sex. I don't deserve a medal for doing no more than observing decent, normal morals. But the fact that I had to concentrate on subduing immoral urges so often worried the shit out of me. I needed to address my *feelings*.

Feelings were not good.

I absolutely did not want to confront feelings about where I was headed with Pascale. I was failing with Pascale. If I confronted my failures with Pascale, *all* of my failure demons would be released. I couldn't even articulate the connections in my own mind. They were in my gut. Which is no doubt why I reacted to our marriage problems by relying on my universal solution of avoidance – the tools of avoidance being heavy physical training and heavier use of alcohol and drugs. When a dam wall is weak, something has to give under pressure. I was the weakest point and I cracked.

'Blame' for a break-up is a concept that people outside a relationship use to package up and rationalise the parting of seemingly happy couples. I don't buy into it, having been through the terrible pain of losing – and hurting – the love of my life. However, I do understand that assigning blame is human nature. That being so, I accept that I'm to blame for the awful pain I caused Pascale by leaving our marriage. Blame aside, I didn't deal with our issues well. I'm guilty of indecision and cowardice. Pascale deserved much better from me, regardless of the inevitability of our separation.

Quiksilver ran camps in the Canary Islands, based around the stupendous waves at Lanzarote. It was here that I met local girl Christina Abelo D'Galba in '99. She was only twenty, but we shared a sense of humour and a fun-loving attitude. We were at different stages in life, but we made each other happy.

I disguised the affair we began and dithered over leaving Pascale 'softly'. I should have been big enough to handle things immediately, but it was months before I finally instigated a split. I stayed living in the house at Hossegor. She preferred to return to our apartment in Lacanau.

If I had my time again, I would have fought harder for our marriage – for our love of one another. Even at thirty-five years of age, I didn't have the awareness or experience to understand that there were ways to deal with emotional adversity other than to ignore it. I'd dealt with physical adversity and fear by welcoming them and working my way through. Applying similar principles to my emotions was still a bridge too far in 1999.

Regret was just another feeling I wrestled into that overstuffed airtight container of mine.

CHAMPION

The ASP had been sanctioning a 'World Masters Championship' for qualified surfers aged thirty-five and over since 1997. Quiksilver's sponsorship had transformed it from a novelty to a full-blown professional event in '99. Thanks to the training camps I felt as fit and strong as ever that year, so I was pissed off that a regulation about my birthdate precluded me from competing in such a major event for my employer. Although it was fantastic that my great mate and fellow perpetual 'number two' Cheyne Horan was rightfully rewarded with a World Title after suffering behind Mark Richards at the peak of his powers in the early eighties.

I viewed the 2000 World Masters Title as a deeply personal crusade. Not only was it a great distraction from the marital upheavals that I was squashing into the background, but it was also a chance to balance the history books. I couldn't rewrite my ASP World Tour record, but I could definitely claim a World Title for myself against the very same blokes.

I'd always been at my best when there was a 'mission' at hand. I wasn't the self-denying spartan I'd been in the past, but

I did develop a good balance between work and preparation in the first half of 2000. Binging on alcohol and drugs was only 'regular' rather than 'constant'. Quite a health kick.

I was lighter, fitter and stronger than I'd ever been in my adult life. My surfing was at its very best, as good if not *better* than it was at my Tour peak. I put serious consideration into a return to the ASP World Tour and was encouraged to do so by lots of friends and colleagues. In the end, there were just too many very good business and personal reasons to stick to the path I was on. Christina and I had settled into a happy relationship and she split her time between her family in the Canary Islands and me in France. To cap it all off, the ASP World Masters in 2000 was being held in Lafitenia, one of my home breaks in France.

The problem was the mind-blowing quality of the competitors. It was an invitational contest of the highest order. In normal ASP events, the draw is not solely comprised of World Champions, Hawaiian Triple Crown Champions, Pipeline Masters, Sunset World Cup winners and multiple ASP World Tour event victors. Every single surfer in the event had both the credentials to win and the hard-earned respect of the entire surfing community. This was no jaunt or nostalgic longboard exhibition.

There wasn't a beer gut to be seen in a competition jersey. There'd be some heavy celebrations to look forward to afterwards but, until the siren ended the final, there were a lot of proven professional champions bent on beating each other for a World Title. Not to mention considerable prize money and lucrative contract extensions.

Nearly every major rival I'd had was front and centre. It was on for young and old. Or to be precise, it was on for ages thirty-five through forty-nine. The coverage and hype was huge.

Lafitenia cooperated with perfect overhead waves and the draw cooperated by allowing me to face definitive foes such as Derek Ho and Tom Curren. I won by beating Curren in the final.

I was World Champion.

It was reported as a 'popular' win, though I didn't have the wherewithal to appreciate that so many people were so very happy for me until hours after I'd left the water. Something more important than my triumph over Curren happened and it took some coming to terms with.

My feelings burst out. All of them. *Every single fucking one that I'd been storing away for over fifteen fucking years.* They hit me like a ton of bricks as I collapsed to my knees on the beach.

I'd cast the 'runner-up' monkey from my back. In the process I discovered that the battle between 'Kong' and 'Gary' was a silly invention that I'd clung to, a device I'd used to excuse my bad behaviour and motivate my good behaviour. Gary 'Kong' Elkerton was World Champion. One person, with a nickname. No more, no less. 'Kong' wasn't a drinking, drugging surf-culture animal who railed against the best intentions of Gary Elkerton the professional surfer. 'Kong' was just the name given to a kid at Mooloolaba Primary School for the crime of having a hairy ball bag.

Strangely, I was as upset as I was ecstatic. Ugly shit that I'd repressed erupted from within in equal measure to the relief of ultimate acknowledgement for the one thing I was good at. I was so stoked in the moment and yet suddenly so aware of what the moment had cost me. And those who loved me. In the blur of ultimate triumph – in that instant – it became clear that casualties are created by the self-absorption required to be a World Champion in this uniquely individualistic, solo sport. Everything had been about 'me' from my mid-teens onward. How could I possibly thank the long list of everyone I'd hurt for carrying me to a World Title?

The three awful second places crashed into my mind. So this is what the alternative feels like! I mourned my losses while I embraced my win. Fate wasn't against me after all. I'd at last started repaying everyone for their love and faith by claiming a World Title. It wasn't enough, but it was a step.

These thoughts whirred as I was ushered through the crowd towards the VIP area. I slumped in a chair with a towel over my head. I was left in peace, sobbing for all I was worth. It took this transcendent elation to make me realise how sad I'd really been.

The spell was broken by someone hugging me from behind. A voice whispered into my ear through the towel. 'You deserve this so much, man. Congratulations. I'm so privileged to have surfed with you – thanks, Kong. Take your time, champ … there's no rush.'

It was Kelly, sounding pretty choked up. He really is a class bloke. TC, Curren, Derek, Pottz, and the rest also rallied around. Rabbit gripped me in a bear hug for about five minutes.

By the time I'd composed myself and made it to the podium, I was a changed man. I lifted the trophy skyward and hooted crazily as Tom Curren sprayed the champagne. The long-denied World Champion in me had emerged. And a welcome torrent of pain, sorrow, regret, guilt and disappointment came with him. The seal was broken. I could start dealing with the worst parts of myself as well as the best. For better or worse, I was liberated.

I was whole.

THE GOOD LIFE

Celebrations may have gone a tad over the top, judging by the industrial-strength clean-up effort that was required to return my poor house into livable condition. You'd be forgiven for thinking I'd hosted a festival, not a party, in the weeks after my Masters win. In due course I was back to work, burning the candle at both ends as promotional host at openings and trade shows, training the team and surfing for the cameras, all the while using the defence of my World Masters Title as a focal point.

The years 2001 to 2003 were good ones. I defended my Title successfully at Bundoran, Ireland in '01. What a sensational part of the world. Great waves, great town, great people. It was a mistake to wear board shorts in the finals though. It may have been a top idea to promote the latest summer styles in images worldwide, but it would have backfired had I died of hypothermia, which I thought was certain at one stage. The medicinal effects of Irish whiskey got my blood flowing again and cajoled my tortured gonads back from their snug hiding place behind my tortured liver. I lived to savour my back-to-back World Masters Title success.

The ASP didn't run the event in '02 for some reason, so I was reigning Champion as the collection of legends gathered at Makaha on Oahu's west side for the '03 Masters. It was a moving expression of aloha by the Hawaiian surfing community to open their closely protected home to the contest. There were plenty of foreign surfers in attendance who'd never even seen Makaha, let alone surfed it, such is the difficulty of obtaining an invite there and so severe the consequences of rocking up unannounced.

Christina and I enjoyed a warm and relaxed couple of weeks with many of my old Hawaiian friends, who embraced us as family in the beautiful way that only Hawaiians can. I was determined to win the contest as a way of thanking these many 'brothers' who'd taken me under their beefy wings so many years ago when they didn't really have to.

It was a sweetly sentimental victory at large, tricky, *historic* Makaha. And it was made all the more memorable because the final was against California's Brad Gerlach, a man I like, respect and admire in the water and out.

I've never completely healed what was wounded by the drama and controversy of my three ASP World Tour second-place finishes. But my three consecutive ASP World Masters titles went a long way to help me feel that the self-belief that drove me from Bull's trawler as a teen was justified. I could look back on a career in which the heartbreak had been balanced – at least to a degree – by fulfilment. There was nothing tragic about having 'three-time ASP World Masters Champion' attached to my name in perpetuity.

I was terribly disappointed when the ASP removed the Masters from its schedule after '03. Something about funding, not intent, apparently. The only upside was that I remained 'undefeated' reigning Champion right through until 2011!

Quiksilver International launched a program called the 'Quiksilver Crossing' in the early 2000s. Innovative as ever, the company used a large ocean-going vessel, the *Indies Trader*, to voyage around the globe with an ever-changing crew of pro surfers seeking new waves, engaging local communities, and educating all and sundry about caring for our oceans. There's an outside chance that the company may have also detected the possibility of promotional return on investment for their efforts. Just maybe.

My shifts on the program were outstanding. I enjoyed the deep-ocean voyaging as much as the surfing. Most surfers' 'boat trips' are inshore or close-shore ventures. This baby was traversing a lot of ocean. The best part was getting to hang out with four-time World Champion, former rival and personal hero Mark Richards. We were scheduled together for a few shifts.

I'd always enjoyed a nice friendship with the hero from my bedroom wall, but the close confines of our shared cabin on the *Indies Trader* deepened my personal affection and respect for Mark. Though the outer limits of mateship and hero worship were tested.

MR suffered viciously from seasickness. One particularly violent storm had me wading barefoot through the great man's ghastly sloshing vomit up to my ankles, just to exit our cabin. The 'Seagull' was fucking 'Wounded' alright. I never get seasick, but slipping face first – hungover – into a pool of someone else's vile spew was enough to make me lose the previous evening's beer and tuna. Mark found it funny; I couldn't see the light side, to be honest. At least we agreed that beating me in the final at Sunset in '86 wasn't the worst thing he could do to me. Disgusting as it was, such things tend to create lasting bonds.

Mark and I often worked for Quiksilver at the same shows and promos. Fancy being mates with both MR and Rabbit! If I'd had a crystal ball when I was twelve years old I would've returned it as faulty. MR is every bit the complete gentleman and ornamental champion that he appears to be in the media. Even if he is given to coating his companions in vomit on occasion.

NEW HORIZONS IN OLD PLACES

It's given in life that you won't 'click' personally with everyone you meet. Not 'clicking' with a person doesn't necessarily mark them as a dickhead. Friendship and empathy between some people is simply not meant to be.

I've never 'clicked' less with a person – ever – than I did with Pierre Agnes, who was appointed as managing director of Quiksilver Europe in late 2003. From the moment we met, his distaste for me was palpable. I can handle people not liking me – that's never been a problem. However, I expect them to make some sort of effort to get to know me first.

I could speculate as to why Agnes felt the way he did. I'm an outspoken, brash kind of person who tends to be blunt and undiplomatic. I've not disguised, rationalised or excused my more unsavoury habits and behaviours. I tend to be suspicious of authority and regulations. I'm not deferential to people based solely on the position they hold. I guess I would be shithouse in the army for that reason.

Agnes definitely didn't know me well enough to measure

these failings against the importance I place on reciprocating loyalty, and the commitment I always had to returning value for my sponsors and backers. And these were just business issues. I'd have liked the opportunity to display my personal character before my personal character was judged as good or bad.

I was given the clear impression that Agnes wanted me out. I'm sure I wasn't rude or disrespectful to him, but I should have been more deferential. In the huge corporate hierarchy that now prevailed within what was once a genuine surfers' business, I was a square peg in a round hole. A relic. But the fact was that I was employed by Quiksilver as a veteran professional surfer and multiple World Champion who would promote the label and impart my considerable knowledge and experience to their up-and-coming team of surfers. I was demonstrably succeeding on all fronts, whether the MD 'liked' me or not.

Pierre hauled me over the coals a couple times because of my boisterous behaviour – exaggerated, I might add. I pointed out that this was the surf industry. The world, the town, the region, the industry, the sport and indeed our very own company was populated by many perfectly decent, functional people who harboured various private appetites and proclivities which would preclude them from employment at the Vatican. As I remarked to Pierre, Quiksilver is not the Holy See.

It's not, you know. I checked.

Part of my promotional work was to 'be Kong'. These promo events weren't tea parties. There were lots of people around before, during and after these functions who were doing anything but drinking tea and nibbling cucumber fucking sandwiches. If the company didn't want me associated with 'indulgence', stop fucking sending me, I thought.

Besides, outside of work functions, what I did on my own time was my concern, was it not? I dismissed this 'disciplining' as lightweight crap. I was nowhere near the drug-fucked wreck I'd been in the distant past. Being singled out by management rankled me.

I was philosophical about Agnes's problems with me because I knew I still had the support of 'originals' like Al, Harry and Jeff. I passed off the MD's personal enmity as an unfortunate case of two people not 'clicking'. He was just doing his job as he saw fit. I continued to focus on doing mine.

Despite my abiding love and connection to France, I wasn't French. Let alone Basque. I suppose I was like a haole in Hawaii – notwithstanding the depth of my connection, I would always be somewhat foreign. It wasn't that I wasn't loved as a *personne locale* by my adoptive family of friends, but I was, after all, an Aussie. A fiercely proud one at that. I hadn't lived full-time in Australia for nearly twenty years. Homesickness crept up on me in 2004 as I made my way to Bells Beach to support the team.

The gnawing discomfort was exacerbated by the claustrophobia of working within the internal politics of a big corporation. The only thing separating my employer from any other global corporation were the widgets it produced. Manoeuvring, arse-kissing and career strategising were never going to be my strong points. Though the politicking typical of any decent-sized business was draining me, the work itself –

especially the coaching – remained a pleasure. I took great pride in it.

I'd spoken about my homesickness a number of times with Christina. She had not been particularly at ease with leaving tiny Lanzarote for Hossegor, let alone contemplating a move all the way down to Australia. It became clear that the age gap between us had finally placed us on divergent paths in life. I sensed a new stage approaching, as thoughts of a family and a home for once began to form in earnest.

Ross Clarke-Jones and his wife, Marcia, threw a pre-Bells party at their home in Jan Juc. It was there that I met Rozane 'Neca' Lazzari.

Neca is a Brazilian beauty from the equally beautiful city of Porto Alegre, near the border with Argentina. She is also an intelligent, outspoken, fun-loving, successful businesswoman whose energy, confidence and sexiness captured me from the first conversation we had.

After the Bells contest, we spent a few days together in St Kilda up in Melbourne before she had to return to Bondi, where she was living and running her business, Brazil Body Activewear. I was booked to fly home to France, but I had no commitments for a week or so. She invited me to Bondi. I accepted. We fell in love.

Meeting Neca clinched the deal. I was going to move back to Australia. I just had to make sure that my career with Quiksilver – my only income – wasn't put at risk. Despite my misgivings about how I fitted into the company, I stayed committed and pinned my future to Quik. Not everyone loves their boss. And not everyone loved their job as much as I did either. Time to knuckle down.

Harry Hodge was supportive of my move to Australia, as was Al Green. Very little happened in Europe during winter anyway, so I was free to move, provided I was in France and available for surfing, promo and coaching for at least five months during summer. Great! It was agreed. Harry was even nice enough to give me space in his own shipping container to move my things. He was also heading back Down Under.

I moved in with Neca in Bondi and the arrangements worked out well for the first European summer. It seemed as though the move suited my employers at Quiksilver Europe as much as it suited me. Neca and I lived as man and wife. We wanted the same things in life and had already begun planning a family.

After the trauma and disappointment of one failed pregnancy, we were blessed when Neca fell pregnant again at the start of 2005. All was bliss. Business was going great guns for us both, and we were enjoying the closeness of our compatibility and the wonder of expecting a baby for the first time.

THE BEST THING

Lunna Holly Elkerton was born in Bondi on 7 September 2005 to overjoyed parents. And to *very* doting grandparents, Bull and Joan. Not to mention a small army of loving uncles, aunties and cousins in both Australia and Brazil.

Every cliché applied to me as a first-time father of a new daughter. I could barely stop crying for a week. Everything that Lunna learnt from the day she was born, I was learning with her ... seeing the world through her eyes. Early on, there were whole days when I couldn't put her down. I just loved her too much to part with her. Neca even had to wrestle Lunna from my arms at feeding time!

Neca's business was in good shape and I had some savings too. I was determined that hectic Bondi was not the ideal place to raise Lunna and I eventually convinced Neca that a move 'up north' was the thing to do. With the proceeds of the sale of my home in Hossegor, we relocated to Ocean Shores in far northern New South Wales, just a stone's throw away from Bull's old stomping grounds with the Brunswick Heads prawn fleet. Our new home was even closer, as it happens, to Bull's favourite pub. The Billinudgel Hotel hasn't changed a bit since Dad first set foot in it as a teenager. Like father, like son. Neca will tell you we're a little *too* close to the 'Billi'.

We liked the idea of great open spaces, beautiful bushland and pristine, uncrowded beaches as an environment for Lunna to grow up in. Just quietly, it ain't too shabby for surfing or motocross either.

Home was now only an hour's drive away from my old mates on the Gold Coast at Mt Woodgee, where I received venomous competition in ping-pong, and also my treasured surfboards. We were also smack-bang in the middle of the region containing the extended Elkerton and Lowe families.

Lunna brings such joy to me that any happiness I'd felt before her arrival seems shallow by comparison. My girls – Lunna and Neca – are the lights in my life. They've been the perfect antidote for the self-centredness that grows around a driven solo athlete.

In March 2005, Craig Stevenson was the boss at Quiksilver Australia. I really like him. He is no surf industry 'barnacle', that's for sure. So, I had no qualms when Craig phoned me from Victoria to say that he wanted to pop up to the Gold Coast for a meeting with me. I looked forward to seeing him. Perhaps Quiksilver Australia were set to take over my contract from Europe? More likely, we'd be planning some coaching and tow-surfing promotions, or something of the sort.

When I met with Craig at the Rainbow Bay Surf Club, I knew what was happening the second I saw the ashen look on his normally smiling face. He gave me a letter on Quik letterhead which read like a dismissal notice that an eighteen-year-old manager at Burger King gives to a fourteen-year-old subordinate. A couple of sentences. I don't even think it was signed. It just had the words 'termination' and 'immediate' in it.

I thundered indignantly at poor Craig until I remembered that it was not his doing. As a matter of fact, he is such a high-quality person that he volunteered to deliver the news from Quiksilver Europe personally, rather than have me open such an abrupt and *cowardly* letter.

The letter did not offer an explanation. Nor did Craig, because it basically had nothing to do with him. With impressive bravery and professionalism, he told me that one thing he could say for sure was that the decision was definitely irreversible. It says a lot about Craig that I would hold him in even higher regard after this most upsetting meeting than I did before. He had the integrity to front me face to face with a decision that wasn't even his.

I rang everyone – Harry, Al, Jeff, Tommy, Ross. I even called Bob McKnight. They all spoke with me, but nobody could (or would) give me an exact answer as to precisely why I'd been axed so unceremoniously. No-one would admit to making the call, which left me to assume that the one person who wouldn't speak to me had made the decision. Good old Pierre.

Once I'd been cut loose from Europe, I would've had to be employed in either Australia or the US to have a future with the company. I guess the 'old man' roster was full elsewhere. There was no squeezing in with Ross and Tommy's tow-in team, that's for sure!

I sulked and raged for a while, I'll admit. Here was a company I had genuinely helped as a promotional centrepiece, long before there were such things as 'global HQs' and listings on stock exchanges. I headlined in many of their groundbreaking films. I'd won them a Hawaiian Triple Crown and three World Masters titles. And after telling me I was doing valuable work, they erased me with a two-line letter that contained not a hint of 'thanks and best wishes'. Like I was a temporary accounts clerk. If it weren't for Craig Stevenson, I would have pulled the letter from my mailbox and that would have been that.

Unattributed rumours eventually circulated about my 'over' love of a good time. Working in promotions – in surfing! Oh boy … that's a good one. I must really stand out like a bull's tits amongst *that* particular selection of choirboys! They were easy rumours to ignore.

Being fired from Quiksilver could have been well deserved. Until I get a decent explanation from someone, I'll never know.

It's pointless to have hard feelings against an inorganic company. In short order, I took stock of the lessons I'd learnt from when I first parted with them almost twenty years before. These guys have a job to do. Was I still helping to move t-shirts? Business is business. I told myself to stop being such a sook and I got over it. Even now, I still wish my many remaining friends at Quiksilver well and marvel at the transformations in the business since its humble beginnings.

Regardless of reasons and explanations, I was left with a family to support and I had no job. At forty-one, I was qualified to surf, coach surfing and trawl for prawns.

Neca and I spoke at length about our immediate future. After much soul searching we decided that this horrible development actually created some opportunities for positive change. I could've networked myself into a role with another big surf company as a tow-specialist, coach and promotional advocate. But was that what I truly wanted any more? I'd already become wearied by fitting into a big business. Should I open myself – ourselves – to more disappointment down the track? Surely if I started up a role with another surf corporation I was only delaying the inevitable?

The time had come for genuine reinvention.

The following years have proven that getting the boot from Quiksilver was actually the best thing that could have happened.

KONG FOR KIDS

I picked up some scaffolding work on the Goldie through a mate. It was a matter of considerable hilarity that I actually stuck to the task for a while. The last labouring job I'd had – fresh off the trawler as a kid – lasted all of one week.

We booked Lunna in for swimming lessons as soon as we could. One day, while I was observing a lesson in which few children seemed to be having fun, the idea struck me that I could teach these kids way better and far less stressfully. Thanks to my lifetime in the water and our status as new parents, Neca and I became passionate about teaching kids to swim and surf. Kong for Kids was born.

With the help and support of many close friends, especially business mentors Rick Cassidy (my dear friend, astute entrepreneur and pool landlord) and Nick Anagnostou, my second career in construction came to an early (and welcome) end. Kong for Kids Swim School opened in a custom-made indoor facility in Billinudgel in mid-2008. Since then, it's been the great satisfaction and achievement of my working life to have taught so many kids of all ages swimming and water safety. I teach up to 270 kids a week and I'm stoked to pass on lasting skills and the fun of life in the water to each and every one of them.

Thanks to having formed bonds with so many parents, many of my swim students go on to take coaching in ocean safety and surfing. Some of these have become successful junior competitive surfers, who I continue to mentor. All of them have the thrill of riding waves absorbed into their lives, just like I did when I was a grommet.

Not long after my move north, I connected with ASP World Title contender, fellow Mt Woodgee team rider and North Stradbroke Island local Bede Durbidge, and became his coach. Bede and I have quite an interlocking history in many ways. And in addition to his incredible talent, Bede is simply one of the highest-quality individuals there is. He's like family to me. I love him like a brother and I'll move heaven and earth to help him become World Champion. There could not be a more deserving person of the Title.

I also occupy myself with hosting surf tours to various parts of the world. It goes without saying that this doesn't feel like a job! More like meeting a bunch of new friends from all walks of life and sharing a week or two of fun in far-flung places.

I have myself a richly rewarding, busy and diverse working life, which would never have happened had fate not turned the way it did in 2005. I'm so glad that love and encouragement from Neca and family and friends helped me embrace the change.

As busy as I am, there's still plenty of time to hang on the beach with Lunna and Neca – the very best of all the simple pleasures.

FINAL THOUGHTS

Surfing as a professional, competitive sport is pretty weird. Great, but weird.

There are few – if any – other sports that are so symbiotically entwined with pure corporate marketing and sales processes. Of course, all professional sports rely on complex sponsorships and media arrangements for survival. But the influence of these arrangements generally stops once the 'white line' is crossed – when the athletes are actually doing their thing on the field or on the court.

When football players battle it out, the full-time score definitively tells you who the best team was. Tennis players exchange shots across the net until the winner is decided within a clear set of rules. Mixed martial artists pummel each other until one combatant is standing and one isn't. Basketball goes end-to-end-to-end-to-end until someone has more points when the buzzer goes off. The team with the most runs wins a baseball game. The player who uses the fewest strokes to put the ball in the hole eighteen times prevails in a round of golf.

Most professional sports are driven by the passion of fans for the simplicity and traditions of the contest itself, and the purpose of most sports is to produce a champion. Corporations attach themselves to this purpose by sponsoring individuals, teams or whole competitions. The selling of consumer goods is a by-product of the contest to produce winners.

Surfing is different. In professional surfing, the production of winners may be perceived as a by-product of the selling of consumer goods and the mighty battle between a small handful of highly invested gigantic corporations.

Imagine if the tennis racquet and clothing manufacturer Yonex only had two major competitors, say Head and Wilson, for example. Imagine that these three companies owned many enterprises in tennis, from the production of clothes and equipment, to sales and distribution, to retail. Imagine that few top tennis tournaments could exist without the financial support of one of these corporations or a business owned or partially owned by one of these corporations.

If you can, also try to imagine that Yonex, Head or Wilson were then given the media rights to each tournament as part of their sponsorship arrangements. To further stretch your creative thinking, conjure up the notion that these tournaments were decided on court by subjective judgments regarding the power and beauty of the stroke play, rather than by tennis balls landing physically within lines.

Since it would be too unlikely, I won't ask you to imagine that tennis didn't use WADA to test its athletes.

Chances are that professional tennis may not get much mainstream corporate support outside of Yonex, Head and Wilson if the game was as we've conceived it above. Might be a bit tough to sell the sport to overarching, mainstream global media too. Maybe even tougher for a potentially excellent pro tennis player to get to the top if he used racquets, clothes and shoes that were outside the promotional 'loop'.

You don't have to imagine this closed-club version of tennis. You need only behold pro surfing as it is today.

I love the sport of professional surfing with a passion. It has a massive, largely latent following of recreational surfers and non-surfers alike around the world. Its potential is enormous. However, until these followers are treated as 'fans' first and 'consumers' second, and until the quality of competition and the best interests of its athletes are put before the selling of t-shirts, professional surfing will forever be a 'closed club'. Shut off to the kind of growth and potential that comes with broad interest from a broad scope of potential stakeholders. It just isn't an ideal model for a professional sports organisation. At present, it's more like a sub-unit of a sales and marketing division.

One low point in the history of pro surfing is the heartbreaking, tragic death of Andy Irons. An unbelievably talented surfer and competitor. A terrific, fun-filled, caring, engaging person who was respected and loved by all who knew him. A multiple World Champion, adored by fans worldwide. Also, Andy was well known in surfing circles to have had his battles with drug and alcohol addiction. That he wound up passing away, alone, when it was common knowledge that he wasn't well is shatteringly sad. 'Blame' is not the appropriate response, of course. There's no blame. None at all. But there is shame on us all, in a way, thanks to our surfing culture of freedom and acceptance.

I had problems similar to Andy's during several stages of my career in the spotlight. I was lucky that there was always someone with an eye on me or I could easily have died in a similar way, especially in 1985. Self-evidently, not much has changed behind the scenes in the long years between my overdoses in 1985 and Andy's death in 2010.

How I wish this wonderful man had the luck that I was blessed with. God rest Andy Irons and here's hoping that some peace can be found in the years ahead for his family and loved ones. Of all the unnecessary losses in the surfing community over the years, Andy's may be the most bitterly felt by us all.

If the sport, the 'industry' and the culture of surfing doesn't have the collective courage to confront its demons as a result of Andy's passing, then it doesn't deserve any more respect than the 'closed club' status it has now. There are good, well-intentioned people involved administratively, managerially and corporately in the sport. Always has been. All that's needed is the right expertise and the necessary impetus for change in the right places. The structural, operational and cultural shortcomings can be remedied, I'm sure of it, but it will take some hard-headed, brave people at the top to get the changes underway.

I lead a serene life these days. There's still a lot of excitement. There are still a lot of mistakes and bumps on the road. I still have an unstoppable need to push myself to the limits with surfing, towing and motocross. While I'll often be surprised by a new level of adrenalin in tow-surfing or on my bike, I'm just as likely to be stimulated by taking on a new business venture or coaching project.

I've accepted that – like it or not – 'safety' is not my thing. Accepting that fact has given me serenity – 'serenity in chaos'. Maybe I need therapy! Amongst the chaos, there's now a feeling of peace that took a long time coming.

In 2009 I joined 'the heroes on my bedroom wall' when I was inducted into the Surfing Hall of Fame. I'm humbled by the honour and grateful for the recognition, not just for my own sake but also for every single person who's ever helped and supported me.

I thrive on the stability and love that surrounds my home life. Lunna and Neca take me back to simpler times on the boat with Bull and Mum and my siblings – the 'rocks' that I left behind when I threw myself into the global madness of the pro Tour as a teen. Lunna and Neca mean everything to me. After years of putting the demands of my career before all else, they've given more to live for than I'd ever dreamt was possible.

I love hosting surf trips around the world. The easy camaraderie between surfers of all standards, and the diversity of experiences and backgrounds amongst the friends I make on these journeys, is priceless. As rewarding and as meaningful as the hurly-burly of my days on Tour.

I love teaching kids to swim and surf. It's deeply sentimental to introduce little kids to the sheer fun and lifetime possibilities of life in the water. Water has been so instrumental in my life – what could it hold ahead for my tiny students?

And I look at the talented kids I coach in surfing. It's impossible to be cynical when I take a grommet under my wing. I can't help but be optimistic about the sport of surfing when my young charges help me see it through the eyes I had when I caught my first wave at Kingscliff all those many years ago. I can be a hard taskmaster, but from World Title contenders all the way through to my youngest students, I espouse the wisdom of the oldest saying in surfing. It binds me to the newest friends I make on my hosted surf trips as much as it binds me to my many friends, loved ones, mentors and ex-rivals alike.

'The best surfer is the one with the biggest smile.'

Sometimes the most well-worn sayings are also the truest. I'm counting on smiling for a good while yet, come what may.

AFTERWORD

Joan Mary Elkerton passed away on 11 February 2012, two weeks before the final draft of this book was completed. She was surrounded by loved ones whom *she* comforted – in typical fashion – right to the end.

My biggest supporter. My friend. *My mum.*

'Love' just doesn't explain it.

Now in the company of St Brendan, no doubt, and still watching over us …

NOTES AND ACKNOWLEDGEMENTS

I've made personal admissions regarding drugs frequently throughout this book. Unless I've specifically referred (by name) to someone using specific drugs, it should not be assumed that any or all of my friends, or any individual at all in my company or otherwise mentioned, was also using the same substances. 'Guilt by association' in context with any individual is not implied or intended. Though there are generalisations, no inference regarding drug use about an individual who is not specifically mentioned by name as taking drugs is made or intended.

I'd like to give love and thanks to: Dad and Mum, Neca and Lunna, David and Bernadette, Al Green, Nick Anagnostou, Jack McCoy, John 'Seaweed' Tragere, Paul Pascoe, Mick Hopper, Reid Pinder, Wayne 'Rabbit' Bartholomew, James 'Chappy' Jennings, Tommy Carroll, Ross Clarke-Jones and Martin Potter. And Kelly Slater for the kind words. John Dunfey from Shimano has been a much appreciated friend and supporter. Also, special mention to all of my Hawaiian friends and mentors, and to everyone I've ever pulled on a jersey against – thanks for making my ride such a memorable one.

Then there's Pete McGuinness. He spent a couple of years living in my skin. Pete and I spent hundreds of hours together recording my life, though he invested way more time than that putting my voice into written form. Words that *exactly* reflect how I speak, who I am, what I feel, what I think and what I've done. He sacrificed a lot of time with his own lovely family to make himself part of mine forever. Only a truly gifted writer, a great person and a bloody good surfer with his kind of patience and insight could have done it.

www.garykongelkerton.com

WRITER'S NOTE

The real beauty of 'Kong' is that he truly doesn't put himself above anyone. Not even above a bloke like me who can't dream of drawing lines on an unbroken wave with even one per cent of his majestic fluidity or power. He's a rare salt-of-the-earth character who has achieved global fame without collecting the slightest pretence along the way, despite his deserved reputation as a cocky, hard-arsed competitor.

Like most of the world's surfers, I've watched Gary's performances in films like *Kong's Island* and – in particular – the Sunset Beach sequences in *Mad Wax* and *The Performers* with nothing short of genuine awe. It doesn't take any special insight to deduce that Gary is plainly one of the most individualistic and gifted surfers of all time.

I got to know Gary through mutual friends at Mt Woodgee Surfboards. He's a natural yarn teller and I'm a writer, so it was inevitable, perhaps, that we'd form the idea that I could help him with an autobiography. I've since learnt that a more profound privilege than watching him surf is to be invited to share in his incredible life, of which surfing has been a part but by no means the whole. The process of distilling a life so diverse that it may well have been led by ten men has been a rollicking adventure, though surprisingly touching – even wrenching at times. All the while, it has been thoroughly enjoyable.

I thank Gary for placing his trust in me. He has been his usual courageous self by leaving nothing unsaid in this book. I'm sure you've enjoyed sharing in his remarkable story as much as I have.

I'd like to acknowledge Noel Snr, Brow, Dools, Dez, Mick D, Anthony, Eno and Nick's ayyoupi. They know why. Also Patrick Kidd and Tim Baker for their early encouragement, and Amruta Slee and Brigitta Doyle from HarperCollins for believing in the project. Likewise, Kit and the lads from the Triple Crown in New York for keeping me sane a long way from home.

I'm especially grateful to Melissa, Jordan, Montana and my darling little Kitty for loving me despite – or maybe because of – all the writing and surfing. Whatever the reasons, I'm a very lucky man.

Peter McGuinness, 2012